P9-DVU-994

Best Jobs *For* Ex-Offenders

Ron Krannich, Ph.D.

DISCARD
L.C.C.C. LIBRARY

IMPACT PUBLICATIONS
Manassas Park, VA

Copyright © 2009 by Ron Krannich. All rights reserved. Printed in the United States of America. No part of this book may be used or reproduced in any manner whatsoever without written permission of the publisher: IMPACT PUBLICATIONS, 9104 Manassas Drive, Suite N, Manassas Park, VA 20111, Tel. 703-361-7300 or Fax 703-335-9486.

Warning/Liability/Warranty: The author and publisher have made every attempt to provide the reader with accurate, timely, and useful information. However, given the rapid changes taking place in today's economy and job market, some of our information will inevitably change. The information presented here is for reference purposes only. The author and publisher make no claims that using this information will guarantee the reader a job or a satisfying career. The author and publisher shall not be liable for any losses or damages incurred in the process of following the advice in this book.

ISBN: 978-1-57023-284-8 (13-digit); 1-57023-284-9 (10-digit)

Library of Congress: 2008936724

Publisher: For information on Impact Publications, including current and forthcoming publications, authors, press kits, online bookstore, newsletters, downloadable catalogs, and submission requirements, visit the left navigation bar on the front page of our main company website: www.impactpublications.com.

Publicity/Rights: For information on publicity, author interviews, and subsidiary rights, contact the Media Relations Department: Tel. 703-361-7300, Fax 703-335-9486, or email: query@impactpublications.com.

Sales/Distribution: All special sales inquiries should be directed to the publisher: Sales Department, IMPACT PUBLICATIONS, 9104 Manassas Drive, Suite N, Manassas Park, VA 20111-5211, Tel. 703-361-7300, Fax 703-335-9486, or email: query@impactpublications. com. All bookstore sales go through Impact's trade distributor: National Book Network, 15200 NBN Way, Blue Ridge Summit, PA 17214, Tel. 1-800-462-6420.

Quantity Discounts: We offer generous quantity discounts (up to 60 per cent) on bulk purchases. Please review our discount schedule for this book at www.impactpublications. com, refer to the discounts listed on the inside front cover of this book, or contact the Special Sales Department, Tel. 703-361-0255.

The Author: For more than 25 years, Ron Krannich has been one of America's leading career and travel writers. Author and co-author of more than 80 books, he has written such bestsellers as *The Ex-Offender's Job Hunting Guide, High Impact Resumes and Letters, Interview for Success, No One Will Hire Me!, Nail the Resume, Job Interview Tips for People With Not-So-Hot Backgrounds, Give Me More Money!, You Should Hire Me!, Jobs for Travel Lovers, I Want to Do Something Else, But I'm Not Sure What It Is,* and *Change Your Job, Change Your Life.* Ron can be contacted through the publisher: krannich@impactpublications.com.

Acknowledgments: Special thanks goes to the many correctional educators, ex-offenders, and community leaders who shared their insights into the employment issues facing ex-offenders, especially the transitional employment experiences (Chapter 2) and barriers to employment (Chapter 3) incorporated into this book. Individual job descriptions (Chapters 4-10) are based on the U.S. Department of Labor's 2008-2009 edition of the *Occupational Outlook Handbook* (www.bls.gov/oco).

Contents

1

What Are the Best Jobs for You?

"You're largely on your own in navigating a job market that is not so friendly to ex-offenders. Knowing the best jobs in general, and those for ex-offenders in particular, can help you quickly jump-start your new life in the free world."

I T'S WELL DOCUMENTED and not surprising to most observers familiar with America's sprawling criminal justice and correctional systems – ex-offenders face numerous difficulties in finding and keeping jobs. Unfortunately, most become re-offenders. In fact, we do a relatively mediocre job of managing our corrections system – from arresting, convicting, and locking up criminals – and a very poor job in changing mindsets and behaviors to ensure that offenders don't become repeat offenders after release from prisons, jails, and detention centers. It's a costly, incendiary, and mind-numbing "lockup and wait" body-holding program that often promotes more failures and collateral damage. An amazing system, it seems to work against everyone's best interests.

A Bankrupt But Hopeful System

America's annual correctional and recidivism statistics are staggering – 2.3 million people locked up in state and federal prisons (up from 330,000 in 1960), 10-12 million people circulating in and out of jails and detention centers, and over 5 million people on parole and probation. Because of the "war on drugs" and tough sentencing laws and practices since the 1980s, it's not surprising to learn that the majority of today's prisoners are nonviolent drug offenders who mostly engaged in victimless crimes. But it's still crime.

Being convicted and incarcerated is often a ticket to purgatory as well as a big red flag for employers. Yes, mother was right – getting sent to prison or jail will ruin your life – or at least make your future more difficult and challenging. Indeed, nearly two-thirds of all ex-offenders return to prison within three years. From all objective indicators, we live in a dangerous society where public safety is a major concern. And no one seems to agree on what to do to make these correctional numbers go down significantly. Simply amazing!

If this system were a business, it would have been declared bankrupt and closed long ago. But it's not a business – it's a classic government service and construction program preoccupied with expanding facilities, personnel, and technology in order to warehouse more bodies mandated by the courts. It simply doesn't work beyond temporarily keeping some offenders off the streets and locked up for a while. Not surprisingly, they'll be back!

While getting tough on crime may make for great photo opportunities for politicians and public officials, in reality this system is very costly when it produces negative results for everyone involved – victims, offenders, and taxpayers. The direct and collateral costs of this system – probably over $1 trillion dollars a year – are simply astounding. If taxpayers knew the true costs of this "get-tough-on-crime" system, they might become outraged and cynical about those who claim to be trusted and cost-effective gatekeepers.

Many people have lots of good ideas on what needs to be done, and several experimental re-entry programs with strong employment components have demonstrated excellent "lessons learned." Indeed, there is hope for a better day when this system begins to get serious about the whole **re-entry process** by developing re-entry programs with strong employment components that really work. In the meantime, most ex-offenders are on their own in navigating a challenging job market that is not too receptive to their backgrounds. After all, who wants to hire and nurture an ex-offender?

Believe it or not, many employers do hire ex-offenders. As you will see throughout this book, certain jobs are very ex-offender-friendly. Knowing what jobs are best suited for ex-offenders can get you started in the right direction as you re-enter the free world.

Jobs and Re-Offending

The failure to find steady and rewarding employment, along with decent and affordable housing, is one of the key factors explaining why so many ex-offenders don't make it on the outside. Unable to support themselves, many ex-offenders return to old habits that initially got them into trouble. Within three years, nearly two-thirds of the more than 650,000 ex-offenders who are released into society each year return to prison. Both the human and economic costs of such a high recidivism rate are horrendous.

Knowing various job options should help you better develop a pre-release resume as well as target your job search in the days ahead.

As we've documented in *The Ex-Offender's Job Hunting Guide*, on www.exoffenderreentry.com, and on pages 19-28, ex-offenders face many barriers to employment. Some are legal, such as the prohibition from working in certain occupations, but most relate to knowledge, skills, education, and training. Many ex-offenders lack basic literacy skills – unable to read, write, and communicate at satisfactory workplace levels. Others have little work experience and few job skills. And still others don't have a clue as to what types of jobs best fit their interests, skills, and abilities. Their biggest barriers tend to be their own attitudes and mindsets – **things they can change**.

It's this latter group that this book is primarily aimed at – those who have basic workplace skills but who need more information on the types of jobs that are most appropriate for their present level of interests, skills, and abilities as well as their red flag background. Knowing various job options available for someone with their backgrounds should help them better develop a pre-release resume as well as target their job search in the days ahead.

On Your Own on the Outside

If you want to make it on the outside for good, you need useful knowledge about the realities on the outside – especially on how to find a rewarding job, decent housing, and a good support system. Put aside any **illusions** about the free world. You need to become job-smart by identifying jobs and employers that best fit your interests, skills, and abilities. If you lack education, training, and basic workplace skills, you'll need to start somewhere – perhaps in a low-paying entry-level position – and work your way up by getting more education, training, and work experience. You'll have to take a great deal of initiative to make it on the outside – no one else can do it better than you. You need knowledge about the best jobs for ex-offenders to quickly jump-start your new post-prison life . . . for good!

Consider New Options

If you have been incarcerated for more than a year, this is a good time to reassess what you want to do with the rest of your work life. Do you want to go back to what you were once doing, or do you feel there may be other things you would like to do? Perhaps you would like to pursue one of today's fastest growing or hottest jobs. For example, the U.S. Department of Labor's Bureau of Labor Statistics every two years updates its employment outlook for the coming decade and publishes the results in the November issue of the *Monthly Labor Review* as well as in the latest edition of the biannual *Occupational Outlook Handbook*. For the latest statistics and projections relating to several tables presented in this chapter, please visit the website of the Bureau of Labor Statistics: http://stats.bls.gov. You also can access online the complete text of the popular *Occupational Outlook Handbook* through this website: www.bls.gov/oco.

Assuming a moderate rate of economic growth in the decade ahead – not boom-and-bust cycles – the U.S. Department of Labor projects an average growth rate of nearly 15 percent for all occupations in the coming decade. Technical and service occupations will grow the fastest, as indicated in this table:

Fastest Growing Occupations, 2002-2012
(Numbers in thousands of jobs)

Occupational Title	Employment 2002	2012	Percent Change	Postsecondary Education or Training
▪ Medical assistants [3]	365	579	59	Moderate-term on-the-job training
▪ Network systems and data communications analysts [1]	186	292	57	Bachelor's degree
▪ Physician assistants [3]	63	94	49	Bachelor's degree
▪ Social and human service assistants [3]	305	454	49	Moderate-term on-the-job training
▪ Home health aides [4]	580	859	48	Short-term on-the-job training
▪ Medical records and health information technicians [3]	147	216	47	Associate degree
▪ Physical therapist aides [3]	37	54	46	Short-term on-the-job training
▪ Computer software engineers, applications [1]	394	573	46	Bachelor's degree
▪ Computer software engineers [1]	281	409	45	Bachelor's degree
▪ Physical therapist assistants [2]	50	73	45	Associate degree

▪ Fitness trainers and aerobics instructors [3]	183	264	44	Postsecondary vocational award
▪ Database administrators [1]	110	159	44	Bachelor's degree
▪ Veterinary technologists and technicians [3]	53	76	44	Associate degree
▪ Hazardous materials removal workers [2]	38	54	43	Moderate-term on-the-job training
▪ Dental hygienists [1]	148	212	43	Associate degree
▪ Occupational therapist aides [3]	8	12	43	Short-term on-the-job training
▪ Dental assistants [3]	266	379	42	Moderate-term on-the-job training
▪ Personal and home care aides [4]	608	854	40	Short-term on-the-job training
▪ Self-enrichment education teachers [2]	200	281	40	Work experience in a related occupation
▪ Computer systems analysts [1]	468	653	39	Bachelor's degree
▪ Occupational therapist assistants [2]	18	26	39	Associate degree
▪ Environmental engineers [1]	47	65	38	Bachelor's degree
▪ Postsecondary teachers [1]	1,581	1,284	38	Doctoral degree
▪ Network and computer systems administrators [1]	251	345	37	Bachelor's degree
▪ Environmental science and protection technicians, including health [2]	28	38	37	Associate degree
▪ Preschool teachers, except special education [4]	424	577	36	Postsecondary vocational award
▪ Computer and information systems managers [1]	284	387	36	Bachelor's or higher degree plus work experience
▪ Physical therapists [1]	137	185	35	Master's degree
▪ Occupational therapists [1]	82	110	35	Bachelor's degree
▪ Respiratory therapists [2]	86	116	35	Associate degree

[1] Very high average annual earnings ($42,820 and over)
[2] High average annual earnings ($27,500 to $41,780)
[3] Low average annual earnings ($19,710 to $27,380)
[4] Very low average annual earnings (up to $19,600)

Occupations With the Largest Job Growth, 2002-2012
(Numbers in thousands of jobs)

Occupational Title	Employment		Percent Change	Postsecondary Education or Training
	2002	2012		
▪ Registered nurses [1]	2,284	2,908	27	Associate degree
▪ Postsecondary teachers [1]	1,581	2,184	38	Doctoral degree
▪ Retail salespersons [4]	4,076	4,672	15	Short-term on-the-job training
▪ Customer service representatives [3]	1,894	2,354	24	Moderate-term on-the-job training

• Combined food preparation and service workers, including fast food [3]	1,990	2,444	23	Short-term on-the-job training
• Cashiers, except gaming [4]	3,432	2,886	13	Short-term on-the-job training
• Janitors and cleaners, except maids and housekeeping cleaners [4]	2,267	2,681	18	Short-term on-the-job training
• General and operations managers [1]	2,049	2,425	18	Bachelor's or higher degree + experience
• Waiters and waitresses [4]	2,097	2,464	18	Short-term on-the-job training
• Nursing aides, orderlies, and attendants [3]	1,375	1,718	25	Short-term on-the-job training
• Truck drivers, heavy and tractor-trailer [2]	1,767	2,104	19	Moderate-term on-the-job training
• Receptionists and information clerks [3]	1,100	1,425	29	Short-term on-the-job training
• Security guards [4]	995	1,313	32	Short-term on-the-job training
• Office clerks, general [3]	2,991	3,301	10	Short-term on-the-job training
• Teacher assistants [4]	1,277	1,571	23	Short-term on-the-job training
• Sales representative, wholesale and manufacturing, except technical and scientific products [1]	1,459	1,738	19	Moderate-term on-the-job training
• Home health aides [4]	580	859	48	Short-term on-the-job training
• Personal and home care aides [4]	608	854	40	Short-term on-the-job training
• Truck drivers, light or delivery services [3]	1,022	1,259	23	Short-term on-the-job training
• Landscaping and grounds-keeping workers [3]	1,074	1,311	22	Short-term on-the-job training
• Elementary school teachers, except special education [2]	1,467	1,690	15	Bachelor's degree
• Medical assistants [3]	365	579	59	Moderate-term on-the-job training
• Maintenance and repair workers, general [2]	1,266	1,472	16	Moderate-term on-the-job training
• Accountants and auditors [1]	1,055	1,261	19	Bachelor's degree
• Computer systems analysts [1]	468	653	39	Bachelor's degree
• Secondary school teachers, except special and vocational education [1]	988	1,167	18	Bachelor's degree
• Computer software engineers [1]	394	573	46	Bachelor's degree
• Management analysis [1]	577	753	30	Bachelor's or higher degree, plus work experience
• Food preparation workers [4]	850	1,022	20	Short-term on-the-job training

▪ First-line supervisors/ managers of retail sales workers [2]	1,798	1,962	9	Work experience in a related occupation

[1] Very high average annual earnings ($42,820 and over)
[2] High average annual earnings ($27,500 to $41,780)
[3] Low average annual earnings ($19,710 to $27,380)
[4] Very low average annual earnings (up to $19,600)

Fastest Growing Industries, 2002-2012
(Numbers in thousands of jobs)

Industry Description	Jobs		Percent Change	Average annual rate of change
	2002	2012		
▪ Software publishers	256.0	429.7	173.7	5.3
▪ Management, scientific, and technical consulting services	731.8	1,137.4	405.6	4.5
▪ Community care facilities for the elderly and residential care facilities	695.3	1,077.6	382.3	4.5
▪ Computer systems design and related services	1,162.7	1,797.7	635.0	4.5
▪ Employment services	3,248.8	5,012.3	1,763.5	4.4
▪ Individual, family, community, and vocational rehabilitation services	1,238.8	1,866.6	597.3	3.9
▪ Ambulatory health care services except offices of health practitioners	1,443.6	2,113.4	669.8	3.9
▪ Water, sewage, and other systems	48.5	71.0	22.5	3.9
▪ Internet services, data processing and other information services	528.8	773.1	244.3	3.9
▪ Child day care services	734.2	1,050.3	316.1	3.6

20 Jobs With High Median Earnings and a Significant Number of Job Openings, 2002-2012

Occupation	Average Annual Projected Job Openings, 2002-2012	Median Earnings 2002
▪ Registered nurses	110,119	$48,090
▪ Postsecondary teachers	95,980	$49,090
▪ General and operations managers	76,245	$68,210
▪ Sales representatives, wholesale and manufacturing, except technical and scientific products	66,239	$42,730

- Truck drivers, heavy and tractor-trailer | 62,517 | $33,210
- Elementary school teachers, except special education | 54,701 | $41,780
- First-line supervisors or managers of retail sales workers | 48,645 | $29,700
- Secondary school teachers, except special education | 45,761 | $43,950
- General maintenance and repair workers | 44,978 | $29,370
- Executive secretaries and administrative assistants | 42,444 | $33,410
- First-line supervisors or managers of office and administrative support workers | 40,909 | $38,820
- Accountants and auditors | 40,465 | $47,000
- Carpenters | 31,917 | $34,190
- Automotive service technicians and mechanics | 41,887 | $30,590
- Police and sheriff's patrol officers | 31,290 | $42,270
- Licensed practical and licensed vocational nurses | 29,480 | $31,440
- Electricians | 28,485 | $41,390
- Management analysts | 25,470 | $60,340
- Computer systems analysts | 23,735 | $62,890
- Special education teachers | 23,297 | $43,450

Certain patterns are clearly evident from the U.S. Department of Labor's employment projections for the coming decade:

1. The hot occupational fields are in health care and computers and involve increased technical education and training on an ongoing basis.

2. Education is closely associated with earnings – the higher the education, the higher the average annual earnings.

3. Many of the fastest growing jobs require short- or moderate-term education.

4. Two-year associate degrees in several medical-related fields offer some of the best paying jobs.

5. Nearly 50 percent of the fastest growing jobs that generate relatively high median earnings, such as carpenters, truck drivers, repair workers, and auto mechanics, do not require a four-year degree. Many of these jobs are open to ex-offenders.

Identify the "Best" Jobs for You

The fastest growing occupational fields may not be the best ones for you. The best job and career for you will depend on your particular mix of skills, interests, and work and lifestyle values. At the same time, certain jobs may be off limits to you because of legal restrictions relating to your criminal background. Money, for example, is only one of many determiners of whether or not a particular job or career would be a desirable one to pursue. A job may pay a great deal of money, but it also may be very stressful, insecure, found in an undesirable location, involve long hours, and require extensive travel, including a long commute each day. The "best" job for you will be one you find rewarding in terms of your own unique criteria and priorities.

If you know what you do well and enjoy doing – information you can obtain through various self-assessment tests and exercises – you will have a better idea which jobs best fit you. Indeed, we strongly recommend conducting a self-assessment in conjunction with the information included on the various jobs profiled in this book. For details on how to identify your best fit, see our separate self-assessment volume, *I Want to Do Something Else, But I'm Not Sure What It Is* (Impact Publications, 2005).

Periodically some observers of the labor market attempt to identify what are the best, the worst, the hottest, the most lucrative, or the most promising jobs and careers of the decade. One of the most ambitious attempts to assemble a list of the "best" jobs in America is presented in the *Jobs Rated Almanac*. Similar in approach to *Places Rated Almanac* for identifying the best places to live in America, the latest edition (2002) of this book evaluates and ranks 250 jobs in terms of six primary "job quality" criteria: income, stress, physical demands, environment, outlook, and security. According to this analysis, the 25 highest ranking ("best") jobs by accumulated score of these criteria are:

The Best Jobs in America

Job title	Overall rank
Biologist	1
Actuary	2
Financial planner	3
Computer system analyst	4
Accountant	5
Software engineer	6
Meteorologist	7
Paralegal assistant	8
Statistician	9
Astronomer	10
Mathematician	11
Parole officer	12
Hospital administrator	13
Architectural drafter	14
Physiologist	15
Dietician	16
Website manager	17
Physicist	18
Audiologist	19
Agency director (nonprofit)	20
Industrial designer	21
Chemist	22

- Medical laboratory technician   23
- Archeologist   24
- Economist   25

The 20 worst jobs, or those that rank at the very bottom of the list of 250, include the following:

The Worst Jobs in America

Job title	Overall rank
Fisherman	250
Roustabout	249
Lumberjack	248
Cowboy	247
Ironworker	246
Garbage collector	245
Construction worker (laborer)	244
Taxi driver	243
Stevedore	242
Welder	241
Roofer	240
Dancer	239
Firefighter	238
Dairy farmer	237
Seaman	236
Farmer	235
Boilermaker	234
Carpenter	234
Sheet metal worker	232
Butcher	231

Many of these jobs are ones that ex-offenders tend to gravitate toward – often low-paying jobs that others don't want. For the relative rankings of all 250 jobs as well as the ratings of each job on individual criterion, consult the latest edition of the *Jobs Rated Almanac*, which should be available in your local library or bookstore.

One of the most recent examinations of the best jobs in the decade ahead – those offering high pay, fast growth, and the most new jobs – is found in Ferguson's *25 Jobs That Have It All* (Chicago, IL: Ferguson Publishing Co.). This book identifies 25 jobs as the top ones:

- Advertising account executives
- Business managers
- College professors
- Computer network administrators
- Computer systems programmers/analysts
- Database specialists
- Dental hygienists
- Graphic designers
- Health care managers

- Management analysts and consultants
- Medical record technicians
- Occupational therapists
- Paralegals
- Pharmacy technicians
- Physician assistants
- Police officers
- Public relations specialists
- Registered nurses
- Secondary school teachers
- Software designers
- Software engineers
- Special education teachers
- Speech-language pathologists and audiologists
- Technical support specialists
- Writers and editors

Look for Exciting New Occupations

In the early 1980s the auto and related industries – steel, rubber, glass, aluminum, railroads, and auto dealers – accounted for one-fifth of all employment in the United States. Today that percentage continues to decline as service occupations further dominate America's occupational structure.

New occupations for the decade ahead will center around information, energy, high-tech, health care, and financial industries. Today we have blue-collar and white-collar jobs. Tomorrow we are likely to have more and more green-collar jobs related to promising new jobs and careers in the alternative energy industries. We should see a new occupational structure and vocabulary relating to green technologies, computers, the Internet, robotics, biotechnology, nanotechnology, lasers, and fiber optics. By 1999, for example, the Internet reportedly was responsible for 1.3 million new jobs within a four-year period that generated more than $300 billion in business. Those numbers have more than tripled in the past nine years. And as these fields begin to apply new technologies to developing innovations, they in turn will generate other new occupations in the decades ahead. While most new occupations are not major growth fields – because they do not initially generate a large number of new jobs – they will present individuals with fascinating new opportunities to become leaders in pioneering new fields and industries.

Futurists agree that most new occupations in the coming decade will have two dominant characteristics:

- **They will generate fewer new jobs** in comparison to the overall growth of jobs in hundreds of more traditional service fields, such as sales workers, office clerks, truck drivers, and janitors.

- **They require a high level of education and skills** for entry into the fields as well as continuing training and retraining as each field develops and transforms itself into an additional growth field.

If you plan to pursue an emerging occupation, expect to first acquire highly specialized skills which may require years of higher education and training.

Implications of Future Trends for You

Most growth industries and occupations require training and experience. Moving into one of these fields will require knowledge of job qualifications, the nature of the work, and sources of employment. Fortunately, the U.S. Department of Labor publishes several useful sources of information available in most libraries to help you. These include the *O*NET Dictionary of Occupational Titles*, which identifies over 1,100 job titles. The *Occupational Outlook Handbook* provides an overview of current labor market conditions and projections, as well as discusses nearly 250 occupations that account for 107 million jobs, or 87 percent of the nation's total jobs, according to several useful informational categories: nature of work; working conditions; employment; training, other qualifications, and achievement; job outlook; earnings; related occupations; and sources of additional information.

During the past eight years, the U.S. Department of Labor overhauled its traditional job classification system, which was based on an analysis of the U.S. job market of the 1960s, 1970s, and 1980s. This system had generated over 13,000 job titles as outlined in the *Dictionary of Occupational Titles* and numerous related publications. Known as the O*NET project (The Occupational Information Network), this new occupational classification system more accurately reflects the structure of today's new job market; it condenses the 13,000+ job titles into over 1,100 job titles. The new system is being gradually introduced into career education to replace the job classification system that has defined most jobs in the U.S. during the past four decades.

Anyone seeking to enter or re-enter the job market or change careers should initially consult the U.S. Department of Labor publications as well as access information on the new O*NET (www.onetcenter.org). The Department of Labor only makes this data available online (http://online.onetcenter.org). A commercial version of this system, published in book form, also is available. You should be able to find it in your local library. If not, the *O*NET Dictionary of Occupational Titles* can be ordered from Impact Publications by completing the form at the end of this book or through Impact's online bookstore: www.impactpublications.com.

However, remember that labor market statistics are for industries and occupations **as a whole**. They tell you little about the shift in employment emphasis **within the industry**, and nothing about the outlook of particular jobs for you, **the individual**. For example, employment in agriculture was projected to decline by 14 percent between 1985 and 2000, but the decline consisted of an important shift in employment emphasis within the industry: there would be 500,000 fewer self-employed workers but 150,000 more wage and salary earners in the service end of agriculture. The employment statistics also assume a steady state of economic growth with consumers having more and more disposable income to stimulate a wide variety of service and trade industries.

Therefore, be careful how you interpret and use this information in making your own job and career decisions. If, for example, you want to become a substance abuse counselor, and the data tells you there will be a 10-percent decline in this occupation during the next 10 years, this does not mean you would not find employment, as well as advance, in this field. It merely means that, on the whole, competition may be keen for these jobs, and that future advancement and mobility in this occupation may not be very good – **on the whole**. At the same time, there may be numerous job opportunities available in a declining occupational field as many individuals abandon the field for more attractive occupations. In fact, you may do much better in this declining occupation than in a growing field depending on your interests, motivations, abilities, job search savvy, and level of competition. And if the decade ahead experiences more boom-and-bust cycles, expect most of these U.S. Department of Labor statistics and projections to be invalid for the economic realities of this decade.

Use this industrial and occupational data to expand your awareness of various job and career options. By no means should you make critical education, training, and occupational choices based upon this information alone. Such choices require additional types of information about you, the individual, based upon an assessment of your interests, skills, and values. If identified and used properly, this information will help clarify exactly which jobs are best for you.

The Ex-Offender's Hopeful Job Journey

As an ex-offender trying to survive on the outside with little money, a spotted past, and an official record, you face many challenges most other job seekers take for granted. You may, for example, lack housing, transportation, appropriate clothing, a phone, Internet access, and other basic resources for conducting an effective job search. In addition, you need to disclose your criminal record – a big red flag that may quickly knock you out of the competition. In fact, compared to other groups with difficult backgrounds, employers are least likely to risk hiring an ex-offender. Maybe such discrimination is unfair in your special case, but that's just a fact of life you must deal with. After all, life in general is unfair. Don't get angry – deal with it by presenting your best self. You've got to move on.

Needing immediate employment upon release, many ex-offenders look for low-skill and low-paying jobs with employers who ask few questions about their backgrounds. Not surprisingly, these also tend to be high-turnover positions as janitors, cleaners, lawn maintenance workers, construction laborers, roofers, movers, warehouse workers, home health care workers, food preparers and servers, packers, car washers, and retail salespeople. The construction trades, manufacturing, transportation, and lodging and food industries tend to be most receptive to hiring ex-offenders. While many such positions are actually dead-end jobs, they are at least a **starting point**. They offer one of the most important ingredients in your new life – **hope**. While difficult and sometimes depressing (see our "Worst Jobs" on page 9), nonetheless, such jobs can be key steppingstones to a brighter and more rewarding future. In the end, you may discover that there was actually a **purpose** in taking such a **first job out** – it leads to a more promising second and third job out!

If you want to find a job with a good future, you may need to acquire additional education and training. Try to quickly land your first job out in order to get work experience. Demonstrate that you are an excellent worker who has been rehabilitated and who is very productive. But also keep an eye on some of the promising jobs outlined in this book. A few may become your second and third job out – ones that have a future for those who have the necessary education, training, experience, motivation, and drive to move ahead in their careers.

*   *   *

The following pages outline some of the best jobs for ex-offenders re-entering the workforce. Depending on your occupational interests, these jobs offer many opportunities for starting or advancing a career. Use these pages as a reference for exploring various job and career options. Descriptions and references to additional resources should give you basic information for further exploring the best jobs for you.

2

Transitional Employment Experiences

*"Employers want recent **proof of performance** as well as **evidence of rehabilitation** relevant to the workplace. Transitional employment experiences are excellent ways to present the character and work sides of yourself to potential employers."*

WOULDN'T IT BE GREAT if you could leave prison and jail with a piece of paper or diploma that literally certifies you as being rehabilitated and ready for productive employment? Employers would then snap you up as a very desirable future employee who poses few risks, and you could go on to achieving a very successful career.

Well, this is not going to happen, because no one wants to get into such a sticky business. To do so would create new liabilities for those in charge of certifying so-called rehabilitated ex-offenders.

Taking Initiative, Encountering Reality

Since many ex-offenders lack a stable work history, you are well advised to acquire some type of transitional employment experience while incarcerated or while participating in a work release program. In fact, employers who hire ex-offenders are more impressed with such transitional work experiences than with work experiences that took place three, five, or 10 years ago. The most recent work experiences give employers some immediate proof of performance as well as evidence of rehabilitation relevant to the workplace.

But let's also be very frank about what you are likely to encounter in the outside employment world, especially when it comes to transitional jobs. If you have a similar background to many other ex-offenders – low education level, few work skills, language and cognitive problems, anger and substance abuse issues, part of a dysfunctional street culture, and few job- or career-related goals – you'll be drawn toward very low-level, unstable, and temporary jobs that may only pay minimum wages and offer few benefits.

You'll gravitate toward **hard jobs** no one else may want, such as a day laborer, roofer, mover, or trash hauler. These are heavy lifting and hot physical jobs best suited for young and strong people who can best tolerate the demands of such jobs.

If you have higher level skills appropriate for the health care, fiber optics, and biotech industries, you may end up working in an **underground economy** with subcontractors who offer few if any benefits. Even jobs in the promising hospitality industry may be limited to back-of-the-house positions, which involve few direct contacts with customers and the public.

But you must find work and embrace it as the first of many steppingstones on a path to re-entry, recovery, and renewed career success. Since you must start somewhere, at least from the bottom you can look up and dream of a much brighter future. My advice – take that transitional job and run with it. Make the most of what may not seem to be a very interesting or worthwhile job at the time. It's **experience** you are getting. As you may eventually discover, there is a **purpose** to all of this, and it too will pass as you move toward re-entry success. Impress upon the employer that you are someone who is very special. You have the motivation, enthusiasm, drive, and skills to become a highly desirable employee. Above all, you want to start creating a **new record** of success that employers will find most attractive.

> *Take that transitional job and run with it. There is a purpose to all of this, and it too will pass.*

What Employers Really Want – Proof of Performance

Regardless of how much you believe you can do a job and become a trusted employee, employers want evidence that you can do a job well. In addition to possessing specific work skills, employers also are looking for many of these major characteristics when they hire someone new:

▪ Accurate	▪ Fair	▪ Purposeful
▪ Adaptable	▪ Focused	▪ Reliable
▪ Careful	▪ Good-natured	▪ Resourceful
▪ Competent	▪ Happy	▪ Respectful
▪ Considerate	▪ Helpful	▪ Responsible
▪ Cooperative	▪ Honest	▪ Self-motivated
▪ Dependable	▪ Intelligent	▪ Sensitive
▪ Determined	▪ Loyal	▪ Sincere
▪ Diligent	▪ Nice	▪ Skilled
▪ Discreet	▪ Open-minded	▪ Tactful
▪ Educated	▪ Patient	▪ Team player
▪ Efficient	▪ Perceptive	▪ Tenacious
▪ Empathic	▪ Precise	▪ Tolerant
▪ Energetic	▪ Predictable	▪ Trustworthy
▪ Enthusiastic	▪ Prompt	▪ Warm

What employers don't want are employees who lack initiative and who are undependable, untrustworthy, unpredictable, and make excuses for irresponsible behaviors as expressed in these attitudes:

1. No one told me.	11. I don't know how to do it.
2. I did what you said.	12. That's your problem.
3. Your directions were bad.	13. It wasn't very good.
4. It's not my fault.	14. Maybe you did it.
5. She did it.	15. I thought I wrote it down.
6. It just seemed to happen.	16. That's not my style.
7. It happens a lot.	17. He told me to do it that way.
8. What did he say?	18. I've got to go now.
9. I had a headache.	19. Where do you think it went?
10. I don't understand why.	20. We can talk about it later.

Above all, employers who hire ex-offenders want **evidence of rehabilitation and proof of performance** – that you have the right skills, including attitudes and inter- personal behaviors, to get the job done. Rather than rely solely on impressive but self- serving commentary about yourself during a job interview (*"I'm very dependable and can be trusted"*), prospective employers want to look at your most recent job performance record. In other words, when faced with the possibility of hiring an ex-offender, employers say to themselves the following cautionary words:

> *"Don't just tell me about yourself – show me the evidence that backs up your claims of performance and rehabilitation. Do you have some type of certification that will convince me that I'm making a wise hiring decision, or is this a lot of persuasive talk to convince me to hire you despite my reservations to the contrary?"*

If you have no such evidence, then you become a very risky hire. An employer will have to hire you on the basis of **faith** – a gut feeling that you might over time become a good employee.

The evidence that you offer employers can come in several forms. You might, for example, assemble a **character and performance portfolio**, which includes letters of recommendation from people who you've worked with and know you well. While these letters are obviously self-serving and very selective, nonetheless, they provide some evidence about your skills and character. If you do graphic, artistic, or other types of show- and-tell work, your portfolio might also include samples of your work.

Assuming that you will be assembling a character and performance portfolio to present to employers, complete the following exercise:

What evidence can you give to employers as proof of rehabilitation and job performance?

1. My proof of rehabilitation: _____

_____

_____

_____

_____

_____

_____

_____

2. My proof of job performance: _____

_____

_____

_____

_____

_____

_____

If you have difficulty completing this exercise, chances are you lack sufficient experience to provide such evidence and proof. So what are you planning to do to fill in this important gap in your life? What action can you take now to ensure that you'll be able to present evidence of your rehabilitation and proof of your work-related performance?

Importance of Transitional Work Experiences

Employers who hire ex-offenders report the importance of recent transitional work experiences in their hiring decision. While they can routinely scrutinize an application and resume, listen to a candidate's answers to interview questions, and check out references in the process of making judgments about the suitability or "fit" of a candidate, what really impresses them the most is the evidence provided in recent transition work experiences. Such experiences are the closest ex-offenders can get to being **certified** as trustworthy and competent. Pre-incarceration work experiences have less credibility than incarceration and half-way house experiences simply because these latter factor in prison and post-prison experiences – extremely important and presumably life-changing experiences that are a much sounder basis for making hiring decisions than pre-incarceration experiences.

Creating Your New Record

Depending on where you serve time, many prisons, jails, and detention centers offer important transitional work experiences in the form of half-way houses, job readiness training, and transitional jobs programs, which are often contracted out to a variety of community-based nonprofit organizations. As part of their transition to communities, many ex-offenders are offered subsidized job training and wage-paid temporary work with wrap-around supports and services. These work experiences may be with government agencies, nonprofit organizations, or local businesses, especially in the construction, manufacturing, food preparation, hospitality, printing, transportation, warehousing, and distribution industries. Some jobs may be more seasonal and unpredictable, such as landscaping, construction, and transportation/moving. Many ex-offenders may find work with local governments as uniformed street sweepers and trash haulers.

Your prison, jail, or detention center may partner with community groups that offer transitional job programs for youth, the homeless, welfare recipients, and ex-offenders. In addition to half-way houses, one of the major groups offering transitional job programs is Goodwill Industries. Ex-offenders participating in such programs as part of their probation may receive two weeks of job readiness training followed by 10 weeks of paid work experience. Once they complete the program, they are ostensibly ready to enter the world of unsubsidized employment. Most important of all, they will have created a recent employment training and work **record** that employers may view as a form of certification relating to rehabilitation and work-place behavior. They should be able to consult with program managers who can give them feedback on the candidate's suitability for a new workplace.

> *You want to communicate to employers a recent **work record** – not your prison record or rap sheet.*

It would be unfair to imply that all is well with transitional employment programs. They have their own set of issues that is often troubling for everyone involved. Many programs, for example, encounter difficulties with employers who may take advantage of tax credits by only offering temporary employment as well as failing to offer decent wages and benefits. Many transitional jobs are low-paying entry-level jobs that may not have much of a future beyond the temporary half-way house experience. Nonetheless, one should view these jobs as a new starting point – a place to get some direct work experience however limiting it may be.

Other programs may lack strong support services for helping ex-offenders transition to full-time unsubsidized employment. Many ex-offenders are not mentally ready for the ups and downs attendant with looking for employment, encountering rejections, and ending up unemployed or underemployed. In some communities ex-offenders may be competing with illegal immigrants who will work for very low wages and no benefits and with no complaints. And there are always the issues of housing, transportation, and clothing that can complicate the employability of ex-offenders. Indeed, keeping that job can be difficult!

It's this **transitional employment record** you want to create and communicate to employers – not your other record or rap sheet. Your **new record** will go a long way to off-setting the many red flags that may scream from your criminal record.

Whatever you do, try to get transitional employment experience prior to going out into the free world with your criminal record. Trust me on this one – this new record may well become your ticket to re-entry success, especially if you take the transitional work experience very seriously, treating it as a major steppingstone to a brighter future!

Best Approaches for Ex-Offenders

Counselors and program managers who work in transitional employment programs will tell you the inside secrets of what separates the best participants from all the others. **First,** they look at the employers and will tell you what they really hate – high **turnover** of personnel. It's one of their biggest headaches, and ex-offenders often contribute to the problem. Employee turnover is very costly to employers who must recruit and train new employees. They want to hire people who are relatively talented and who know what they want to do – not just anyone who needs a job for wages and benefits. They are not looking for beggars – only bright-eyed, enthusiastic, and loyal workers.

Second, ex-offenders who work the best with employers **know their interests and skills** and communicate them through **enthusiasm and drive**. They let employers know that they have **goals** and say so by indicating what they really want to do today, tomorrow, next week, next month, next year, or five years from now. If, for example, an individual is being interviewed for a warehouse position, he might indicate to the interviewer that what he eventually wants to do – maybe next year – is to drive the big yellow forklift that's parked near the bay door. This type of conversation indicates the prospective employee probably plans to stay around for a while, especially since he wants to move up in the company to become a forklift driver.

> *Employee turnover is one of the biggest headaches, and ex-offenders often contribute to the problem.*

The problem is this: If you don't know where you want to go, you'll probably end up somewhere after learning where you don't want to go! As noted motivation guru Earl Nightingale observes,

> *"People with goals succeed because they know where they are going. It's as simple as that."*

This simple notion of **goal-driven success** is perhaps best stated in reverse logic:

> *If you don't know where you're going, you're impulsive, and you're not in control, chances are you'll end up somewhere unintended, such as where you are today! That's not good.*

Not surprisingly, goal-oriented people also make good impressions on potential employers.

Third, the most successful ex-offenders break out of the temporary job mode and focus on permanent jobs with a promising future. They have immediate income needs, but they understand their future depends on the smart decisions they make today and tomorrow.

Fourth, the best employees have the **right attitude and motivation** to succeed in the workplace. They communicate in complete sentences and use proper grammar – not low-class street language that marks them as unreformed ex-offenders who still hang around with the wrong crowd. The best employees incorporate many of the positive workplace characteristics we discussed on page 14. Above all, they communicate well with others.

Fifth, the best employees have a **new mindset** that focuses on the value of hard work and performance. It's not about them – it's about fellow workers, the employer, customers, and clients. They become other-directed by constantly asking themselves what they can do to be more helpful to others rather than be self-centered and concerned with how to cut corners and take advantage of others and the workplace for their own personal satisfaction. Whatever you do, learn the value and power of this new mindset. It will serve you well throughout what is hopefully a very long, purposeful, productive, and happy life!

3

Job Restrictions Affecting Ex-Offenders

"Don't ever think you're just a poor victim of a so-called 'system' that discriminates against ex-offenders who served their time and should now be on an even playing field. That's simply delusional. It's not how the world works. In many respects, being incarcerated is a life sentence. Barriers to your employment come from both within you and outside you. You need to understand how both may work against you, and what you need to do to tackle those barriers that are within your power to overcome."

FOR PURPOSES OF DISCUSSION, let's assume that most ex-offenders want to get out and stay out for good. Despite their past mistakes, bad luck, and all the craziness that goes on in prisons and jails, they still want to change their lives for the better. Above all, they want to forget the past and live a new life complete with a decent job, good housing, a terrific family, supportive friends, and lots of "stuff."

Perhaps this is not a realistic assumption, especially when you look around at all the weird body art that someday will be staring at potential employers who will say *"Tell me about yourself"* and then ask *"Why should I hire you?"* Nonetheless, this is a good working assumption, because it gives us all hope for a brighter future. And **hope** is what motivates many ex-offenders to keep on moving toward a better place in life.

I've Fallen Down and . . .

Ex-offenders really don't want to talk, much less tell the whole ugly truth, about the red flags in their background. They know about the importance of **disclosure**, but they know telling the truth is often a set-up for **rejection**. When asked by a potential employer if they have ever been convicted of a crime, they may hesitate, trying to decide whether to tell the whole truth, parse the truth, or just lie-and-pray their rap sheet away, hoping it won't come back to bite them in the rear end. They want to start fresh without that "Big Brother" computerized record following them everywhere they go. It's tough knowing what best to do when employers pop that killer question.

Not surprisingly, there's no place to hide these days. "Big Brother" does a real good job keeping an eye on your record for employers, landlords, and others who bother to do a little checking on your background. And it keeps getting better at doing that job.

Therefore, since you're unlikely to beat the system, it's best to tell the **truth**, especially sharing a compelling story about your **rehabilitation**. If you're a reservoir for lots of scary body art and decorative body piercings, it's probably a good idea to consider some painful removals. Done at one time as an expression of selfish freedom, your body art and realignments probably only look good to you and a few weird buddies. They don't impress employers in a positive way.

Asking for a second chance at freedom is a lot to ask for, but it's something many ex-offenders manage to do and with positive results. Indeed, this revised take on the old adage about falling down and getting up is very appropriate for ex-offenders:

> It's not how far, hard, or often you've fallen that's important. What's really important is how well you get up, dust yourself off, and move on toward achieving dreams that relate to your purpose and legacy in life. If you're unwilling to get up and try your best to move ahead toward a meaningful goal, you'll probably be in serious trouble for the rest of your life! Some day you simply won't be able to get up. Worst of all, no one will want to extend you another helping hand.

Perhaps you've fallen many times. Now it's time to get up, dust yourself off, and start moving in the right direction for good. If others can do it, why can't you? Each day take a good look at yourself. Tell that person exactly what he or she needs to do to stay up and keep moving ahead. If you have a copy of *The Ex-Offender's Re-Entry Success Guide*, complete its many exercises that will help propel you to re-entry success.

Barriers to Employment From Within Yourself

Let's look at the challenging profile of ex-offenders as a statistical group, which many employers know all too well:

- 70 percent are high school dropouts
- 50 percent are functionally illiterate
- 2-3 percent have AIDS or are HIV positive
- 18 percent have hepatitis C
- 15-18 percent have some type of emotional disorder

For employers, this means that ex-offenders as a whole are **risky business**, because they come to the workplace with these potential work-related problems:

- Limited education and cognitive skills (difficult to train, makes mistakes)
- Little work experience (requires lots of training, workplace adjustments)
- Unstable work history (potential job-hopper, disloyal)
- Limited workplace skills (may not show up on time, undependable)
- Few on-the-job skills (problems operating equipment, communicating)
- Many physical and mental health issues (frequent absences, endangers others)
- Substance abuse and addictive behaviors (negatively affects work output)
- Anger and rage issues (threatens boss, fellow workers, customers)
- A rap sheet with a seemingly predictable negative pattern of behavior

While some of these problems are created by several undiagnosed and untreated mental health issues, such as ADD (Attention Deficit Disorder), ADHD (Attention Deficit and Hyperactivity Disorder), bipolarism, depression, and borderline personality disorders, others are simply problems related to individual **choice and judgment**. In fact, the act of dropping out of high school – an extremely common first step toward entering the criminal justice system – is often related to reading, learning, and bullying problems precipitated by undiagnosed ADD or ADHD. As adults with ADHD, they have difficulty concentrating, following instructions, and getting and staying organized. Ex-offenders with ADHD make poor initial impressions on employers who are looking for people who listen and appear interested in the job – all nonverbal clues adults with ADHD have difficulty managing for very long.

Studies show that employers would much prefer hiring a poor and relatively unskilled welfare recipient than an ostensibly risky ex-offender who is likely to become another recidivism statistic. Frankly, many employers view ex-offenders as losers or the dregs of society. They are often seen as human trash that gets recycled every three years when they predictably re-offend and get locked up again. While forgiveness and mercy are fine, and giving someone a second change is commendable, who wants to take such risks in the face of these disappointing recidivism statistics?

Most employers are businesses – not social experiments. They have employees and a bottom line to protect. You must **understand** – not be embittered by – the choices facing employers who may want to give you a second chance but still can't bring themselves to take the risks. In fact, while Title VII of the Civil Rights Act prohibits discriminating in employment decisions (hiring, firing, promoting) based solely on one's conviction record, at the same time, it's legal for employers to refuse to hire an ex-offender if it can be shown there is a "business necessity" in not hiring someone with a conviction record.

> *Most employers are businesses – not social experiments. They have employees and a bottom line to protect. You must first understand where they are coming from.*

Regardless of attempts by state and local governments to **incentivize** the hiring of ex-offenders with special tax credits and bonding arrangements, most employers are still reluctant to take on what they see as the unnecessary **liability** that may come with hiring ex-offenders. In fact, studies show that when employers are sued by employees for endangering the workplace by employing an ex-offender who injured fellow workers, the employees usually win. The average judgment against the employer has been $1.6 million – a cost most employers are unwilling to bear through a risky hire. Indeed, it would be stupid to employ an ex-offender unless that ex-offender could be certified by the state as being rehabilitated – something many states have talked about doing but thus far have been unwilling to do. In the meantime, employers aren't dumb – hiring an ex-offender is a risky crap-shoot. Employers tend to be very conservative gamblers – only play with very good odds.

Take another look at the above list of "facts" about ex-offenders as a whole. Most of these facts are barriers to employment, which are largely the **responsibility** of the ex-offender. In other words, they did these things to themselves through their many short-sighted **choices**. For example, they chose to drop out of high school. They chose to get involved with alcohol and drugs. The chose a troubled crowd to hang around with. They chose to commit a crime. These are all things they can **change**, but only if they are sufficiently **motivated** to make the changes. For example, they can get a GED, stop substance abuse, control their anger, acquire job skills, and get more work experience. They can reduce these barriers significantly by taking the right actions to improve themselves. In other words, they have to **take responsibility and ownership** for their own future by finding a job that's right for them. No one else can or will do this for them.

External Barriers to Employment

On the other hand, many employment barriers are beyond the control of ex-offenders. Most are in the hands of the legal system that mandates what an ex-offender can and can't do after leaving prison or jail. Some are laws passed by federal, state, and local representatives while others are bureaucratic and/or policy interpretations made by federal, state, and local agencies. The overall effect of such actions is to create a special class of restrictive employment for ex-offenders.

Federal Restrictions

The first thing you need to know about such external barriers to employment are the differences in federal, state, and local laws affecting the employability of ex-offenders. While Title VII of the Civil Rights Act prohibits discrimination based on criminal history, nonetheless, several federal laws also restrict ex-offenders from entering certain types of occupations:

- **Banking/commodities/securities:** Anyone convicted of dishonesty, breach of trust, or money laundering is disqualified from working for banking and related institutions insured by the Federal Deposit Insurance Corporation (FDIC). However, there are exceptions to this blanket prohibition. The FDIC, for example, can grant waivers for certain types of convictions. Unknown to some financial institutions, they can submit a waiver request to the FDIC on behalf of the job applicant. For more information on this prohibition, visit this relevant website: http://www.fdic.gov/regulations/laws/rules/5000-1300.html.

- **Insurance:** Certain classes of felons are prohibited from working in the insurance industry, unless they receive permission from insurance regulatory officials.

- **Unions:** Certain classes of felons (robbery, bribery, drug violations, murder) are prohibited for at least 13 years from holding positions in unions or other organizations that manage employee benefit plans. This restriction also applies to serving as a union officer or director of a union governing board.

- **Health care:** Any health care service receiving Medicare payments is prohibited from hiring ex-offenders convicted for certain crimes. Many ex-offenders also are prohibited from working in the generic drug industry.

- **Child care:** Federal law requires criminal background checks for anyone working in the child care industries. To facilitate criminal background checks, the Federal Child Protection Act authorizes states to do mandatory or voluntary fingerprinting of individuals intending to work in this field.

- **Transportation of prisoners:** Federal regulations prohibit individuals with a felony conviction or domestic violence conviction from being employed with a company providing prisoner transportation. Such employees are required to undergo criminal background checks and pre-employment drug testing.

- **Defense contractors/subcontractors:** Five-year prohibition for those with fraud or felony conviction.

- **Aviation:** FAA regulations restrict ex-offenders from working in many airport jobs that give them access to airplanes and affect airline security.

- **Military, Job Corps, or AmeriCorps:** Felons are prohibited from becoming members of these groups. However, the military (especially the Army) is generous in issuing "moral waivers," which allow them to recruit ex-offenders, including felons – controversial exceptions that have allowed the military to reach its recruitment goals in recent years (over 100,000 moral waivers issued between 2003 and 2006).

Certain occupations requiring federal licenses may be closed to ex-offenders: custom broker's license, export license, locomotive engineer's license, merchant marine license.

State and Local Restrictions

But most employment restrictions on ex-offenders are found at the state and local levels. Indeed, employment prohibitions vary from state to state. Depending on the state to which you are paroled, you will be restricted from working in particular jobs. In fact, the restrictions tend to relate to:

- particular occupations
- places of work

For example, in many states you may be prohibited from working as a barber (an occupation) – a vocational skill taught in many prisons. At the same time, you may be barred from working in a day care center (a place).

Before deciding on what job you wish to pursue and where, you need to understand the laws, rules, and regulations restricting and governing your employment in the particular state or locality you may wish to live in after release. At the same time, you need to understand any exceptions to the rules. Restrictions tend to relate to certain types or classes of convictions, such as felonies, violent crimes, or robbery. In some cases "waivers" can be issued if someone appears to be rehabilitated or the nature of the crime or the time that has passed was such that the person longer appears to pose a potential public safety issue. Therefore, it is incumbent upon **you** to acquire such information on job restrictions.

Take, for example, working in correctional settings. Most states permit ex-offenders who have been convicted of nonviolent crimes to apply for certain jobs in prisons and jails. A study of state department of corrections (DOCs) in 2002 conducted by the National Institute of Corrections found that 81 percent of DOCs had formal policies on hiring ex-offenders. Thirty-six DOCs permanently barred people convicted of certain crimes from correctional employment. Thirty-one DOCs prohibited employment to anyone convicted of any felony. Fourteen DOCs specified bans on correctional officer and security positions or any position requiring the possession of firearms. Some DOCs prohibited hiring in cases of domestic violence convictions; misdemeanor drug offices; class A misdemeanors; misdemeanors involving personal injury, perjury, or moral turpitude; and misdemeanors involving jail time. Many DOCs also put time-limited restrictions on hiring people with criminal convictions, which could range from 1 to 15 years. Here are some examples of these time limits in reference to the type of offense committed:

Time Required	Offense Type
1 year from:	• Misdemeanor conviction, for peace officer positions (California • Driving offenses (Ohio, Vermont) • Sentence served in facility in which employment sought (Tennessee) • Marijuana use/experimentation (Alaska, Arizona)
2 years from:	• Disposition of single misdemeanor offense (Connecticut) • DUI conviction, or marijuana misdemeanor, i.e., use (Utah)
3 years from:	• Felony conviction for non-custody position (Missouri) • Three or more Class A misdemeanors (i.e., maximum of two misdemeanors within 3 years) • Misdemeanor convictions (Nebraska, North Carolina) • Conviction of any kind (Rhode Island) • Misdemeanor involving property (Vermont) • Misdemeanor involving vehicular negligence (Vermont)
4 years from:	• Non-substance-abuse related misdemeanor conviction (Utah)
5 years from:	• Hard drug use conviction (Utah) • Felony conviction involving property, felony vehicular negligence, or misdemeanor conviction involving violence against a person (Vermont) • Completion of felony sentence, including any form of supervision (Wyoming, Nebraska, Oregon) • Conviction, if pardon granted (Canada) • Class A or B misdemeanor conviction (Texas) • Drug offenses other than marijuana (Arizona)
7 years from:	• Any conviction (Guam) • Experimentation with drugs other than marijuana (Arizona) • Completion of sentence for multiple misdemeanor incarcerations (Connecticut)
10 years from:	• Felony conviction (North Carolina, South Carolina) • Possession or use of drugs other than marijuana (Alaska)
15 years from:	• Felony conviction, for specified positions (Texas)

The following employment restrictions affect ex-offenders in many states where they cannot become:

- Teachers – if convicted of violent crimes or crimes against children
- Police or correctional officers – if convicted of a felony
- Public office holder – if convicted of a felony
- Private investigator and/or detective
- Security guard
- Security alarm installer
- Caregivers (depends on offense/conviction)

What You Need to Do

In preparation for finding a job appropriate for your background, you need to do two things as soon as possible:

1. **Review your RAP Sheet.** This is your Record of Arrest and Prosecution (RAP). It's your history of arrests based upon your fingerprints. Here's how it works. Every time you are fingerprinted by a law enforcement agency, a record of your arrest, along with its final disposition, goes to a central repository in that state. If you've committed crimes in more than one state, your current state rap sheet may indicate that a record also is on file with the Interstate Identification Index, a repository maintained by the Federal Bureau of Investigation (FBI).

   It's very important that you examine your rap sheets at both the federal and state levels in order to (1) understand what employers are likely to access when they do a background check (you need to deal with the whole truth that's represented on your rap sheets!), (2) understand whether or not any of your arrests and convictions will bar you from certain federal, state, and local jobs, and (3) check on the accuracy of your rap sheet (sometimes there are mistakes that need to be corrected).

   For information on how to get a copy of your state rap sheet, check out the relevant state requirements at http://www.hirenetwork.org/resource.html. You'll need to do a request under the Freedom of Information Act to get a copy of your FBI rap sheet. You can do this by sending a letter, under your signature, along with your name, date and place of birth, a full set of fingerprints (you can get fingerprint cards through your local police precinct or a fingerprint service), and a certified check or money order for $18.00 to:

   U.S. Department of Justice
   Federal Bureau of Investigation Information Services Division
   ATTN: SCU, Mod. D-2
   1000 Custer Hollow Road
   Clarksburg, WV 26306

2. **Explore useful state resources:** You should also explore the many state-by-state resources available through the National H.I.R.E. Network – www.hirenet work.org/resource.html. This organization closely monitors developments at the state level for ex-offenders. Take, for example, this entry for the state of Alabama:

ALABAMA

Alabama Department of Labor
P.O. Box 303500
Montgomery, AL 36130
334-242-3460
334-240-3417 fax

Information about State Department of Labor resources may be of interest to:
- potential employers looking for incentives to hire individuals with criminal histories;
- service providers and individuals with criminal histories who are looking for assistance in finding employment; and
- researchers and policy makers looking at current programs to ascertain what programs are effective and serve their intended purpose.

A. Federal Bonding Program
The Federal Bonding Program provides fidelity bonding insurance coverage to individuals with criminal histories and other high-risk job applicants who are qualified, but fail to get jobs because regular commercial bonding is denied due to their backgrounds.

CONTACT:
Federal Bonding Program
Alabama State Employment Service
Industrial Relations Building, Room 246
649 Monroe Street
Montgomery, AL 36131
334-242-8039
334-242-8585 fax

B. Tax Credits

The Work Opportunity Tax Credit (WOTC) is a federal tax credit to reduce the federal tax liability of private for profit employers to be used as an incentive for employers to hire individuals from eight different targeted groups: TANF recipients, veterans, ex-felons, high risk youth, summer youth, Food Stamp recipients, SSI recipients, and vocational rehabilitation referrals.

CONTACT:
Robert E. Langley
Employment Service Division
Alabama Department of Industrial Relations
Finance Department
649 Monroe Street
Montgomery, AL 36131
334-242-8303
334-242-8299 fax
E-mail: EEO@dir.alabama.gov
Website: http://dir.alabama.gov/business/

C. Unemployment Insurance Office

Unemployment compensation is a social insurance program designed to provide benefits to most individuals out of work, generally through no fault of their own, for periods between jobs. In order to be eligible for benefits, jobless workers must demonstrate that they have worked, usually measured by amount of wages and/or weeks of work, and must be able and available for work.

The unemployment compensation program is based upon federal law, but administered by states under state law.

CONTACT:
Alabama Department of Industrial Relations
649 Monroe Street
Montgomery, AL 36131
334-242-8025
334-242-8021 fax
E-mail: uc@dir.alabama.gov
Website: http://dir.alabama.gov/uc

II. Criminal Record Repository

This is the agency individuals may contact to obtain a copy of their state rap sheet and learn about the process of sealing, expunging, or cleaning it up. The criminal record repository can also tell the individual who else is legally entitled to have access to his or her record.

An individual or employer must call or write the Bureau of Investigations to request a release form. The release form must be signed by the individual whose record is being requested along with a $25 fee. Searches for a criminal record can be done based on a name or a set of fingerprints. Each procedure costs $25.

CONTACT:
Alabama Department of Public Safety
Bureau of Investigations
301 South River Street
P.O. Box 1511
Montgomery, AL 36104
334-353-1100

III. State Attorney General

Employers and service providers may obtain information from the state attorney general regarding occupational bars, the licensing of individuals with criminal records in certain jobs, and whether the state has laws that limit what employers may ask job applicants or protections against employment discrimination based on a criminal record.

CONTACT:
Office of the Attorney General
11 South Union Street
Montgomery, AL 36130
334-242-7300
Website: www.ago.state.al.us

IV. State Department of Corrections

CONTACT:
Alabama Department of Corrections
301 South Ripley Street
P.O. Box 301501
Montgomery, AL 36130-1501
334-353-3883
E-mail: pio@doc.state.al.us
Website: www.doc.state.al.us

V. State Department of Parole/Probation

The Alabama Board of Pardons and Paroles provides adult probation and parole services in Alabama.

CONTACT:
Alabama Board of Pardons and Paroles
301 South Ripley Street
P.O. Box 301501
Montgomery, AL 36130-2405
334-242-8700
E-mail:
  questions4pardonsandparoles@alabpp.gov
Website: www.paroles.state.al.us

VI. Legal Assistance

Free or low-cost legal resources, both in civil and criminal law, are helpful to individuals with criminal histories in learning about relevant state laws governing the expungement or sealing of criminal histories or addressing other legal issues resulting from having a criminal history.

A. State Public Defender

There is no state Public Defender office in Alabama. Defense attorneys are appointed by judges when necessary to provide legal counsel for indigent clients.

B. Legal Services

Alabama's legal services programs are independent, non-profit organizations that provide qualifying low-income families with legal assistance in civil matters.

CONTACT:
Legal Services Corporation of Alabama, Inc.
600 Bell Building
Suite 1200
207 Montgomery Street
Montgomery, AL 36104
334-832-4570
334-241-8683 fax
Website: www.alabamalegalservices.org

C. State Bar Association

CONTACT:
Alabama State Bar
415 Dexter Avenue
Montgomery, AL 36104
334-269-1515
334-261-6310 fax
Website: www.alabar.org

Explore the many state-by-state resources available through the National H.I.R.E. Network – www.hirenetwork. org/resource.html. This organization closely monitors developments at the state level for ex-offenders.

VII. Local Service Providers

Community agencies are available to assist individuals with criminal records find employment. This information will inform individuals with criminal records about government agencies and community-based organizations that assist with employment, education or vocational training. Researchers and policy makers may find this information useful in identifying agencies and service providers in order to evaluate the effectiveness of these programs.

One-Stop Center

The One-Stop Center is also known as the Alabama Department of Industrial Relations local office.

CONTACT:
Employment Services Division
Alabama Department of Industrial Relations
649 Monroe Street
Montgomery, AL 36131
Website: http://dir.alabama.gov

Aid to Inmate Mothers (AIM)

Aid to Inmate Mothers provides services to promote the successful reintegration of women with criminal records by helping them become gainfully employed, obtain clothing, and secure housing.

CONTACT:
Aid to Inmate Mothers
P.O. Box 986
Montgomery, AL 36101
800-679-0246 or 334-262-2245
Website: www.inmatemoms.org

Re-Entry Ministries, Inc.

Re-Entry Ministries, Inc. works with persons with criminal records and offers limited services to prisoners. Programs include support groups for people with criminal records and families of prisoners, church services, job assistance, and Alcoholics Anonymous meetings.

CONTACT:
Re-Entry Ministries, Inc.
2224 3rd Avenue North
Birmingham, AL 35210
205-320-2101

Renascence, Inc.

Renascence, Inc. assists in the transition of non-violent, male ex-offenders from prison to steady employment and responsible living. Renascence provides housing, appropriate monitoring, interpersonal and life skills programs, recovery support groups, as well as access to employment, health, and educational services / opportunities.

CONTACT:
Renascence, Inc.
215 Clayton Street
Montgomery, AL 36104
334-832-1402
E-mail: renascence@bellsouth.net

What Employers Know About Your Record

It's true – there's no place in America to hide these days. If you can move abroad to some Third World country, perhaps you can start all over again. But, then, you'll probably have difficulty getting a passport and visas (felons have international travel restrictions, and few countries issue visas to such ex-offenders). And escaping to another country may not be such a great idea after all, especially after encountering cultural shock and discovering there's not much you can do there to make a decent living. Finding an "offshore" job to start a new life is often a fantasy, not a reality. Even if you manage to get into another country, the authorities may quickly discover your record and deport you as an undesirable. Nonetheless, www.escapeartist.com may give you some useful ideas.

If you think you can make your record go away by lying or parsing the truth, think again. In today's high-tech society, employers have a high probability of uncovering the **truth about you**. However, small companies (under 50 employees) that lack their own human resources departments may not do a very good job of screening candidates with criminal backgrounds. As a result, many ex-offenders seek out such "few questions asked" companies because they know these places may allow them to get in under the radar.

Employers have three sources of information for uncovering your criminal record:

1. **Information you provide employers on applications and in interviews:** Most states permit employers to ask applicants about their criminal history. Ten states (California, Connecticut, Hawaii, Michigan, Montana, New York, Ohio, Rhode Island, Utah, Wisconsin) prohibit questions about **arrests**. All states permit employers to ask questions about **convictions**. In other words, there is a legal difference between these two questions: *"Have you ever been arrested?"* versus *"Have you ever been convicted of a crime?"* You are well advised to tell the truth since the truth will most likely come out from other information sources available to the employer.

2. **Information employers gather from background checks:** Most employers can inexpensively conduct background checks on applicants. For less than $75.00, they can quickly access through several private firms – many operating via the Internet – information on your criminal, employment, and credit history.

3. **Information employers gather from your references:** Most employers check references. However, references often provide little useful information other than verify employment dates. But some are very forthcoming when faced with these two frequently asked reference questions?

   "Is there anything in this candidate's background that might disqualify him or her for this position?"

   "Knowing what you do about this person, would you hire him or her again?"

Again, before setting your sights on particular jobs or careers you might love to pursue, be sure you fully understand the **limitations** you may face given federal, state, and local laws prohibiting or restricting ex-offenders from working in particular jobs. If you face restrictions, you need to know whether you are eligible for **waivers**. And above all, tell the truth about **you**. Develop a compelling story about your rehabilitation **and** performance!

4

Construction Trades and Related Jobs

"The construction trades are relatively open to ex-offenders. While many day laborer jobs attract ex-offenders, these are primarily stop-gap jobs without a promising future. Some of the best construction jobs involve on-the-job training, apprenticeships, and advancement to positions of responsibility, including starting a construction trade business."

THE CONSTRUCTION TRADES offer numerous job opportunities for people re-entering the workforce, changing careers, or jump-starting their lives. Indeed, ex-offenders disproportionately are drawn to many entry-level, high-turnover construction positions, especially construction laborer jobs. These jobs appeal to people without a four-year degree, those with unstable work histories, people with mental health (bipolarism, depression, personality, addiction, anger) and learning disability (ADD and ADHD) issues, small-time owner/operators, and those seeking temporary or part-time work. Since many of these jobs require basic education skills, on-the-job training, and/or apprenticeships, these jobs can become important steppingstones to more stable and professional jobs as well as to owning one's own construction trade business. Just getting one of these jobs with an eye toward enhancing your skills can be a great way to jump-start your life on the outside. Let's look at some important options for doing so.

Promising Opportunities, Unstable Future

Ex-offenders re-entering growing communities often quickly find jobs in the construction trades. Many start at the very bottom in minimum-wage and relatively unskilled positions where they must demonstrate their ability to show up on time, be dependable, follow orders, and avoid making costly mistakes. Not surprisingly, such laborers also discover they are working next to individuals with similar interests, skills, and backgrounds – people with spotted pasts – as well as those who work in the underground economy, especially undocumented Hispanic-speaking immigrants.

However, there is a certain boom/bust quality to many construction and related jobs that is not as prevalent elsewhere in the job market. When the economy is hot and new commercial and residential construction is booming, many construction jobs will be in high demand. These jobs disproportionately attract young people with a high school education or less, undocumented immigrants, job-hoppers, day laborers, and ex-offenders. When the economy softens, which it dramatically did for the construction trades in 2007-2008, many high-demand construction jobs disappear and companies may go out of business. Unemployment will be high among relatively unskilled construction workers who don't know what else to do with their lives given their limited interests, skills, and once comfortable incomes.

Wages, benefits, and work hours for construction jobs can vary greatly depending on the projects, weather conditions, and labor-management relationships. In general, most people working in construction only get paid when they work. If, for example, you expect to get wages for a 40-hour week (at $15.00 an hour that would come to $600.00 for the week) but weather conditions knock out 20 hours for the week, you'll only get paid for the actual 20 hours you work ($300.00). You'll also need to factor in the costs of transportation (getting to and from work sites) and benefits, such as health insurance, that may be limited with many construction jobs. In this sense, construction jobs often become temporary or part-time jobs. Benefits may be severely limited as employers try to get by with paying only basic hourly wages.

Turnover Occupations

The construction trades have always been cyclical occupational fields. When economic times are good, individuals in these fields have plenty of work, and their skills command top dollar. However, during recessions many of these workers have difficulty finding full-time employment, and some leave their trade for other types of employment. In fact, it may be a good idea to view many construction jobs as temporary stop-gap positions that hopefully will lead to other more stable and rewarding employment in the future. Many people have a tough time developing a stable career in construction given the volatility of the work, which is tied to the state of local economies.

Working in the construction trades often involves hard work, uncomfortable working conditions, stressful projects, and unpredictable employment. Many people drop out of these trades because of unhappy experiences. Given the constant turnover of construction workers, opportunities regularly open for skilled and enterprising workers.

Recession-Proof Trades

But if you are very skilled and enjoy this type of work, you'll find excellent opportunities in the construction and related trades. Indeed, you may be pleasantly surprised how well you can do in these jobs, especially ones that require specialty skills and are relatively recession-proof. After all, construction, repairing, and remodeling continue even during bad economic times. The skills of electricians, plumbers, and heating and air-conditioning specialists – three very well paid trades (some make six-figure incomes) – are always in demand, more so than carpenters and heavy machine operators. In fact, electricity, plumbing, heating, and air conditioning are constants in everyone's life. These are critical residential and commercial systems that must be maintained and repaired. Indeed, when you consider jobs and careers in the

> *You may want to focus on trades that are relatively recession proof, especially ones that lead to long-term and stable careers.*

construction trades, you may want to focus on those that are relatively recession proof. Such trades can lead to very rewarding long-term careers, including owning your own electrical, plumbing, or HVAC business.

Many people without a four-year degree enter these trades because doing so is based more on interests, skills, and on-the-job training than on education requirements. Many individuals with or without a high school diploma initially break into the building and construction trades through **apprenticeship programs**, where they acquire the necessary skills and experience to advance into their respective trades. Many apprenticeships are sponsored by unions.

Useful Online Resources

Individuals interested in job and career opportunities in the construction and related trades should explore the following websites:

- **Construction Jobs**   www.constructionjobs.com
- **Construction Job Store**   www.constructionjobstore.com
- **Architect Jobs**   www.architectjobs.com
- **Carpenter Jobs**   www.carpenterjobs.com
- **ConstructionGigs.com**   www.constructiongigs.com
- **Construction Manager Jobs**   www.constructionmanagerjob.com
- **Electrician Jobs**   www.electricianjobs.com
- **Engineering Employment**   www.engineeremployment.com
- **Estimator Jobs**   www.estimatorjobs.com
- **iHireConstruction**   www.ihireconstruction.com
- **New Home Sales Jobs**   www.newhomesalesjobs.com
- **PlumberJobs**   www.plumberjobs.com
- **Project Manager Jobs**   www.projectmanagerjobs.com
- **Trade Jobs Online**   www.tradejobsonline.com

Brickmasons, Blockmasons, and Stonemasons

- ⇨ **Annual Earnings:** $42,972
- ⇨ **Education/Training:** Experience, vocational education, and apprenticeships
- ⇨ **Outlook:** Very good

Employment Outlook: Employment opportunities for brickmasons, blockmasons, and stonemasons are expected to be very good in the decade ahead, especially for those with restoration skills. Many openings will result from the need to replace workers who retire, transfer to other occupations, or leave these trades for other reasons. There may be fewer applicants than needed because many potential workers prefer to work under less strenuous, more comfortable conditions. Employment in these trades is expected to increase about as fast as the average for all occupations as population and business growth create a need for new houses, industrial facilities, schools, hospitals, offices, and other structures. Employment of brickmasons, blockmasons, and stonemasons, like that of many other construction workers, is sensitive to changes in the economy. When the level of construction activity falls, workers in these trades can experience periods of unemployment.

Nature of Work: Brickmasons, blockmasons, and stonemasons work in closely related trades creating attractive, durable surfaces, and structures. The work varies in complexity, from laying a simple masonry walkway to installing an ornate exterior on a high-rise building. Brickmasons and blockmasons – who often are called simply **bricklayers** – build and repair walls, floors, partitions, fireplaces, chimneys, and other structures with bricks, precast masonry panels, concrete block, and other masonry materials. Some brickmasons specialize in installing firebrick linings in industrial furnaces. Stonemasons build stone walls, as well as set stone exteriors and floors. They work with two types of stone – natural cut stone, such as marble, granite, and limestone, and artificial stone made from concrete, marble chips, or other masonry materials. Stonemasons usually work on nonresidential structures, such as houses of worship, hotels, and office buildings.

Working Conditions: Brickmasons, blockmasons, and stonemasons usually work outdoors and are exposed to the elements. They stand, kneel, and bend for long periods and often have to lift heavy materials. Common hazards include injuries from tools and falls from scaffolds, but these can often be avoided when proper safety equipment is used and safety practices are followed.

Education, Training, & Qualifications: Most brickmasons, blockmasons, and stonemasons pick up their skills informally, observing and learning from experienced workers. Many others receive training in vocational education schools or from industry-based programs that are common throughout the country. Another way to learn these skills is through an apprenticeship program, which generally provides the most thorough training. Individuals who learn the trade on the job usually start as helpers, laborers, or mason tenders. These workers carry materials, move scaffolds, and mix mortar.

Earnings: Median hourly earnings of brickmasons and blockmasons in 2006 were $20.66 (around $42,972 in annual earnings). The middle 50 percent earned between $15.96 and $26.26. Median hourly earnings in the industries employing the largest number of brickmasons in 2002 were:

- Foundation, structure, and
  building exterior contractors $20.57
- Masonry contractors $20.67

Median hourly earnings of stonemasons in 2006 were $17.26. The middle 50 percent earned between $13.12 and $22.04.

Earnings for workers in these trades can be reduced on occasion because poor weather and downturns in construction activity limit the time they can work.

Key Contacts: For information on the work of brickmasons, blockmasons, or stonemasons, contact:

- **Associated Builders and Contractors:** Workforce Development Department, 4250 N. Fairfax Drive, 9th Floor, Arlington, VA 22203. Website: www.trytools.org.

- **International Union of Bricklayers and Allied Craftworkers, International Masonry Institute National Training Center:** 17101 Science Dr., Bowie, MD 20715. Website: www.imiweb.org/training/training_center

- **Mason Contractors Association of America:** 33 S. Roselle Rd., Schaumburg, IL 6019 3. Website: www.masoncontractors.org.

- **Brick Industry Association:** 1850 Centennial Park Dr., Suite 301, Reston, VA 20191. Website: www.gobrick.com.

- **National Association of Home Builders:** 1201 15th Street NW, Washington, DC 20005. Website: www.nahb.org.

- **National Concrete Masonry Association:** 13750 Sunrise Valley Drive, Herndon, VA 20171-4662. Website: www.ncma.org.

Carpenters

⇨ **Annual Earnings:** $36,545
⇨ **Education/Training:** Combination of on-the-job and classroom training
⇨ **Outlook:** Average
⇨ **Self-employed:** 32% (largest percent in construction trade)

Employment Outlook: Job opportunities for carpenters are expected to be about average for occupations as a whole given average job growth along with replacement needs. Because there are no strict training requirements for entry, many people with limited skills take jobs as carpenters but eventually leave the occupation because they dislike the work or cannot find steady employment. Construction activity should increase in response to new housing and commercial and industrial plants and the need to renovate and modernize existing structures. A strong home remodeling market will create increased demands for carpenters. Construction of roads and bridges as well as restaurants, hotels, and other businesses will increase the demand for carpenters in the coming decade. Carpenters can experience periods of unemployment because of the short-term nature of many construction projects and the cyclical nature of the construction industry.

Nature of Work: Carpenters are involved in many different kinds of construction activity. They cut, fit, and assemble wood and other materials for the construction of buildings, highways, bridges, docks, industrial plants, boats, and many other structures. Carpenters' duties vary by type of employer. Builders increasingly are using specialty trade contractors who, in turn, hire carpenters who specialize in just one or two activities. Such activities include setting forms for concrete construction, erecting scaffolding, or doing finishing work, such as interior and exterior trim. However, a carpenter directly employed by a general building contractor often must perform a variety of the tasks associated with new construction, such as framing walls and partitions, putting in doors and windows, building stairs, laying hardwood floors, and hanging kitchen cabinets. Carpenters employed outside the construction industry perform a variety of installation and maintenance work. They may replace panes of glass, ceiling tiles, and doors, as well as repair decks, cabinets, and other furniture.

Working Conditions: As is true of other building trades, carpentry work is sometimes strenuous. Prolonged standing, climbing, bending, and kneeling often are necessary. Carpenters risk injury working with sharp or rough materials, using sharp tools and power equipment, and working in situations where they might slip or fall. Many carpenters work outdoors. Some change employers each time they finish a construction job. Others alternate between working for a contractor and working as contractors themselves on small jobs.

Education, Training, & Qualifications: Carpenters learn their trade through on-the-job training, as well as formal training programs. Most pick up skills informally by working under the supervision of experienced workers. Many acquire skills through vocational education. Others participate in employer training programs or apprenticeships. Most employers recommend an apprenticeship as the best way to learn carpentry. Apprenticeship programs are administered by local point union-management committees of the United Brotherhood of Carpenters and Joiners of America, the Associated General Contractors of America, Inc., and the National Association of Home Builders.

Earnings: Median hourly earnings of carpenters were $17.57 ($36,545 in annual earnings).

The middle 50 percent earned between $13.55 and $23.85 an hour. Median hourly earnings in the industries employing the largest numbers of carpenters in 2006 were:

- Residential building construction $17.39
- Foundation, structure, and building exterior contractors $17.03
- Nonresidential building construction $15.12
- Building finishing contractors $13.76

Earnings can be reduced on occasion, because carpenters lose work time in bad weather and during recessions when jobs are unavailable. Some carpenters are members of the United Brotherhood of Carpenters and Joiners of America.

Key Contacts: For information on training opportunities and carpentry in general, contact:

- **Associated Builders and Contractors:** 4250 N. Fairfax Drive, 9th Floor, Arlington, VA 22203. Website: www.trytools.org.

- **Associated General Contractors of America, Inc.:** 2300 Wilson Blvd., Suite 400, Arlington, VA 22201. Website: www.agc.org.

- **National Association of Home Builders:** 1201 15th St., NW, Washington, DC 20005. Website: www.nahb.org.

- **United Brotherhood of Carpenters and Joiners of America, Carpenters Training Fund:** 6801 Placid Street, Las Vegas, NV 89119. Website: www.carpenters.org.

Carpet, Floor, & Tile Installers & Finishers

- ⇨ **Annual Earnings:** $34,570
- ⇨ **Education/Training:** Combination of on-the-job training, apprenticeships, and classroom instruction
- ⇨ **Outlook:** Slower than average

Employment Outlook: Overall employment is expected to grow by 4 percent between 2006 and 2016, more slowly than the average for all occupations. Tile and marble setters, the largest specialty, will experience faster than average job growth because population and business growth will result in more construction of shopping malls, hospitals, schools, restaurants, and other structures in which tile in used extensively.

Carpet installers, the second largest specialty, will have little or no job growth as residential investors and homeowners increasingly choose hardwood floors because of their durability, neutral colors, and low maintenance, and because owners feel these floors will add to the value of their homes. Workers who install other types of flooring, including laminate, cork, rubber, and vinyl, should experience rapidly declining employment because these materials are used less often and are often laid by other types of construction workers.

In 2006 appropriately 196,000 people worked in these occupations by the following specialties:

- Tile and marble setters   79,000
- Carpet installers   73,000
- Floor layers, except carpet,
  wood, and hard tiles   29,000
- Floor sanders and finishers   14,000

Nature of Work: Carpet, tile, and other types of floor coverings not only serve an important basic function in buildings, but their decorative qualities also contribute to the appeal of the buildings. Carpet, floor, and tile installers and finishers lay floor coverings in homes, offices, hospitals, stores, restaurants, and many other types of buildings. Tile also may be installed on walls and ceilings.

Carpet installers inspect surfaces to be covered to determine their condition and, if necessary, correct any imperfections that could show through the carpet or cause the carpet to wear unevenly. They install wall-to-wall carpet using a combination of padded cushion or underlay, tacks, and tackless strips. Using a power stretcher, they stretch the carpet, hooking it to the tackless strip to hold it in place. They finish the edges using a wall trimmer.

Floor installers and floor layers lay floor coverings such as laminate, linoleum, vinyl, cork, and rubber for decorative purposes, or to deaden sounds, absorb shocks, or create airtight environments. When installing linoleum or vinyl, they may use an adhesive to cement the material directly to the floor. For laminate floor installation, workers may unroll and install a polyethylene film which acts as a moisture barrier, along with a thicker, padded underlayer which helps reduce noise.

Floor sanders and finishers complete the work done by floor installers by smoothing any imperfections in the wood and applying finish coats of varnish or polyurethane.

Tile installers, tilesetters, and marble setters apply hard tile and marble to floors, walls, ceilings, countertops, patios, and roof decks. Prior to installation, tilesetters use measuring devices and levels to ensure that the tile is placed in a consistent manner. Spacers are used to maintain exact distance between tiles.

Working Conditions: Carpet, floor, and tile installers and finishers usually work indoors and have regular daytime hours. However, when floor covering installers need to work in occupied stores or offices, they may work evenings and weekends to avoid disturbing customers or employees. Installing these materials is labor intensive; workers spend much of their time bending, kneeling, and reaching – activities that require endurance. The work can be very hard on workers' knees and back. Carpet installers frequently lift heavy rolls of carpet and may move heavy furniture, which requires strength and can be physically exhausting.

Education, Training, Qualifications: The vast majority of carpet, floor, and tile installers and finishers learn their trade informally on the job. A few, mostly tilesetters, learn through formal apprenticeship programs, which include classroom instruction and paid on-the-job training. Informal training for carpet installers often is sponsored by individual contractors. Workers start as helpers, and begin with simple assignments, such as installing stripping and padding, or helping to stretch newly installed carpet. Tile and marble setters also learn their craft mostly through on-the-job training. Other floor layers also learn on the job and begin by learning how to use the tools of the trade. They next learn to prepare surfaces to receive flooring. As they progress, they learn to cut and install the various floor coverings.

Skills needed to become carpet, floor, and tile installers and finishers include manual dexterity, eye-hand coordination, physical fitness, and a good sense of balance and color. The ability to solve basic arithmetic problems quickly and accurately also is required. In addition, reliability and a good work history are viewed favorably by contractors.

Earnings: In May 2006, the median hourly earnings of wage and salary workers in the following specialties included:

- Carpet installers $16.62
- Floor layers except carpet,
  wood, and hard tiles $16.44
- Tile and marble setters $17.59

Apprentices and other trainees usually start out earning about half of what experienced workers earn; their wage rates increase as they advance through the training program.

Key Contacts: For general information about the work of carpet installers and floor layers, contact:

- **Floor Covering Installation Contractors Association:** 7439 Milwood Drive, West Bloomfield, MI 48322. Website: www.fcica.com.

Additional information on training for carpet installers and floor layers is available from:

- **Finishing Trades Institute, International Union of Painters and Allied Trades:** 1750 New York Avenue, NW, Washington, DC 20006. Website: www.finishingtradesinstitute.org/about.htm.

For general information about the work of tile installers and finishers, contact:

- **International Union of Bricklayers and Allied Craftworkers,** International Masonry Institute, The James Brice House, 42 East St., Annapolis, MD 21401. Website: www. imiweb.org/about/contact.php.

For general information about tile setting and tile training, contact:

- **National Tile Contractors Association:** P.O. Box 13629, Jackson, MS 39236. Website: www.tile-assn.com.

For information concerning training of carpet, floor, and tile installers and finishers, contact:

- **United Brotherhood of Carpenters and Joiners of America:** 50 F Street, NW, Washington, DC 20001. Website: www.carpenters.org.

Construction and Building Inspectors

- ○ **Annual Earnings:** $46,850
- ○ **Education/Training:** Experience, certificate, associate degree
- ○ **Outlook:** Good – faster than average

Employment Outlook: Employment of construction and building inspectors is expected to grow about as fast as the average for all occupations in the coming decade. Growing concern for public safety and improvements in the quality of construction should continue to stimulate demand for construction and building inspectors. In addition to the expected employment growth, some job openings will arise from the need to replace inspectors who transfer to other occupations or leave the labor force. Inspectors are involved in all phases of construction, including maintenance and repair work, and are therefore less likely to lose jobs when new construction slows during recessions. As the population grows and the volume of real estate transactions increases, greater emphasis on home inspections should result in strong demand for home inspectors. In 2006 construction and building inspectors held 110,000 jobs. Local governments – primarily municipal or county building departments – employed 41 percent. Approximately 26 percent of construction and building inspectors work for architectural and engineering services firms.

Nature of Work: There are many types of specialized inspectors related to the construction and repair processes: building, plan, electrical, elevator, mechanical, plumbing, public works, specification, and home inspectors. Construction and building inspectors examine the construction, alteration, or repair of buildings, highways and streets, sewer and water systems, dams, bridges, and other structures to ensure compliance with building codes and ordinances, zoning regulations, and contract specifications. Building codes and standards are the primary means by which building construction is regulated in the United States for health and safety of the general public. Building inspectors inspect the structural quality and general safety of buildings. Some specialize in such areas as structural steel or reinforced concrete structures. Home inspectors conduct inspections of newly built or previously owned homes. Home inspection has become a standard practice in the home purchasing process. Although inspections are primarily visual, inspectors may use tape measures, survey instruments, metering devices, and test equipment such as concrete strength measurers. They keep a log of their work, take photographs, file reports, and, if necessary, act on their findings. Many inspectors also investigate construction or alterations being done without proper permits.

Working Conditions: Construction and building inspectors usually work alone. However, several may be assigned to large, complex projects, particularly because inspectors tend to specialize in different areas of construction. Although they spend considerable time inspecting construction worksites, inspectors also spend time in a field office reviewing blueprints, answering letters or telephone calls, writing reports, and scheduling inspections. Inspection sites are dirty and may be cluttered with tools, materials, or debris. Inspectors may have to climb ladders or many flights of stairs, or crawl around in tight spaces. Although their work generally is not considered hazardous, inspectors, like other construction workers, wear hard hats and adhere to other safety requirements while at a construction site. Inspectors normally work regular hours. However, they may work additional hours during periods when a lot of construction is taking place.

Education, Training, & Qualifications:

Although requirements vary considerably depending upon where one is employed, construction and building inspectors should have a thorough knowledge of construction materials and practices in either a general area, such as structural or heavy construction, or in a specialized area, such as electrical or plumbing systems, reinforced concrete, or structural steel. Applicants for construction or building inspection jobs need several years of experience as a construction manager, supervisor, or craftworker. Many inspectors previously worked as carpenters, electricians, plumbers, or pipefitters. Because inspectors must possess the right mix of technical knowledge, experience, and education, employers prefer applicants who have formal training as well as experience. Most employers require at least a high school diploma or equivalent, even for workers with considerable experience. Construction and building inspectors usually receive much of their training on the job, although they must learn building codes and standards on their own. Most states and cities require some type of certification for employment. To become certified, inspectors with substantial experience and education must pass stringent examinations on code requirements, construction techniques, and materials.

Earnings:

Median annual earnings for construction and building inspectors were $46,570 in May 2006. The middle 50 percent earned between $36,610 and $58,780. Median annual earnings in the industries employing the largest numbers of construction and building inspectors in 2006 were:

- Local government $46,040
- Architectural, engineering, etc. $46,850
- State government $43,680

Generally, building inspectors, including plan examiners, earn the highest salaries. Salaries in large metropolitan areas are substantially higher than those in small jurisdictions.

Key Contacts:

For information on careers and certification, contact the following organizations:

- **International Code Council:** 500 New Jersey Ave., NW, 6th Floor, Washington, DC 20001-2070. Website: www.iccsafe.org.

- **Association of Construction Inspectors:** 1224 North 19th Avenue, Suite C-2, Phoenix, AZ 85027. Website: www.aci-assoc.org.

- **International Association of Electrical Inspectors:** 901 Waterfall Way, Suite 602, Richardson, TX 75080-7702. Website: www.iaei.org.

- **American Society of Home Inspectors:** 932 Lee Street, Suite 101, Des Plaines, IL 60016. Website: www.ashi.org.

- **National Association of Home Inspectors:** 4248 Park Glen Road, Minneapolis, MN 55416. Website: www.nahi.org.

Construction Equipment Operators

⇨ **Annual Earnings:** $36,900++
⇨ **Education/Training:** On-the-job training and apprenticeships
⇨ **Outlook:** Average growth

Employment Outlook:

Average job growth, reflecting increased demand for their services, and the need to replace workers who leave the occupation should result in very good job opportunities for construction equipment operators. Employment of construction equipment opportunities is expected to increase 8 percent between 2006 and 2016, about as fast as average for all occupations.

In 2006 construction equipment operators held about 494,000 jobs. They were found in every section of the country and were distributed among various types of operators as follows:

- Operating engineers and other construction equipment operators   424,000
- Paving, surfacing, and tamping equipment operators   64,000
- Pile-driver operators   5,600

Nature of Work:

Construction equipment operators use machinery to move construction materials, earth, and other heavy materials at construction sites and mines. They operate equipment that clears and grades land to prepare it for construction of roads, buildings, and bridges. They use machines to dig trenches to lay or repair sewer and other pipelines and hoist heavy construction materials. They may even work off-shore constructing oil rigs. Construction equipment operators also operate machinery that spreads asphalt and concrete on roads and other structures.

These workers also set up and inspect the equipment, make adjustments, and perform some maintenance and minor repairs. Construction equipment operators control equipment by moving levers, foot pedals, operating switches, or joysticks. Included in the construction equipment operator occupation are paving, surfacing, and tamping equipment operators; piledriver operators; and operating engineers. All use specialized equipment.

Working Conditions: Construction equipment operators work outdoors, in nearly every type of climate and weather condition, although in many areas of the country, some types of construction operations much be suspended in winters. Bulldozers, scrapers, and especially tampers and piledrivers are noisy and shake or jolt the operators. Operating heavy construction equipment can be dangerous.

Operators may have irregular hours because work on some construction projects continues around the clock or must be performed late at night or early in the morning.

Education, Training, & Qualifications: Construction equipment operators usually learn their skills on the job, but formal apprenticeship programs provide more comprehensive training. Employers of construction equipment operators generally prefer to hire high school graduates, although some employers may train non-graduates to operate some types of equipment. On the job, workers may start by operating light equipment under the guidance of an experienced operator. Later, they may operate heavier equipment, such as bulldozers and cranes. Technologically advanced construction equipment with computerized controls and improved hydraulics and electronics requires more skill to operate. Operators of such equipment may need more training and some understanding of electronics.

Earnings: Earnings for construction equipment operators vary. In May 2006, median hourly earnings of wage and salary operating engineers and other construction equipment operations were $17.74. Medium hourly earn-

ings in the industries employing the largest numbers of operating engineers were:

- Highway, street, and bridge construction $19.88
- Utility system construction $18.62
- Other specialty trade contractors $18.00
- Local government $15.95

Median hourly earnings of wage and salary paving, surfacing, and tamping equipment operators were $15.05 and piledriver operators were $22.20 in May 2006.

Key Contacts: For general information about the work of construction equipment operators, contact:

- **Associated General Contractors of America:** 2300 Wilson Blvd., Suite 400, Arlington, VA 22201. Website: www.agc.org.

- **International Union of Operating Engineers:** 1125 17th St., NW, Washington, DC 20036. Website: www.iuoe.org.

- **National Center for Construction Education and Research:** 3600 NW 43rd Street, Building G, Gainesville, FL 32606. Website: www.nccer.org.

- **Pile Driving Contractors Association:** P.O. Box 66208, Orange Park, FL 32065. Website: www.piledrivers.org.

Construction Laborers

- ➪ **Annual Earnings:** $26, 333
- ➪ **Education/Training:** On-the-job training and apprenticeships
- ➪ **Outlook:** Average growth

Employment Outlook: Employment is expected to grow about as fast as the average – about 11 percent between 2006 and 2016. In many areas, there will be competition for jobs, especially for those requiring limited skills. Laborers who have specialized skills or who can relocate near new construction projects should have the best opportunities. Construction laborer jobs will be adversely affected by automation as some jobs are replaced by new machinery and equipment that improves productivity and quality. Also, laborers will be increasingly employed by staffing agencies that will contract out laborers to employers on a temporary basis, and in many areas employers will continue to rely on day laborers instead of full-time laborers on staff. Employment of construction laborers, like that of many other construction workers, is sensitive to the fluctuations on the economy.

Nature of Work: Construction laborers can be found on almost all construction sites performing a wide range of tasks from the very easy to the potentially hazardous. They can be found at building, highway, and heavy construction sites; residential and commercial sites; tunnel and shaft excavations; and demolition sites. Many of the jobs they perform require physical strength, training, and experience. Other jobs require little skill and can be learned in a short amount of time. While most construction laborers specialize in a type of construction, such as highway or tunnel construction, some are generalists who perform many different tasks during all stages of construction.

Construction laborers clean and prepare construction sites. They remove trees and debris, tend pumps, compressors and generators, and build forms for pouring concrete. They erect and disassemble scaffolding and other temporary structures. They load, unload, identify, and distribute building materials to the appropriate location according to project plans and specifications. La borers also tend machines – mix concrete using a portable mixer or tend a machine that pumps concrete, grout, cement, sand, plaster, or stucco through a spray gun for application to ceilings and walls. They often help other craftworkers, including carpenters, plasterers, operating engineers, and masons.

Working Conditions: Most laborers do physically demanding work. They may lift and carry heavy objects, and stoop, kneel, crouch, or crawl in awkward positions. Some work at great heights, or outdoors in all weather conditions. Some jobs expose workers to harmful materials or chemicals, fumes, odors, loud noise, or dangerous machinery.

Construction laborers generally work eight-hour shifts, although longer shifts are common. Overnight work may be required with working on highways. In some parts of the country, construction laborers may work only during certain seasons.

Education, Training, & Qualifications: Many construction laborer jobs require a variety of basic skills, but others require specialized training and experience. Most construction laborers learn on the job, but formal apprenticeship programs provide the most thorough preparation.

While some construction laborer jobs have no specific educational qualifications or entry-level training, apprenticeships for laborers require a high school diploma or equivalent. High school classes in English, mathematics, physics, mechanical drawing, blueprint reading, welding, and general shop can be helpful.

Most workers start by getting a job with a contractor who provides on-the-job training. Increasingly, construction laborers find work through temporary help agencies that send laborers to construction sites for short-ter m work.

Laborers need manual dexte rity, eye-hand coordination, good physical fitness, a good sense of balance, and an ability to work as a member of a team. Military service or a good work history is viewed favorably by contractors.

Earnings: Median hourly earnings of wage and salary construction laborers in May 2006 were $12.66 ($26,333 on an annual basis if working a steady 40-hour week, 52 weeks a year). The middle 50 percent earned between $9.95 and $17.31. Median hourly earnings in the industries employing the largest number of construction laborers were as follows:

- Nonresidential building
  construction $13.62
- Other specialty trade contractors $12.93
- Residential building construction $12.82
- Foundation, structure, and
  building exterior contractors $12.41

Key Contacts: For information about jobs as a construction laborer, contact local building or construction contractors, local joint labor-management apprenticeship committees, apprenticeship agencies, or the local office of your state employment service.

For information on education programs for laborers, contact:

- **Laborers Learning Education and Resource Network:** 37 Deerfield Road, P.O. Box 37, Pomfret Center, CT 06259. Website: www. laborerslearn.org.

- **National Center for Construction Education and Research:** 3600 NW 43rd Street, Building G, Gainesville, FL 32606. Website: www.nccer.org.

Drywall Installers, Ceiling Tile Installers, and Tapers

⇨ **Annual Earnings:** $36,150
⇨ **Education/Training:** Experience and apprenticeships
⇨ **Outlook:** Good

Employment Outlook: Job opportunities for drywall installers, ceiling tile installers, and tapers are expected to be good in the decade ahead – to grow about average for all occupations, reflecting increases in new construction and remodeling projects. Employment is expected to grow by 7 percent between 2006 and 2016. In addition to jobs involving traditional interior work, drywall workers will find employment opportunities in the installation of insulated exterior wall systems, which are becoming increasingly popular. Many jobs will open up each year because of the need to replace workers who transfer to other occupations or leave the labor force. Some drywall installers, ceiling tile installers, and tapers with limited skills leave the occupation when they find that they dislike the work or fail to attain steady employment. Since most of their work is done indoors, these workers lose less work time because of inclement weather than do some other construction workers. Nevertheless, they may be unemployed between construction projects and during downturns in construction activity.

Nature of Work: There are two kinds of drywall workers – installers and tapers – although many workers do both types of work. Installers, also called applicators or hangers, fasten drywall panels to the inside framework of residential houses and other buildings. Tapers, or finishers, prepare these panels for painting by taping and finishing joints and imperfections. Ceiling tile installers, or acoustical carpenters, apply or mount acoustical tiles or blocks, strips, or sheets of shock-absorbing materials to ceilings and walls of buildings to reduce reflection of sound or to decorate rooms. Lathers fasten metal or rockboard lath to walls, ceilings, and partitions of buildings.

Working Conditions: As in many other construction trades, the work sometimes is strenuous. Drywall installers, ceiling tile installers, and tapers spend most of the day on their feet, either standing, bending, or kneeling. Some tapers use stilts to tape and finish ceiling and angle joints. Installers have to lift and maneuver heavy panels. Hazards include falls from ladders and scaffolds and injuries from power tools and from working with sharp materials. Because sanding a joint compound to a smooth finish creates a great deal of dust, some finishers wear masks for protection.

Education, Training, & Qualifications: Most drywall installers, ceiling tile installers, and tapers start as helpers and learn their skills on the job. Installer helpers start by carrying materials, lifting and holding panels, and cleaning up debris. Within a few weeks they learn to measure, cut, and install materials. Eventually they become fully experienced workers. Some drywall installers, ceiling tile installers, and tapers learn their trade in an apprenticeship program. The United Brotherhood of Carpenters and Joiners of America, in cooperation with local contractors, administers an apprenticeship program both in drywall installation and finishing and in acoustical carpentry. Apprenticeship programs consist of at least three years, or 6,000 hours, of on-the-job training and 144 hours a year of related classroom instruction. In addition, local affiliates of the Associated Builders and Contractors and the National Association of Home Builders conduct training programs for nonunion workers. The International Union of Painters and Allied Trades conducts an apprenticeship program in drywall finishing that lasts two to three years. Employers prefer high school graduates who are in good physical condition, but they frequently hire applicants with less education. High school or vocational school courses in carpentry provide a helpful background for drywall work. Drywall installers, ceiling tile installers, and tapers with a few years of experience and with leadership ability may become supervisors. Some workers start their own contracting businesses.

Earnings: In May 2006, the median hourly earnings of drywall and ceiling tile installers were $17.38 (annual earnings of $36,150). The middle 50 percent earned between $13.60 and $22.58. The median hourly earnings in the industries employing the largest numbers of drywall and ceiling tile installers in 2006 were:

- Foundation, structure, and
  building exterior contractors $18.10
- Drywall and insulation contractors $17.42
- Nonresidential building
  construction $17.26
- Residential building construction $17.26

In 2006, median hourly earnings of tapers were $19.85. The middle 50 percent earned between $14.65 and $25.70 an hour. Trainees usually started at about half the rate paid to experienced workers and received wage increases as they became more highly skilled.

Key Contacts: For information about work opportunities in drywall application and finishing and ceiling tile installation, contact local drywall installation and ceiling tile installation contractors, a local of the building unions, a local joint union-management apprenticeship committee, a state or local chapter of the Associated Builders and Contractors, or the nearest office of the state employment service or apprenticeship agency.

For details about job qualifications and training programs in drywall application and finishing and ceiling tile installation, contact:

- **Associated Builders and Contractors:** 4250 N. Fairfax Drive, 9th Floor, Arlington, VA 22203. Website: www.trytools.org.

- **National Association of Home Builders:** 1201 15th Street NW, Washington, DC 20005. Website: www.nahb.org.

- **International Union of Painters and Allied Trades:** 1750 New York Avenue NW, Washington, DC 20006. Website: www.iupat.org.

- **United Brotherhood of Carpenters and Joiners of America, Carpenters Training Fund:** 6801 Placid Street, Las Vegas, NV 89119. Website: www.carpenters.org.

Electricians

⇨ **Annual Earnings:** $43,618
⇨ **Education/Training:** Apprenticeship program (3-5 years)
⇨ **Outlook:** Very good – above average

Employment Outlook: Job opportunities for electricians are expected to be good. Numerous openings will arise each year as experienced electricians leave the occupation. In addition, many potential workers may choose not to enter training programs because they prefer work that is less strenuous and has more comfortable working conditions. Employment of electricians is expected to grow faster than the average for all occupations in the coming decade. As the population and economy grow, more electricians will be needed to install and maintain electrical devices and wiring in homes, factories, offices, and other structures. New technologies also are expected to continue to stimulate the demand for these workers.

Nature of Work: Electricians install, connect, test, and maintain electrical systems for a vari-

ety of purposes, including climate control, security, and communications. They also may install and maintain the electronic controls for machines in business and industry. Although most electricians specialize in construction or maintenance, a growing number do both. Electricians work with blueprints when they install electrical systems in factories, office buildings, homes, and other structures. Blueprints indicate the locations of circuits, outlets, load centers, panel boards, and other equipment. Electricians must follow the National Electric Code and comply with the building codes of states and localities when they install these systems. Maintenance work varies greatly, depending on where the electrician is employed. Maintenance electricians spend much of their time doing preventive maintenance. They periodically inspect equipment, and locate and correct problems before breakdowns occur. Electricians use hand tools such as screwdrivers, pliers, knives, hacksaws, and wire strippers. They also use a variety of power tools as well as testing equipment such as oscilloscopes, ammeters, and test lamps.

Working Conditions: Electricians' work is sometimes strenuous. They bend conduits, stand for long periods, and frequently work on ladders and scaffolds. Their working environment varies, depending on the type of job. Some may work in dusty, dirty, hot, or wet conditions, or in confined areas, ditches, or other uncomfortable places. Electricians risk injury from electrical shock, falls, and cuts. Most electricians work a standard 40-hour week, although overtime may be required. Those in maintenance work may work nights or weekends, and be on call.

Electricians held about 705,000 jobs in 2006. More than one-quarter of wage and salary workers were employed in the construction industry. The remainder worked as maintenance electricians outside the construction industry. About one in 10 electricians was self-employed.

Education, Training, & Qualifications: Most people learn the electrical trade by completing an apprenticeship program lasting three to five years. Apprenticeship gives trainees a thorough knowledge of all aspects of the trade and generally improves their ability to find a job. Although electricians are more likely to be trained through apprenticeship than are workers in other construction trades, some still learn their skills informally on the job. Others train to be residential electricians in a three-year program. Apprenticeship programs may be sponsored by joint training committees made up of local unions of the International Brotherhood of Electrical Workers and local chapters of the

National Electrical Contractors Association; company management committees of individual electrical contracting companies; or local chapters of the Associated Builders and Contractors and the Independent Electrical Contractors Association. The typical large apprenticeship program provides at least 144 hours of classroom instruction and 2,000 hours of on-the-job-training each year. Those who do not enter a formal apprenticeship program can begin to learn the trade informally by working as helpers for experienced electricians.

Earnings: In 2006, median hourly earnings of electricians were $20.97 ($43,618 per year). The middle 50 percent earned between $16.07 and $27.71. Median hourly earnings in the industries employing the largest numbers of electricians in 2006 were:

- Motor vehicle parts manufacturing $31.90
- Electric power generation,
  transmission, and distribution $26.32
- Local government $23.80
- Nonresidential building
  construction $20.58
- Electrical contractors $20.47
- Plumbing, heating, and
  air-conditioning contractors $19.56
- Employment services $17.15

Depending on experience, apprentices usually start at between 40 and 50 percent of the rate paid to fully trained electricians.

Key Contacts: For details about apprenticeships or other work opportunities in this trade, contact the offices of the state employment service, the state apprenticeship agency, local electrical contractors or firms that employ maintenance electricians, or local union-management electrician apprenticeship committees. For information about union apprenticeship programs, contact:

- **National Joint Apprenticeship Training Committee:** 301 Prince George's Blvd., Upper Marlboro, MD 20774. Website: www. njatc.org.

- **National Electrical Contractors Association:** 3 Bethesda Metro Center, Suite 1100, Bethesda, MD 20814. Website: www.neca net.org.

- **International Brotherhood of Electrical Workers:** 900 Seventh St., NW, Washington, DC 20001. Website: www.ibew.org.

For information about independent apprenticeship programs, contact:

- **Associated Builders and Contractors:** Workforce Development Department, 4250 North Fairfax Drive, 9th Floor, Arlington, VA 22203. Website: www.trytools.org.

- **Independent Electrical Contractors, Inc.:** 4401 Ford Avenue, Suite 1100, Alexandria, VA 22302. Website: www.ieci.org.

- **National Association of Home Builders:** 1201 15th Street NW, Washington, DC 20005. Website: www.nahb.org.

- **Home Builders Institute:** 1201 15th Street, NW, 6th Floor, Washington, DC 20005. Website: www.hbi.org.

Elevator Installers and Repairers

⇨ **Annual Earnings:** $63,627
⇨ **Education/Training:** Apprenticeships
⇨ **Outlook:** Excellent

Employment Outlook: Employment of elevator installers and repairers is expected to increase 9 percent during the 2006-2016 decade, about as fast as the average for all occupations. Demand for additional elevator installers depends greatly on growth in nonresidential construction, such a commercial office buildings and stores that have elevators and escalators.

Nature of Work: Evaluator installers and repairers – also called *elevator constructors* or *elevator mechanics* – assemble, install, and replace elevators, escalators, chairlifts, dumbwaiters, moving walkways, and similar equipment in new and old buildings. Once the equipment is in service, they maintain and repair it as well. They also are responsible for modernizing older equipment.

A service crew usually handles major repairs – for example, replacing cables, elevator doors, or machine bearings.

The most highly skilled elevator installers and repairers, called "adjusters," specialize in fine-tuning all the equipment after installation. Adjusters make sure that an elevator works according to specifications and stops correctly at each floor within a specified time. Adjusters need a thorough knowledge of electricity, electronics, and computers to ensure the newly installed elevators operate properly.

Working Conditions: Elevator installers lift and carry heavy equipment and parts, and they may work in cramped spaces or awkward positions. Potential hazards include falls, electrical shock, muscle strains, and other injuries related to handling heavy equipment. Most of their work is performed indoors in existing buildings or buildings under construction.

Education, Training, & Qualifications: Most elevator installers receive their education and training through an apprenticeship program. High school classes in mathematics, science, and shop may help applicants compete for apprenticeship openings. Most elevator installers and repairers learn their trade in an apprenticeship program administered by local joint educational committees representing the employers and the union – the International Union of Elevator Constructors. In nonunion shops, workers may complete training programs sponsored by independent contractors.

Earnings: Earnings of elevator installers and repairers are among the highest of all construction trades. Median hourly earnings of wage and salary elevator installers and repairers were $30.59 in May 2006. The middle 50 percent earned between $23.90 and $35.76. Median hourly earnings in the building equipment contractors industry were $30.74.

About three out of four elevator installers and repairers were members of unions or covered by a union contract, one of the highest proportions of all occupations. The largest numbers were members of the International Union of Elevator Constructors. In addition to free continuing education, elevator installers and repairers receive basic benefits enjoyed by other workers.

Key Contacts: For further information on opportunities as an elevator installer and repairer, contact:

- **International Union of Elevator Constructors:** 7154 Columbia Gateway Drive, Columbia, MD 21046. Website: www.iuec.org.

- **National Association of Elevator Contractors:** 1298 Wellbrook Circle, Suite A, Conyers, GA 30012. Website: www.naec.org.

Glaziers

⇨ **Annual Earnings:** $34,612
⇨ **Education/Training:** Experience and apprenticeship programs
⇨ **Outlook:** Good

Employment Outlook: Job opportunities are expected to be good for glaziers, growing by 12 percent from 2006 to 2016, largely due to the numerous openings arising each year as experienced glaziers leave the occupation. In addition, many potential workers may choose not to enter this occupation because they prefer work that is less strenuous and has more comfortable working conditions. Employment of glaziers is expected to grow about as fast as the average for all occupations in the coming decade, as a result of growth in residential and commercial construction. Demand for glaziers will be spurred by the continuing need to modernize and repair existing structures and the popularity of glass in bathroom and kitchen design. The need to improve glass performance related to insulation, privacy, safety, condensation control, and noise reduction also is expected to contribute to the demand for glaziers in both residential and nonresidential remodeling. Glaziers held 55,000 jobs in 2006.

Nature of Work: Glaziers are responsible for selecting, cutting, installing, replacing, and removing glass. They generally work on one of several types of projects. Residential glazing involves work such as replacing glass in home windows; installing glass mirrors, shower doors, and bathtub enclosures; and fitting glass for tabletops and display cases. On commercial interior projects, glaziers install items such as heavy, often etched, decorative room dividers or security windows. Glazing projects also may involve replacement of streetfront windows for establishments such as supermarkets, auto dealerships, or banks. In the construction of large commercial buildings, glaziers build metal framework extrusions and install glass panels or curtain walls.

Working Conditions: Glaziers often work outdoors, sometimes in inclement weather. At times, they work on scaffolds at great heights. They do a considerable amount of bending, kneeling, lifting, and standing. Glaziers may be injured by broken glass or cutting tools, by falls from scaffolds, or by improperly lifting heavy glass panels.

Education, Training, & Qualifications: Many glaziers learn the trade informally on the job. They usually start as helpers, carrying glass and cleaning up debris in glass shops. They often practice cutting on discarded glass. After a while, they are given an opportunity to cut glass for a job. Eventually, helpers assist experienced workers on simple installation jobs. By working with experienced glaziers, they eventually acquire the skills of a fully qualified glazier. Employers recommend that glaziers learn the trade through a formal apprenticeship program that lasts three to four years. Apprenticeship programs, which are administered by the National Glass Apprenticeship and local union-management committees or local contractors' associations, consist of on-the-job training and a minimum of 144 hours of classroom instruction or home study each year. On the job, apprentices learn to use the tools and equipment of the trade; handle, measure, cut, and install glass and metal framing; cut and fit moldings; and install and balance glass doors.

Earnings: In May 2006, median hourly earnings of glaziers were $16.64 ($34,612 per year). The middle 50 percent earned between $12.85 and $22.18. Median hourly wage and salary earnings in the foundation, structure, and building exterior contractors industry were $17.03. Median hourly earnings for glaziers employed by building materials and supply dealers were $15.51.

Glaziers covered by union contracts generally earn more than their nonunion counterparts. Apprentice wage rates usually start at between 40 and 50 percent of the rate paid to experienced glaziers and increase as apprentices gain experience in the field.

Key Contacts: For more information about glazier apprenticeships or work opportunities, contact local glazing or general contractors, a local of the International Union of Painters and Allied Trades, a local joint union-management apprenticeship agency, or the nearest office of the state employment service or state apprenticeship agency. For information about the work and training of glaziers, contact:

- **International Union of Painters and Allied Trades:** 1750 New York Ave., NW, Washington, DC 20006. Website: www. iupat.org.

- **National Glass Association:** Education and Training Department, 8200 Greensboro Drive, Suite 302, McLean, VA 22102-3881. Website: www.glass.org.

Hazardous Materials Removal Workers

⇨ **Annual Earnings:** $35,444
⇨ **Education/Training:** High school diploma and training
⇨ **Outlook:** Excellent

Employment Outlook: Job opportunities are expected to be excellent for hazardous materials removal workers. The occupation is characterized by a relatively high rate of turnover, resulting in a number of job openings each year. Many potential workers are not attracted to this occupation, because they prefer work that is less strenuous and under safer working conditions. Employment of hazardous materials removal workers is expected to grow much faster than the average for all occupations in the decade ahead, reflecting increasing concern for a safe and clean environment. Special-trade contractors will have strong demand for the largest segment of these workers, namely, asbestos abatement and lead abatement workers; lead abatement should offer particularly good opportunities. Mold remediation is an especially rapidly growing part of the occupation at the present time, but it is unclear whether its rapid growth will continue. Employment of decontamination technicians, radiation safety technicians, and decommissioning and decontamination workers is expected to grow in response to increased pressure for safer and cleaner nuclear and electric generator facilities.

Nature of Work: Hazardous materials workers identify, remove, package, transport, and dispose of various hazardous materials, including asbestos, lead, and radioactive and nuclear materials. The removal of hazardous materials, or "hazmats," from public places and the environment also is called abatement, remediation, and decontamination. Hazardous materials removal workers use a variety of tools and equipment, depending on the work at hand. Equipment ranges form brooms to personal protective suits that completely isolate workers from the hazardous materials. The equipment required varies with the threat of contamination and can include disposable or reusable coveralls, gloves, hard hats, shoe covers, safety glasses or goggles, chemical-resistant clothing, face shields, and devices to protect one's hearing. Most workers also are required to wear respirators while working, to protect them from airborne particles. Asbestos abatement workers and lead abatement workers remove asbestos, lead, and other materials from buildings scheduled to be renovated or demolished. Using a variety of hand and power tools, such as vacuums and scrapers, these workers remove the asbestos and lead from surfaces. Emergency and disaster response workers clean up hazardous materials after train derailments and trucking accidents. These workers also are needed when an immediate cleanup is required, as would be the case after an attack by biological or chemical weapons. Decommissioning and decontamination workers remove and treat radioactive materials generated by nuclear facilities and power plants.

Treatment, storage, and disposal workers transport and prepare materials for treatment or disposal. Nearly 39,000 hazardous materials removal workers held jobs in 2006.

Working Conditions: Hazardous materials removal workers function in a highly structured environment, to minimize the danger they face. Each phase of an operation is planned in advance, and workers are trained to deal with safety breaches and hazardous situations. Crews and supervisors take every precaution to ensure that the worksite is safe. Whether they work in asbestos, mold, or lead abatement or in radioactive decontamination, hazardous materials removal workers must stand, stoop, and kneel for long periods. Some must wear fully enclosed personal protective suits for several hours at a time. These workers face different working conditions, depending on their area of expertise. Although many work a standard 40-hour week, overtime and shift work are common, especially in asbestos and lead abatement.

Education, Training, & Qualifications: No formal education beyond a high school diploma is required to work in this field. Federal regulations require an individual to have a license to work in the occupation, although, at present, th ere are few laws regulating mold removal. Most employers provide technical training on the job, but a formal 32- to 40-hour training program must be completed if one is to be licensed as an asbestos abatement and lead abatement worker or a treatment, storage, and disposal worker. For decommissioning and decontamination workers employed at nuclear facilities, training is more extensive. Workers in all fields are required to take refresher courses every year in order to maintain their license. Because much of the work is done in buildings, a background in construction is helpful.

Earnings: In 2006, median hourly earnings of hazardous materials removal workers were $17.04 ($35,444 annually). The middle 50 percent earned between $13.31 and $22.78 per hour. The median hourly earnings in remediation and other waste management services, the largest industries employing these workers – were $16.75 in 2006. Treatment, storage, and disposal workers usually earn slightly more than asbestos abatement and lead abatement workers. Decontamination and decommissioning workers and radiation protection technicians, though constituting the smallest group, tend to earn the highest wages.

Key Contacts: For more information on hazardous materials removal workers, including information on training, contact:

- **Laborers Learning Education and Resource Network**: 37 Deerfield Road, Pomfret, CT 06259. Website: www.laborerslearn. org.

Insulation Workers

⇨ **Annual Earnings:** $30,514
⇨ **Education/Training:** Experience and apprenticeships
⇨ **Outlook:** Excellent

Employment Outlook: Job opportunities are expected to be excellent for insulation workers, growing by 8 percent from 2006 to 2016. Because there are no strict training requirements for entry, many people with limited skills work as insulation workers for a short time and then move on to other types of work, creating many job openings. Employment of insulation workers should grow as fast as average for all occupations in the coming decade, due to growth in residential and commercial construction. Demand for efficient use of energy to heat and cool buildings will create an increased demand for these workers in the construction of new residential, industrial, and commercial buildings. Insulation workers in the construction industry may experience periods of unemployment because of the short duration of many construction projects.

Nature of Work: Insulation workers cement, staple, wire, tape, or spray insulation. When covering a steam pipe, for example, insulation workers measure and cut sections of insulation to the proper length, stretch it open along a cut that runs the length of the material, and slip it over the pipe. They fasten the insulation with adhesive, staples, tape, or wire bands. When covering a wall or other flat surface, workers may use a hose to spray foam insulation onto a wire mesh that provides a rough surface to which the foam can cling and which adds strength to the finished surface. In attics or exterior walls of uninsulated buildings, workers blow in loose-fill insulation. In new construction or on major renovations, insulation workers staple fiberglass or rock-wool batts to exterior walls and ceilings before drywall, paneling, or plaster walls are put in place. Insulation workers use common hand tools – tro wels, brushes, knives, scissors, saws, pliers, and stapling guns. They use power saws to cut insulating materials, welding machines to join sheet metal or secure clamps, and compressors to blow or spray insulation.

Insulation workers held about 61,000 jobs in 2006. The construction industry employed 91 percent of workers; 53 percent work for drywall and insulation contractors.

Working Conditions: Insulation workers usually work indoors. They spend most of the workday on their feet, either standing, bending, or kneeling. Sometimes they work from ladders or in tight spaces. The work requires more coordination than strength. Insulation work often is dusty and dirty, and the summer heat can make the insulation worker very uncomfortable. Minute particles from insulation materials, especially when blown, can irritate the eyes, skin, and respiratory system. Workers must follow strict safety guidelines to protect themselves from the dangers of insulating irritants. They keep work areas well ventilated; wear protective suits, masks, and respirators; and take decontamination showers if necessary.

Education, Training, & Qualifications: Most insulation workers learn their trade informally on the job, although some complete formal apprenticeship programs. For entry-level jobs, insulation contractors prefer high school graduates who are in good physical condition and licensed to drive. Applicants seeking apprenticeship positions should have a high school diploma or its equivalent and be at least 18 years old. Trainees who learn on the job receive instruction and supervision from experienced insulation workers. Trainees begin with simple tasks, such as carrying insulation or holding material while it is fastened in place. On-the-job training can take up to two years, depending on the nature of the work.

Earnings: In 2006, median hourly earnings of insulation workers were $14.67 ($30,514 per year). The middle 50 percent earned between $11.26 and $20.00 per hour.

Key Contacts: For information on training programs or other work opportunities in this trade, contact a local insulation contractor, the nearest office of the state employment service or apprenticeship agency, or the following organizations:

- **National Insulation Association:** 99 Canal Center Plaza, Suite 222, Alexandria, VA 22314. Website: www.insulation.org.

- **Insulation Contractors Association of America:** 1321 Duke Street, Suite 303, Alexandria, VA 22314. Website: www.insulate.org.

Painters and Paperhangers

- ⇨ **Annual Earnings:** $31,200
- ⇨ **Education/Training:** Experience and apprenticeships
- ⇨ **Outlook:** Good

Employment Outlook: Job prospects should be good – about as fast as average for all occupations (expected to grow by 11 percent between 2006 and 2016) – as thousands of painters and paperhangers transfer to other occupations or leave the labor force each year. Because there are no strict training requirements for entry, many people with limited skills work as painters or paperhangers for a short time and then move on to other work. Employment of painters and paperhangers is expected to grow about as fast as average for all occupations in the decade ahead, reflecting increases in the level of new construction and in the supply of buildings and others structures that require maintenance and renovation.

Nature of Work: Painters apply paint, stain, varnish, and other finishes to buildings and other structures. They choose the right paint or finish for the surface to be covered, taking into account durability, ease of handling, method of applications, and customers' wishes. Painters first prepare the surfaces to be covered. This may require removing the old coat of paint by stripping, sanding, wire brushing, burning, or water and abrasive blasting. Painters also wash walls and trim to remove dirt and grease, fill nail holes and cracks, sandpaper rough spots, and brush off dust. When working on tall buildings, painters erect scaffolding, including "swing stages," scaffolds suspended by ropes, or cables attached to the roof hood.

Paperhangers cover walls and ceilings with decorative wall coverings made of paper, vinyl, or fabric. They first prepare the surface to be covered by applying "sizing," which seals the surface and makes the covering stick better. When redecorating, they may first remove the old covering by soaking, steaming, or applying solvents. When necessary, they patch holes and take care of other imperfections before hanging the new wall covering. After the surface has been prepared, paperhangers must prepare the paste or other adhesive. Then they measure the area to be covered, check the covering for flaws, cut the covering into strips of the proper size, and closely examine the pattern in order to match it when the strips are hung. The next step is to brush or roll the adhesive onto the back of the covering and then place the strips on the wall or ceiling, making sure the pattern is matched, the strips are hung straight, and the edges are butted together to make tight, closed seams. They finally smooth the strips to remove bubbles and wrinkles, trim the top and bottom with a razor knife, and wipe off any excess adhesive. Painters and paperhangers held 473,000 jobs in 2006; about 98 percent were painters. About 38 percent of painters and paperhangers work for painting and wall covering contractors engaged in new construction, repair, restoration, or remodeling work.

Working Conditions: Most painters and paper hangers work 40 hours a week or less; about one-quarter have variable schedules or work part time. Painters and paperhangers must stand for long periods. Their jobs also require a considerable amount of climbing and bending. These workers must have stamina, because much of the work is done with their arms raised overhead. Painters often work outdoors but seldom in wet, cold, or inclement weather. These workers risk injury from slipping or falling off ladders and scaffolds. They sometimes may work with materials that can be hazardous if masks are not worn or if ventilation is poor. Some painting jobs can leave a worker covered with paint. In some cases, painters may work in a sealed self-contained suit to prevent inhalation of, or contact with, hazardous materials.

Education, Training, & Qualifications: Painting and paperhanging are learned through apprenticeships or informal, on-the-job instruction. Although training authorities recommend completion of an apprenticeship program as the best way to become a painter or paperhanger, most painters learn the trade informally on the job as a helper to an experienced painter. Limited opportunities for informal training exist for paperhangers because few paperhangers need helpers. The apprenticeships for painters and paperhangers consists of two to four years of on-the-job training, in addition to 144 hours of related classroom instruction each year. Apprentices receive instruction in color harmony, use and care of tools and equipment, surface preparation, application techniques, paint mixing and matching, characteristics of different finishes, blueprint reading, wood finishing, and safety. Painters and paperhangers may advance to supervisory or estimating jobs with painting and decorating contractors. Many establish their own painting and decorating businesses.

Earnings: Median annual earnings of painters (construction and maintenance) were $15.00 ($31,200 annually). The middle 50 percent earned between $12.19 and $19.51 an hour. Median hourly earnings in the industries employing the largest numbers of painters in 2006 were:

- Local government $20.11
- Drywall and insulation contractors $16.18
- Nonresidential building
  construction $15.68
- Residential building construction $15.04
- Painting and wall covering
  contractors $11.62

In 2006, median earnings for paperhangers were $16.21. The middle 50 percent earned between $13.12 and $20.62.

Earnings for painters may be reduced on occasion because of bad weather and the short-term nature of many construction jobs. Hourly wage rates for apprentices usually start at 40 to 50 percent of the rate for experienced workers and increase periodically.

Key Contacts: For information about the work of painters and paperhangers, contact local painting and decorating contractors, a local of the International Union of Painters and Allied Trades, a local joint union-management apprenticeship committee, or an office of the state apprenticeship agency or employment services:

- **International Union of Painters and Allied Trades:** 1750 New York Avenue, NW, Washington, DC 20006. Website: www. iupat.org.

- **Associated Builders and Contractors:** Workforce Development Department, 4250 N. Fairfax Drive, 9th Floor, Arlington, VA 22203. Website: www.trytools.org.

- **Painting and Decorating Contractors of America:** 1801 Park 270 Drive, Suite 220, Saint Louis, MO 63146. Website: www.pdca. org.

Pipelayers, Plumbers, Pipefitters, and Steamfitters

⇨ **Annual Earnings:** $42,765
⇨ **Education/Training:** Apprenticeship
⇨ **Outlook:** Very good

Employment Outlook: Job opportunities are expected to be very good, especially for workers with welding experience. Employment of pipelayers, plumbers, pipefitters, and steamfitters is expected to grow 10 percent between 2006 and 2016, about as fast as the average for all occupations. The demand for skilled pipelayers, plumbers, pipefitters, and steamfitters is expected to outpace the supply of workers trained in these crafts. Many potential workers may prefer work that is less strenuous and has more comfortable working conditions. Employment of individuals in these trades is expected to grow about as fast as the average for all occupations in the coming decade. Demand for plumbers will stem from building renovation, including the growing use of sprinkler systems; repair and maintenance of existing residential systems; and maintenance activities for places having extensive systems of pipes, such as power plants, water and wastewater treatment plants, pipelines, office buildings, and factories. Employment of pipelayers, plumbers, pipefitters, and steamfitters generally is less sensitive to changes in economic conditions than is employment of some other construction trades. Even when construction activity declines, maintenance, rehabilitation, and replacement of existing piping systems, as well as the increasing installation of fire sprinkler systems, provide many jobs for pipelayers, plumbers, pipefitters, and steamfitters.

Nature of Work: Although pipelaying, pipefitting, plumbing, and steamfitting sometimes are considered a single trade, workers generally specialize in one of the four areas. Pipelayers lay clay, concrete, plastic, or cast-iron pipe for drains, sewers, water mains, and oil or gas lines. Before laying the pipe, pipelayers prepare and grade the trenches either manually or with machines. Plumbers install and repair the water, waste disposal, drainage, and gas systems in homes and commercial and industrial buildings. Plumbers also install plumbing fixtures – bathtubs, showers, sinks, and toilets – and appliances such as dishwashers and water heaters. Pipefitters install and repair both high- and low-pressure pipe systems used in manufacturing, in the generation of electricity, and in heating and cooling buildings. They also install automatic controls that are increasingly being used to regulate these systems. Some pipefitters specialize in only one type of system. Steamfitters, for example, install pipe systems that move liquids or gases under high pressure. Sprinkler fitters install automatic fire sprinkler systems in buildings.

Pipelayers, plumbers, pipefitters, and steamfitters constitute one of the largest construction occupations, holding about 569,000 jobs in 2006. About 55 percent worked for plumbing, heating, and air-conditioning contractors engaged in new construction, repair, modernization, or maintenance work.

Working Conditions: Because pipelayers, plumbers, pipefitters, and steamfitters must lift heavy pipes, stand for long periods, and sometimes work in uncomfortable or cramped positions, they need physical strength as well as stamina. They also may have to work outdoors in inclement weather. In addition, they are subject to possible falls from ladders, cuts from sharp tools, and burns from hot pipes or soldering equipment. Pipelayers, plumbers, pipefitters, and steamfitters engaged in construction generally work a standard 40-hour week. Those involved in maintenance services under contract may have to work evening or weekend shifts, as well as be on call. These maintenance workers may spend quite a bit of time traveling to and from work sites.

Education, Training, & Qualifications: Virtually all pipelayers, pipefitters, plumbers, and steamfitters undergo some type of apprenticeship training. Many apprenticeship programs are administered by local union-management committees made up of members of the United Association of Journeymen and Apprentices of the Plumbing and Pipefitting Industry of the United States and Canada, and local employers who are members of either the Mechanical Contractors Association of America, the National Association of Plumbing-Heating-Cooling Contractors, or the National Fire Sprinkler Association. Nonunion training and apprenticeship programs are administered by local chapters of the Associated Builders and Contractors, the National Association of Plumbing-Heating-Cooling Contractors, the American Fire Sprinkler Association, or the Home Builders Institute of the National Association of Home Builders. Apprenticeships – both union and nonunion – consist of four or five years of on-the-job training, in addition to at least 144 hours per year of related classroom instruction. As apprentices gain experience, they learn how to work with various types of pipe and how to install different piping systems and plumbing fixtures.

Earnings: Pipelayers, plumbers, pipefitters, and steamfitters are among the highest paid construction occupations. In 2006, median annual earnings of pipelayers were $20.56 ($42,765 per year). The middle 5 0 percent earned between $15.62 and $27.54. Also, in 2006, median hourly earnings of wage and salary pipelayers were $14.58. The middle 50 percent earned between $11.75 and $19.76.

Median hourly earnings in the industries employing the largest numbers of plumbers, pipefitters, and steamfitters in 2006 were:

- Natural gas distribution $24.91
- Nonresidential building
  construction $21.30
- Plumbing, heating, and
  air-conditioning contractors $20.44
- Utility system construction $19.18
- Local government $17.86

Apprentices usually are paid about 50 percent of the wage rate paid to experienced pipelayers, plumbers, pipefitters, and steamfitters.

About 30 percent of pipelayers, plumbers, pipefitters, and steamfitters belonged to a union.

Key Contacts: For information on apprenticeship opportunities for pipelayers, plumbers, pipefitters, and steamfitters, contact:

- **United Association of Journeymen and Apprentices of the Plumbing and Pipefitting Industry of the U.S. and Canada:** 901 Massachusetts Avenue, NW, Washington, DC 20001. Website: www.ua.org.

For more information about training programs for pipelayers, plumbers, pipefitters, and steamfitters, contact:

- **Associated Builders and Contractors:** Workforce Development Department, 4250 North Fairfax Drive, 9th Floor, Arlington, VA 22203. Website: www.trytools.org.

- **Home Builders Institute:** 1201 15th Street NW, Washington, DC 20005. Website: www.hbi.org.

For general information about the work of pipelayers, plumbers, and pipefitters, contact:

- **Mechanical Contractors Association of America:** 1385 Piccard Drive, Rockville, MD 20850. Website: www.mcaa.org.

- **Plumbing-Heating-Cooling Contractors Association:** 180 S. Washington Street, Falls Church, VA 22046. Website: www.phccweb. org.

For general information about the work of sprinkler fitters, contact:

- **American Fire Sprinkler Association:** 12750 Merit Drive, Suite 350, Dallas, TX 75251. Website: www.firesprinkler.org.

- **National Fire Sprinkler Association:** 40 Jon Barrett Road, Patterson, NY 12563. Website: www.nfsa.org.

Plasterers and Stucco Masons

- **Annual Earnings:** $34,695
- **Education/Training:** On-the-job or apprenticeship
- **Outlook:** Average

Employment Outlook: Employment of plasterers and stucco masons is expected to grow about as fast as the average for all occupations as a result of increased appreciation for durability and attractiveness of troweled finishes. Good job prospects are expected.

Employment is expected to grow by 8 percent between 2006 and 2016, about as fast as the average for all occupations. Many potential candidates prefer work that is less strenuous and more comfortable. Additionally, some prospects may be deterred by the lengthy apprenticeships. This creates more opportunity for people who want these jobs.

Nature of Work: Plastering – one of the oldest crafts in the building trades – remains popular due to the durability and relatively low cost of the material. Plasterers apply plaster to interior walls and ceilings to form fire-resistant and relatively soundproof surfaces. They also apply plaster veneer over drywall to create smooth or textured abrasion-resistant finishes. In addition, plasterers install prefabricated exterior insulation system over existing walls – for good insulation and interesting architectural effects – and cast ornamental designs in plaster. Stucco masons apply durable plasters, such as polymer-based acrylic finishes and stucco, to exterior surfaces.

Plasterers and stucco masons should not be confused with drywall installers, ceiling tile installers, and tapers who use drywall instead of plaster to make interior walls and ceilings.

Working Conditions: Most plasterers work indoors, except for the few who apply decorative exterior finishes. Stucco masons, however, work outside when applying stucco or exterior wall insulation. Plasterers and stucco masons may work on scaffolds high above the ground.

Plastering and stucco work is physically demanding, requiring considerable standing, bending, lifting, and reaching overhead, sometimes causing neck and upper back cramps. The work can also be dusty and dirty. It can irritate the skin, eyes, and lungs unless protective masks and gloves are used.

Education, Training, & Qualifications: Becoming a skilled plasterer or stucco mason generally requires 3 or 4 years of training, either informally on the job or through a formal apprenticeship. Preparation for a career as a plasterer or stucco mason can begin in high school, with classes in mathematics, mechanical drawing, and shop. The most common way to get a job is with a contractor who will provide on-the-job training. Entry-level workers usually start as helpers, assisting more experienced workers. They may start by carrying materials, setting up scaffolds, and mixing plaster. Later, they learn to apply the scratch, brown, and finish coats and may also learn to replicate plaster decorations for restoration work. Depending on the region, some employers say a formal apprenticeship is the best way to learn plastering. Apprenticeship programs, sponsored by local joint committees of contractors and unions, usually include 3 or 4 years of paid on-the-job training and 160 hours of classroom instruction each of those years. In class, apprentices learn drafting, blueprint reading, and basic mathematics for layout work. They also learn how to estimate materials and costs and how to cast ornamental plaster designs.

Earnings: In May 2006, median hourly earnings of wage and salary plasterers and stucco masons were $16.68 ($34,695 per year). The middle 50 percent earned between $13.53 and $21.25. The median hourly earnings in the largest industries employing plasterers and stucco masons were $16.92 for drywall and insulation contractors and $15.55 for masonry contractors.

Key Contacts: For general information about the work of plasterers and stucco masons, contact:

- Association of the Wall and Ceiling Industry: 513 W. Broad Street, Suite 210, Falls Church, VA 22046. Website: www.awci.org.

For information about plasterers, contact:

- Operative Plasterers' and Cement Masons' International Association: 11720 Beltsville Drive, Suite 700, Beltsville, MD 20705. Website: www.opcmia.org.

For information on certification and training of plasterers and stucco masons, contact:

- International Union of Bricklayers and Allied Craftworkers, International Masonry Institute, The James Brice House: 42 East Street, Annapolis, MD 21401. Website: www.imiweb.org.

Roofers

⇨ **Annual Earnings:** $32,261
⇨ **Education/Training:** On-the-job and apprenticeships
⇨ **Outlook:** Excellent

Employment Outlook: Most job openings will arise from high turnover, because the work is hot, strenuous, and dirty, causing many people to switch to jobs in other construction trades. In fact, many workers treat roofing as a temporary job until they find other work, which partly explains why many ex-offenders initially gravitate toward this particular occupation.

Faster-than-average employment growth is expected – by 14 percent between 2006 and 2016. Roofs deteriorate faster than most other parts of buildings, and they need to be repaired or replaced more often.

Job opportunities for roofers will arise primarily because of the need to replace workers who leave the occupation. Indeed, the proportion of roofers who leave the occupation each year is higher than in most construction trades.

Nature of Work: A leaky roof can damage ceilings, walls, and furnishings. Roofers repair and install roofs made of tar or asphalt and gravel; rubber or thermoplastic; metal; or shingles to protect buildings and their contents from water damage. Repair and reroofing – replacing old roofs on existing buildings – makes up the majority of work for roofers.

Roofers held about 156,000 jobs in 2006. Almost all salaried roofers worked for roofing contractors. About 20 percent of roofers were self-employed. Many self-employed roofers specialized in residential work.

Working Conditions: Roofing work is strenuous. It involves heavy lifting, as well as climbing, bending, and kneeling. Roofers work outdoors in all types of weather, particularly when making repairs. Workers risk slips or falls from scaffolds, ladders, or roofs or burns from hot bitumen. Roofs can become extremely hot during summer, causing heat-related illnesses. In 2005, the rate of injuries for roofing contractors in construction was almost twice that of workers overall.

Education, Training, & Qualifications: Most roofers learn their skills informally by working as helpers for experienced roofers and by taking classes, including safety training, offered by their employers; some complete three-year apprenticeships.

Earnings: In May 2006, median hourly earnings of wage and salary roofers were $15.51 ($32,261 per year). The middle 5 0 percent earned between $12.12 and $20.79. The median hourly earnings of roofers in the foundation, structure, and building exterior contractors industry were $15.54.

Key Contacts: For information about hte work of roofers, contact:

- **National Roofing Contractors Association:** 10255 W. Higgins Road, Suite 600, Rosemont, IL 60018-5607. Website: www. nrca.net.

- **United Union of Roofers, Waterproofers, and Allied Workers:** 1660 L Street, NW, Suite 800, Washington, DC 20036. Website: www.unionroofers.com.

Sheet Metal Workers

➪ **Annual Earnings:** $37,357
➪ **Education/Training:** Apprenticeship
➪ **Outlook:** Average

Employment Outlook: Employment opportunities are expected to be average – growing by 7 percent between 2006 and 2016 – for sheet metal workers in the construction industry and in construction-related sheet metal fabrication, reflecting both employment growth and openings arising each year as experienced sheet metal workers leave the occupation. In addition, many potential workers may prefer work that is less strenuous and that has more comfortable working conditions, thus limiting the number of applicants for sheet metal jobs. Opportunities should be particularly good for individuals who acquire apprenticeship training.

Employment of sheet metal workers in construction is expected to grow about as fast as the average for all occupations in the decade ahead. This will be in response to growth in the demand for sheet metal installations as more industrial, commercial, and residential structures are built. The need to install energy-efficient air-conditioning, heating, and ventilation systems in the increasing numbers of old buildings and to perform other types of renovation and maintenance work also should boost employment.

Nature of Work: Sheet metal workers make, install, and maintain heating, ventilation, and air-conditioning duct systems, roofs, siding, rain gutters, downspouts, skylights, restaurant equip-

ment, outdoor signs, railroad cars, tailgates, customized precision equipment, and many other products made from metal sheets. They also may work with fiberglass and plastic materials. Although some workers specialize in fabrication, installation, or maintenance, most do all three jobs. Sheet metal workers do both construction-related sheet metal work and mass production of sheet metal products in manufacturing. Sheet metal workers held about 205,000 jobs in 2002. Nearly two-thirds of all sheet metal workers were found in the construction industry. Of those employed in construction, almost half worked for plumbing, heating, and air-conditioning contractors; most of the rest worked for roofing and sheet metal contractors.

Working Conditions: Sheet metal workers usually work a 40-hour week. Those who fabricate sheet metal products work in shops that are well-lighted and well-ventilated. However, they stand for long periods and lift heavy materials and finished pieces. Sheet metal workers must follow safety practices because working around high-speed machines can be dangerous. They also are subject to cuts from sharp metal, burns from soldering and welding, and falls from ladders and scaffolds. They usually wear safety glasses but must not wear jewelry or loose-fitting clothing that could easily be caught in a machine. Those performing installation work do considerable bending, lifting, standing, climbing, and squatting, sometimes in close quarters or in awkward positions.

Sheet metal workers held about 189,000 jobs in 2006. About 66 percent of all sheet metal workers were in the construction industry, including 45 percent who worked for plumbing, heating, and air-conditioning contractors; most of the rest in construction worked for roofing and sheet metal contractors. About 21 percent of all sheet metal workers were in manufacturing industries, such as the fabricated metal products, machinery, and aerospace products and parts industries. Few sheet metal workers are self-employed.

Education, Training, & Qualifications: Apprenticeship generally is considered to be the best way to learn this trade. The apprenticeship program consists of four to five years of on-the-job training and an average of 200 hours per year of classroom instruction. Apprenticeship programs may be administered by local joint committees composed of the Sheet Metal Workers' International Association and local chapters of the Sheet Metal and Air-Conditioning Contractors National Association. On the job, apprentices learn the basics of pattern layout and how to cut, bend, fabricate, and install sheet metal. In the classroom, apprentices learn drafting, plan and specification reading, trigonometry and geometry applicable to layout work, the use of computerized equipment, welding, and the principles of heating, air-conditioning, and ventilating systems.

Some people pick up the trade informally, usually by working as helpers to experienced sheet metal workers. Most sheet metal workers in large-scale manufacturing receive on-the-job training, with additional classwork or in-house training when necessary.

Earnings: In May 2006, median hourly earnings of sheet metal workers were $17.96 which equals $37,357 per year. The middle 50 percent earned between $13.30 and $24.89. The median hourly earnings of the largest industries employing sheet metal workers in 2002 were:

- Building finishing contractors $18.84
- Plumbing, heating, and
  air-conditioning contractors $18.60
- Roofing contractors $17.27
- Architectural and structural
  metals manufacturing $16.60

Apprentices normally start at about 40 to 50 percent of the rate paid to experienced workers.

Key Contacts: For more information on apprenticeships or other work opportunities, contact local sheet metal contractors or heating, refrigeration, and air-conditioning contractors; a local of the Sheet Metal Workers International Association; a local of the Sheet Metal and Air-Conditioning Contractors National Association; a local joint union-management apprenticeship committee; or the nearest office of your state employment service or apprenticeship agency.

For general and training information about sheet metal workers, contact:

- **International Training Institute for the Sheet Metal and Air Conditioning Industry**: 601 N. Fairfax Street, Suite 240, Alexandria, VA 22314. Website: www.sheetmetal-iti.org.

- **Sheet Metal and Air Conditioning Contractors National Association**: 4201 Lafayette Center Drive, Chantilly, VA 20151-1209. Website: www.smacna.org.

- **Sheet Metal Workers International Association**: 1750 New York Avenue, NW, Washington, DC 20006. Website: www.smwia.org.

Structural and Reinforcing Iron and Metal Workers

- ➪ **Annual Earnings:** $40,477
- ➪ **Education/Training:** Apprenticeships
- ➪ **Outlook:** Excellent

Employment Outlook: Employment of structural and reinforcing iron and metal workers is expected to grow about as fast as the average for all occupations in the decade ahead – about 8 percent between 2006 and 2016 – largely on the basis of continued growth in industrial and commercial construction. The rehabilitation, maintenance, and replacement of a growing number of older buildings, factories, power plants, highways, and bridges is expected to create employment opportunities. The number of job openings fluctuates from year to year with economic conditions and the level of construction activity.

Nature of Work: Structural and reinforcing iron and metal workers place and install iron or steel girders, columns, and other construction materials to form buildings, bridges, and other structures. They also position and secure steel bars or mesh in concrete forms in order to reinforce the concrete used in highways, buildings, bridges, tunnels, and other structures. In addition, they repair and renovate older buildings and structures. Even though the primary metal involved in this work is steel, these workers often are known as ironworkers.

Working Conditions: Structural and reinforcing iron and metal workers usually work outside in all kinds of weather. However, those who work at great heights do not work during wet, icy, or extremely windy conditions. Because the danger of injuries due to falls is great, ironworkers use safety devices such as safety belts, scaffolding, and nets to reduce risk. Some ironworkers fabricate structural metal in fabricating shops, which usually are located away from the construction site. These workers usually work a 40-hour week. They held about 102,000 jobs in 2006; structural iron and steel workers held about 72,000 jobs; and reinforcing iron and rebar workers held about 30,000 jobs.

Education, Training, & Qualifications: Most employers recommend a three- or four-year apprenticeship involving on-the-job training and evening classroom instruction as the best way to learn this trade. Apprenticeship programs usually are administered by committees made up of representatives of local unions of the International Association of Bridge, Structural, Ornamental and Reinforcing Iron Workers or the local chapters of contractors' associations. Ironworkers must be at least 18 years old. A high school diploma is preferred by employers and local apprenticeship committees.

Earnings: In 2006, median hourly earnings of structural iron and steel workers in all industries were $19.46 ($40,477 per year). The middle 50 percent earned between $14.11 and $27.08. In 2006, median hourly earnings of reinforcing iron and rebar workers in all industries were $18.36. Median hourly earnings of structural iron and steel workers in 2006 employed by foundation, structure, and building exterior contractors were $20.54, and in nonresidential building construction, $16.76. According to the International Association of Bridge, Structural, Ornamental, and Reinforcing Iron Workers, average hourly earnings, including benefits, for structural and reinforcing metal workers who belonged to a union and worked full time were 34 percent higher than the hourly earnings of nonunion workers.

Key Contacts: For information on apprenticeships or other work opportunities, contact

local general contractors; a local of the International Association of Bridge, Structural, Ornamental, and Reinforcing Iron Workers Union; a local iron workers' joint union-management apprenticeship committee; a local or state chapter of the Associated Builders and Contractors or the Associated General Contractors of America; or the nearest office of your state employment service or apprenticeship agency.

For apprenticeship information, contact:

- **International Association of Bridge, Structural, Ornamental, and Reinforcing Iron Workers:** Apprenticeship Department, 1750 New York Avenue, NW, Suite 400, Washington, DC 20006. Website: www.ironworkers. org.

For general information about ironworkers, contact either of the following sources:

- **Associated Builders and Contractors:** Workforce Development Department, 4250 N. Fairfax Drive, 9th Floor, Arlington, VA 22203. Website: www.trytools.org.

- **Associated General Contractors of America:** 2300 Wilson Blvd., Suite 400, Arlington, VA 22201. Website: www.agc.org.

Ask Yourself

If some of the construction trades described in this chapter appeal to you, ask yourself the following questions:

1. Which construction trades am I most interested in pursuing?

_____

_____

2. What skills do I currently have that would be helpful in landing a job in those trades?

_____

_____

3. What additional education and trading do I need in order to land a job?

_____

_____

4. Where will I get that additional education and training?

_____

_____

5. Who could help me now in landing a job in the trade that interests me?

_____

_____

6. What else do I need to know and do to get into this trade?

_____

_____

_____

_____

*   *   *

When completing the remaining chapters, ask yourself similar questions at the end of each chapter about the particular jobs or occupations featured in that chapter. In so doing, you'll get a better idea of how your interests and skills might best relate to each job. Better still, you'll begin developing an **action plan** for directing your post-release job search. You'll also begin identifying your additional education and training needs and focusing on key individuals who might be willing to extend you a helping hand for getting your career on a positive track.

5

Installation, Maintenance, and Repair Occupations

T HE INCREASED USE OF TECHNOLOGY and machinery requires more and more workers who are experts at installing, maintaining, and repairing equipment. Most of these jobs require some postsecondary education and training, such as attending specialized trade school classes, receiving on-the-job training, and acquiring certification. Individuals entering these fields can expect to regularly acquire additional education and training in order to keep up with the latest developments in their respective fields.

Most of the jobs profiled in this chapter are expected to grow substantially in the decade ahead as well as generate high median earnings for their workers. Many are attractive alternatives for installation- and repair-oriented individuals who are entering the job market but who do not have the requisite education credentials to enter other occupational fields. These also are some of the safest jobs – relatively recession-proof and impossible to offshore. Entry into one of these jobs should lead to a relatively comfortable and secure employment future. Ex-offenders should seriously consider many of these job and career alternatives.

Aircraft and Avionics Equipment Mechanics & Service Technicians

⇨ **Annual Earnings:** $47,736
⇨ **Education/Training:** Trade school, on-the-job training, and certificate
⇨ **Outlook:** Average

Employment Outlook: Opportunities for aircraft and avionics equipment mechanics and service technician jobs should be as fast as the average for all occupations. Job opportunities should be favorable for people who have completed aircraft mechanic training programs. Employment is expected to increase by 10 percent during the 2006-2016 period. Large

numbers of additional job openings should arise from the need to replace experienced mechanics who retire.

Avionics technicians are projected to increase at a slower than average rate. Contributing to favorable future job opportunities for mechanics is the long-term trend towards fewer students entering technical schools to learn maintenance and repair trades. Many of the students who have the ability and aptitude to work on planes are choosing to enter college, work in computer-related fields, or go to other repair and maintenance occupations with better working conditions. If the trend continues, the supply of trained aviation mechanics will not be able to keep up with air transportation industry needs when growth resumes in the industry.

Job opportunities are likely to be best at small commuter and regional airlines, at Federal Aviation Administration (FAA) repair stations, and in general aviation. Commuter and regional airlines are the fastest growing segment of the air transportation industry, but wages in these companies tend to be lower than those in the major airlines, so they attract fewer job applicants. In general, prospects will be best for applicants with experience. Mechanics who keep abreast of technological advances in electronics, composite materials, and other areas will be in greatest demand. The number of job openings for aircraft mechanics in the federal government should decline as the government increasingly contracts out service and repair functions to private repair companies.

Nature of Work: Aircraft and avionics equipment mechanics and service technicians perform scheduled maintenance, make repairs, and complete inspections required by the FAA. Many aircraft mechanics specialize in preventive maintenance. They inspect engines, landing gear, instruments, pressurized sections, accessories – brakes, valves, pumps, and air-conditioning systems, for example – and other parts of the aircraft, and do the necessary maintenance and replacement of parts. Inspections take place following a schedule based on the number of hours the aircraft has flown, calendar days since the last inspection, cycles of operation, or a combination of these factors.

To examine an engine, aircraft mechanics work through specially designed openings while standing on ladders or scaffolds, or use hoists or lifts to remove the entire engine from the aircraft. After taking an engine apart, mechanics use precision instruments to measure parts for wear and use x-ray and magnetic inspection equipment to check for invisible cracks. Worn or defective parts are repaired or replaced. After completing all repairs, they must test the equipment to ensure that it works properly. Mechanics work as fast as safety permits so that the aircraft can be put back into service quickly. Some mechanics work on one or many different types of aircraft, such as jets and helicopters.

Avionics systems are now an integral part of aircraft design and have vastly increased aircraft capability. Avionics technicians repair and maintain components used for aircraft navigation and radio communications, weather radar systems, and other instruments and computers that control flight, engine, and other primary functions. These duties may require additional licenses issued by the Federal Communications Commission (FCC). Because of technological advances, an increasing amount of time is spent repairing electronic systems, such as computerized controls. Technicians also may be required to analyze and develop solutions to complex electronic problems.

Working Conditions: Mechanics usually work in hangars or in other indoor areas, although they can work outdoors – sometimes in unpleasant weather – when hangars are full or when repairs must be made quickly. Mechanics often work under time pressure to maintain flight schedules or, in general aviation, to keep from inconveniencing customers. At the same time, mechanics have a tremendous responsibility to maintain safety standards, and this can cause the job to be stressful.

Frequently, mechanics must lift or pull objects weighing as much as 70 pounds. They often stand, lie, or kneel in awkward positions and occasionally must work in precarious positions on scaffolds or ladders. Noise and vibration are common when engines are being tested, so ear protection is necessary. Aircraft mechanics usually work 40 hours a week on 8-hour shifts around the clock. Overtime is frequent.

Education, Training, & Qualifications: The majority of mechanics who work on civilian aircraft are certificated by the FAA as "airframe mechanic," "powerplant mechanic," or "avionics repair specialist." Mechanics who also have an inspector's authorization can certify work completed by other mechanics and perform required inspections. Uncertified mechanics are supervised by those with certificates.

The FAA requires at least 18 months of work experience for an airframe, powerplant, or avionics repairer's certificate. Completion of a program at an FAA-certified mechanic school can substitute for the work experience requirement. Applicants for all certificates also must pass written and oral tests and demonstrate that they can do the work authorized by the certificate. Few people become mechanics through on-the-job training. Most learn their job in one of about 200 trade schools certified by the FAA. About one-third of these schools award 2- and 4-year degrees in avionics, aviation technology, or aviation maintenance management. Some aircraft mechanics in the military services acquire enough general experience to satisfy the work experience requirements for the FAA certificate. With additional study they may pass the certifying exam. In general, however, jobs in the military services are too specialized to provide the broad experience required by the FAA. In any case, military experience is a great advantage when seeking employment; employers consider trade school graduates who have this experience to be the most desirable applicants.

Aircraft mechanics must do careful and thorough work that requires a high degree of mechanical aptitude. Employers seek applicants who are self-motivated, hard-working, enthusiastic, and able to diagnose and solve complex mechanical problems. Agility is important for the reaching and climbing necessary to do the job. Because they may work on the tops of wings and fuselages on large jet planes, aircraft mechanics must not be afraid of heights.

Earnings: Median hourly earnings of aircraft mechanics and service technicians were about $22.95 in May 2006. The middle 50 percent earned between $18.96 and $28.12. Median hourly earnings in the industries employing the largest numbers of aircraft mechanics and service technicians in May 2006 were:

- Scheduled air transportation $27.46
- Nonscheduled air transportation $23.33
- Federal government $23.19
- Aerospace product and parts
  manufacturing $21.58
- Support activities for air
  transportation $19.57

Median hourly earnings of avionics technicians was about $22.57 in May 2006. The middle 50 percent earned between $19.02 and $26.65. Mechanics who work on jets for the major airlines generally earn more than those working on other aircraft. Airline mechanics and their immediate families receive reduced-fare transportation on their own and most other airlines. Almost 4 in 10 aircraft and avionics equipment mechanics and service technicians are members of or covered by union agreements.

Key Contacts: Information about jobs with a particular airline can be obtained by writing to the personnel manager of the company.

For general information about aircraft and avionics equipment mechanics and service technicians, contact:

- **Professional Aviation Maintenance Association:** 400 Commonwealth Drive, Warrendale, PA 15096. Website: www.pama.org.

For information on jobs in a particular area, contact employers at local airports or local offices of the state employment services.

Automotive Body and Related Repairers

⇨ **Annual Earnings:** $35,194
⇨ **Education/Training:** Technical school or apprenticeship training preferred
⇨ **Outlook:** Good

Employment Outlook: Employment of automotive body and related repairers is expected to grow about as fast as average through the year 2016, and job opportunities are projected to be excellent due to a growing number of retirements in this occupation.

Employment of automotive body repairers is expected to grow 12 percent over the 2006-2016 decade, as compared to 10 percent for all occupations. Demand for qualified body repairers will increase as the number of vehicles on the road continues to grow. Employment growth will continue to be in automotive body, paint, interior, and glass repair shops, with little or no change in automotive dealerships.

Nature of Work: Most of the damage resulting from everyday vehicle collisions can be repaired, and vehicles can be refinished to look and drive like new. Automotive body repairers, often called collision repair technicians, straighten bent bodies, remove dents, and replace crumpled parts that cannot be fixed. They repair all types of vehicles, and although some work on large trucks, businesses, or tractor-trailers, most work on cars and small trucks. They can work alone, with only general direction from supervisors, or as specialists on a repair team. In some shops, helpers or apprentices assist experienced repairers.

Working Conditions: Repairers work indoors in body shops that are noisy with the clatter of hammers against metal and the whine or power tools. Most shops are well ventilated to disperse dust and paint fumes. Body repairers often work in awkward or cramped positions, and much of their work is strenuous and dirty.

Education, Training, & Qualifications: Automotive technology is rapidly becoming more sophisticated, and most employers prefer applicants who have completed a formal training program in automotive body repair or refinishing. Most new repairers complete at least part of this training on the job. Many repairers, particularly in urban areas, need a national certification to advance past entry-level work.

A high school diploma or GED is often all that is required to enter this occupation, but more specific education and training is needed to learn how to repair newer automobiles. Collision repair programs may be offered in high school or in postsecondary vocational schools and community colleges. Courses in electronics, physics, chemistry, English, computers, and mathematics provide a good background for a career as an automotive body repairer. Most training programs combine classroom instructions and hands-on practice.

Certification by the National Institute for Automotive Service Excellence (ASE), although voluntary, is the pervasive industry credential for non-entry-level automotive body repairers.

Earnings: Median hourly wage-and-salary earnings of automotive body and related repairers, including incentive pay, were $16.92 in May 2006. The middle 50 percent earned between $13.00 and $22.33 an hour. Median hourly earnings of automotive body and related repairers were $17.85 in automobile dealerships and $16.66 in automotive repair and maintenance. Median hourly wage-and-salary earnings of automotive glass insta llers and repairers, including incentive pay, were $14.77.

The majority of body repairers employed by independent repair shops and automotive dealers are paid on an incentive basis. Under this system, body repairers are paid a set amount for various tasks, and earnings depend on both the amount of work assigned and how fast it is completed. Employers frequently guarantee workers a minimum weekly salary.

Key Contacts: For general information about automotive body repairer careers, contact the following sources:

- **Automotive Careers Today:** 8400 Westpark Drive, MS#2, McLean, VA 22102. Website: www.autocareerstoday.org.

- **Automotive Service Association:** P.O. Box 929, Bedford, TX 76095. Website: www.asa shop.org.

For information on how to become a certified automotive body repairer, contact:

- **National Institute for Automotive Service Excellence (ASE):** 101 Blue Seal Drive, SE, Suite 101, Leesburg, VA 20175. Website: www.asecert.org.

Automotive Service Technicians and Mechanics

- **Annual Earnings:** $33,772
- **Education/Training:** High school and training
- **Outlook:** Good

Employment Outlook: Employment of automotive service technicians and mechanics is expected to grow faster than average in the decade ahead. Population growth will boost demand for motor vehicles, which will require regular maintenance and service. Growth of the labor force and in the number of families in which both spouses need vehicles to commute to work will contribute to increased vehicle sales and employment in this industry. Growth of personal income will also contribute to families owning multiple vehicles. Employment growth will continue to be concentrated in automobile dealerships and independent automotive repair shops. Many new jobs also will be created in small retail operations that offer after-warranty repairs, such as oil changes, brake repair, air-conditioner service, and other minor repairs. Most persons who enter the occupation can expect steady work, because changes in general economic conditions and developments in other industries have little effect on the automotive repair business.

Nature of Work: The ability to diagnose the source of a problem quickly and accurately requires good reasoning ability and a thorough knowledge of automobiles. The work of automotive service technicians and mechanics has evolved from mechanical repair to a high-tech job. Today, integrated electronic systems and complex computers run vehicles and measure their performance while on the road. Technicians must have the ability to work with electronic diagnostic equipment and computer-based technical reference materials.

Automotive service technicians and mechanics use their high-tech skills to inspect, maintain, and repair automobiles and light trucks that have gasoline engines. The increasing sophistication of automotive technology, including new hybrid vehicles, now requires workers who can use computerized shop equipment and work with electronic components while maintaining their skills with traditional hand tools. Service technicians use a variety of tools in their work – power tools such as pneumatic wrenches to remove bolts quickly; machine tools like lathes and grinding machines to rebuild brakes; welding and flame-cutting equipment to remove and repair exhaust systems; and jacks and hoists to lift cars and engines. They also use common hand tools, such as screwdrivers, pliers, and wrenches, to work on small parts and in hard-to-reach places. Automotive service technicians in large shops have increasingly become specialized.

Automotive service technicians and mechanics held about 773,000 jobs in 2006. Automotive repair and maintenance shops and automotive dealers employed the majority of these workers – 29 percent each.

Working Conditions: About half of automotive service technicians work a standard 40-hour week, but almost 30 percent work more than 40 hours a week. Many of those working extended hours are self-employed technicians. To satisfy customer service needs, some service shops offer evening and weekend service. Generally, service technicians work indoors in well-ventilated and -lighted repair shops. However, some shops are drafty and noisy. Although technicians fix some problems with simple computerized adjustments, they frequently work with dirty and greasy parts, and in awkward positions. They often lift heavy parts and tools. Minor cuts, burns, and bruises are common, but technicians usually avoid serious accidents when the shop is kept clean and orderly and safety practices are observed.

Education, Training, & Qualifications:
Automotive technology is rapidly increasing in sophistication, and most training authorities strongly recommend that persons seeking automotive service technician and mechanic jobs complete a formal training program in high school or in a postsecondary vocational school. However, some service technicians still learn the trade solely by assisting and learning from experienced workers.

Many high schools, community colleges, and vocational and technical schools offer automotive service technician training programs. The traditional postsecondary programs usually provide a thorough career preparation that expands upon the student's high school repair experience. Postsecondary automotive technician training programs vary greatly in format, but normally provide intensive career preparation through a combination of classroom instruction and hands-on practice. Some trade and technical school programs provide concentrated training for six months to a year, depending on how many hours the student attends each week. Community college programs normally spread the training over two years; supplement the automotive training with instruction in English, bas ic mathematics, computers, and other subjects; and award an associate degree or certificate. Some students earn repair certificates and opt to leave the program to begin their career before graduation. Recently, some programs have added to their curricula training on employability skills such as customer service and stress management. Employers find that these skills help technicians handle the additional responsibilities of dealing with the customers and parts vendors.

Most employers regard the successful completion of a vocational training program in automotive service technology as the best preparation for trainee positions. Experience working on motor vehicles in the Armed Forces or as a hobby also is valuable. Because of the complexity of new vehicles, a growing number of employers require the completion of high school and additional postsecondary training.

Earnings: Median hourly earnings of automotive service technicians and mechanics, including those on commission, were $16.24 ($33,779 annually) in May 2006. The highest 10 percent earned more than $27.22. Median annual earnings in the industries employing the largest number of service technicians in 2006 were:

- Local government $19.07
- Automobile dealers $18.85
- Automotive repair and maintenance $14.55
- Gasoline stations $14.51
- Automotive parts, accessories,
  and tire stores $14.38

Many experienced technicians employed by automobile dealers and independent repair shops receive a commission related to the labor cost charged to the customer. Employers frequently guarantee commissioned mechanics and technicians a minimum weekly salary. Some technicians are members of labor unions.

Key Contacts: For more details about work opportunities, contact local automobile dealers and repair shops or local offices of the state employment service. The state employment service may also have information about training programs. A list of certified automotive service technician training programs can be obtained from:

- **National Automotive Technicians Education Foundation:** 101 Blue Seal Drive, Suite 101, Leesburg, VA 20175. Website: www. natef.org.

For a directory of accredited private trade and technical schools that offer programs in automotive service technician training, contact:

- **Accrediting Commission of Career Schools and Colleges of Technology:** 2101 Wilson Blvd., Suite 302, Arlington, VA 22201. Website: www.accsct.org.

For a list of public automotive service technician training programs, contact:

- **SkillsUSA:** P.O. Box 3000, Leesburg, VA 20177-0300. Website: www.skillsusa.org.

Information on automobile manufacturer-sponsored programs in automotive service technology can be obtained from:

- **Automotive Youth Educational Systems (AYES):** 100 W. Big Beaver, Suite 300, Troy, MI 48084. Website: www.ayes.org.

Information on how to become a certified automotive service technician is available from:

- **National Institute for Automotive Service Excellence (ASE):** 101 Blue Seal Drive SE, Suite 101, Leesburg, VA 20175. Website: www.asecert.org.

For general information about a career as an automotive service technician, contact:

- **National Automobile Dealers Association:** 8400 Westpark Drive, McLean, VA 22102. Website: www.nada.org.

Coin, Vending, and Amusement Machine Servicers and Repairers

- ◇ **Annual Earnings:** $28,704
- ◇ **Education/Training:** Prefer high school graduates/on-the-job training
- ◇ **Outlook:** Good

Employment Outlook: Employment of coin, vending, and amusement machine servicers and repairers is expected to decline moderately through the year 2016. Opportunities for these workers, however, should be good for those with the proper training or related experience.

Businesses are expected to install additional vending machines to meet the public demand for snacks and other food items. Establishments that are likely to install additional vending machines include industrial plants, hospitals, stores, schools, and prisons in order to meet the public demand for inexpensive snacks and other food items. Growth of casino slot machines and coin-operated lottery ticket machines will increase the total number of amusement machines as well.

Opportunities should be especially good for those with knowledge of electronics, because electronic circuitry is an important component of vending and amusement machines. If firms cannot find trained or experienced workers for these jobs, they are likely to train qualified route drivers or hire inexperienced people who have acquired some mechanical, electrical, or electronics training by taking high school or vocational courses. However, improved technology in newer machines will reduce employment growth because these machines require less frequent maintenance than do older ones. New machines will need restocking less often and they contain computers that record sales and inventory data, reducing the amount of time-consuming paperwork that otherwise would have to be filled out. The Internet is beginning to play a large role in the monitoring of vending machines from remote locations. Some new machines use wireless transmitters to signal the vending machine company when the machine needs restocking or repairing. This allows servicers and repairers to be dispatched only when needed, instead of having to check each machine on a regular schedule.

Nature of Work: Coin, vending, and amusement machine servicers and repairers install, service, and stock the machines and keep them, in good working order. Vending machine servicers, often called route drivers, visit machines that dispense soft drinks, candy, and snacks, and other items. They collect money from the machines, restock merchandise, and change labels to indicate new selections. They also keep machines clean and appealing. Vending machine repairers, often called mechanics or technicians, make sure that the machines operate correctly. When checking complicated electrical and electronic machines, such as beverage dispensers, they ascertain whether the machines mix drinks properly and whether the refrigeration and heating units work correctly. If the machines are not in good working order, the mechanics repair them. Because many vending machines dispense food, these workers must comply with state and local public health and sanitation standards.

Amusement machine servicers and repairers work on jukeboxes, video games, pinball machines and slot machines. They make sure the various mechanisms function properly so that the games remain fair and the jukebox selections are accurate. Those who work in the gaming industry must adhere to strict guidelines, because federal and state agencies regulate many gaming machines.

Vending machine servicers and repairers employed by small companies may both fill and fix machines on a regular basis. These combination servicers-repairers stock machines, fill coin and currency changers, collect money, and repair machines when necessary. Servicers and repairers also do some paperwork, such as filing reports, preparing repair cost estimates, ordering parts, and keeping daily records of merchandise distributed and money collected. Newer machines with computerized inventory controls reduce the paperwork a servicer must complete.

Working Conditions: Some vending and amusement machine repairers work primarily in company repair shops, but many spend substantial time on the road, visiting machines wherever they have been placed. Repairers generally work a 40 hour week. However, vending and amusement machines operate around the clock, so repairers may be on call to work at night and on weekends and holidays.

Vending and amusement machine repair shops generally are quiet, are well lighted, and have adequate work space. However, when machines are serviced on location, the work may be done where pedestrian traffic is heavy, such as in busy supermarkets, industrial complexes, offices, casinos, or arcades. Repair work is relatively safe, although workers must take care to avoid hazards such as electrical shocks and cuts from sharp tools and other metal objects. They may be expected to move (or assist with moving) heavy vending and amusement machines.

Education, Training, & Qualifications: Although most workers learn their skills on the job, employers prefer to hire high school graduates. High school or vocational school courses in electricity, refrigeration, and machine repair are an advantage in qualifying for entry-level jobs. Employers usually require applicants to demonstrate mechanical ability, either through work experience or by scoring well on mechanical aptitude tests.

Because coin, vending, and amusement machine servicers and repairers sometimes handle thousands of dollars in merchandise and cash, employers hire persons who seem to have a record of honesty. The ability to deal tactfully with people is also important, because the servicers and repairers play a significant role in relaying customers' requests and concerns. A driver's license and a good driving record are essential for most vending and amusement servicer and repairer jobs. Some employers require their servicers to be bonded.

To learn about new machines, repairers and servicers attend training sessions sponsored by manufacturers and distributors that may last from a few days to several weeks. Both trainees and experienced workers sometimes take evening courses in basic electricity, electronics, microwave ovens, refrigeration, and other related subjects to stay on top of new techniques and equipment. Skilled servicers and repairers may be promoted to supervisory jobs or go into business for themselves.

Earnings: Median hourly earnings of coin, vending, and amusement machine servicers and repairers were $13.80 ($28,704 annually) in 2006. Many earned less than $8.77 an hour,

and the highest 10 percent more than $21.35 an hour. Typically, states with some form of legalized gaming have the highest wages. Most coin, vending, and amusement machine servicers and repairers work 8 hours a day, 5 days a week, and receive premium pay for overtime. Some union contracts stipulate higher pay for night work and for emergency repair jobs on weekends and holidays than for regular hours.

Key Contacts: Information on job opportunities in this field can be obtained from local vending machine firms and local offices of each state employment service. For general information on vending machine repair, contact:

- **National Automatic Merchandising Association**: 20 N. Wacker Drive, #3500, Chicago, IL 60606. Website: www.vending.org.

- **Vending Times**: 1375 Broadway, Room 602, New York, NY 10018. Website: www.vending times.com.

Heating, Air-Conditioning, and Refrigeration Mechanics and Installers

- ⇨ **Annual Earnings:** $37,669
- ⇨ **Education/Training:** Technical school or apprenticeship training preferred
- ⇨ **Outlook:** Average

Employment Outlook: Employment of heating, air-conditioning, and refrigeration mechanics and installers is expected to grow fast as average for all occupations through the 2006-2016 period. Job prospects are expected to be good, especially for those with technical school or formal apprenticeship training.

As population and economy grow, so does the demand for new residential, commercial, and industrial climate-control systems. Technicians who specialize in installation work may experience periods of unemployment when the level of new construction activity declines, but maintenance and repair work usually remains stable. In addition, the continuing focus on improving indoor air quality should contribute to the creation of more jobs for heating, air-conditioning, and refrigeration technicians. The growth of businesses that use refrigerated equipment – such as supermarkets and convenience stores – will also add to a growing need for technicians. In addition to openings created by employment growth, thousands of openings will result from the need to replace workers who transfer to other occupations or leave the labor force.

Nature of Work: Heating, air-conditioning, and refrigeration systems consist of many mechanical, electrical, and electronic components, such as motors, compressors, pumps, fans, ducts, pipes, thermostats, and switches. Technicians must be able to maintain, diagnose, and correct problems throughout the entire system. To do this, they adjust system controls to recommended settings and test the performance of the entire system using special tools and test equipment. Although they are trained to do both, technicians often specialize in either installation or maintenance and repair. Some specialize in one type of equipment – for example, oil burners, solar panels, or commercial refrigerators. Technicians may work for large or small contracting companies or directly for a manufacturer or wholesaler. Those working for smaller operations tend to do both installation and servicing, and work with heating, cooling, and refrigeration equipment. Depending on the size of the company, technicians may work solely on residential or commercial projects, although typically they service both. Service contracts – which involve work for particular customers on a regular basis – are becoming more common. Service agreements help to reduce the seasonal fluctuations of this work.

HVACR (heating, ventilation, air-conditioning, and refrigeration) mechanics and installers are adept at using a variety of tools, including hammers, wrenches, metal snips, electric drills, pipe cutters and benders, measurement gauges, and acetylene torches, to work with refrigerant lines and air ducts. They use voltmeters, thermometers, pressure gauges, manometers, and other testing devices to check airflow, refrigerant pressure, electrical circuits, burners, and other components.

Other craftworkers sometimes install or repair cooling and heating systems. For example, on a large air-conditioning installation job, especially where workers are covered by union contracts, duct work might be done by sheet metal workers and duct installers; electrical work by electricians; and installation of piping, condensers and other components by pipelayers, plumbers, pipefitters, and steamfitters.

Working Conditions: Heating, air-conditioning, and refrigeration mechanics and installers work in homes, stores, hospitals, office buildings, and factories – anywhere there is climate-control equipment. They may be assigned to specific job sites at the beginning of each day, or if they are making service calls, they may be dispatched to jobs by radio, telephone, or pager. Increasingly, employers are using cell phones to coordinate schedules.

Technicians may work outside in cold or hot weather or in buildings that are uncomfortable because the air-conditioning or heating equipment is broken. Technicians might have to work in awkward or cramped positions and sometimes are required to work in high places. Hazards include electrical shock, burns, muscle strains, and other injuries from handling heavy equipment. Appropriate safety equipment is necessary when handling refrigerants because contact can cause skin damage, frostbite, or blindness. Inhalation of refrigerants when working in confined spaces also is a possible hazard.

The majority of mechanics and installers work at least a 40-hour week. During peak seasons they often work overtime or irregular hours. Maintenance workers, including those who provide maintenance services under contract, often work evening or weekend shifts and are on call. Most employers try to provide a full workweek year-round by scheduling both installation and maintenance work, and many manufacturers and contractors now provide or even require service contracts. In most shops that service both heating and air-conditioning equipment, employment is stable throughout the year.

Education, Training, & Qualifications: Because of the increasing sophistication of heating, air-conditioning, and refrigeration systems, employers prefer to hire those with technical school or apprenticeship training. Many mechanics and installers, however, still learn the trade informally on the job. Those who acquire their skills on the job usually begin by assisting experienced technicians.

Many secondary and postsecondary technical and trade schools, junior and community colleges, and the military offer month-long to 2-year programs in heating, air conditioning, and refrigeration. Students study theory, design, and equipment construction, as well as electronics. They also learn the basics of installation, maintenance, and repair. Courses in shop math, mechanical drawing, applied physics and chemistry, blueprint reading, and computer applications provide a good background for those interested in entering this occupation. Some knowledge of plumbing or electrical work also is helpful. A basic understanding of electronics is becoming more important because of the increasing use of this technology in equipment controls. Because technicians frequently deal directly with the public, they should be courteous and tactful, especially when dealing with an aggravated customer. They should also be in good physical condition because they sometimes have to lift and move heavy equipment.

Earnings: Median hourly earnings of heating, air-conditioning, and refrigeration mechanics and installers were $18.11 ($37,669 annually) in May 2006. Some earned less than $11.38 an hour, whereas the top 10 percent earned more than $28.57. Apprentices usually begin at about 50 percent of the wage rate paid to experienced workers. In addition to typical benefits such as health insurance and pension plans, some employers pay for work-related training and provide uniforms, company vans, and tools. About 20 percent of workers are members of a union.

Key Contacts: For more information about opportunities for training and employment in this trade, contact local vocational and technical schools; local heating, air-conditioning, and refrigeration contractors; or the nearest office of the state employment service. For information on career opportunities, training, and technician certification, contact:

- **Air Conditioning Contractors of America**: (ACCA) 2800 Shirlington Road, Suite 300, Arlington, VA 22206. Website: www.acca. org.

- **Refrigeration Service Engineers Society**: (RSES) 1666 Rand Road, Des Plaines, IL 60016. Website: www.rses.org.

- **Sheet Metal and Air Conditioning Contractors' National Association**: 4201 Lafayette Center Drive, Chantilly, VA 20151-1209. Website: www.smacna.org.

- **North American Technician Excellence**: 2111 Wilson Blvd., Suite 510, Arlington, VA 22203. Website: www.natex.org.

Home Appliance Repairers

⇨ **Annual Earnings:** $33,862
⇨ **Education/Training:** High school diploma
⇨ **Outlook:** Average growth

Employment Outlook: Good job prospects are expected as job openings will continue to outnumber job seekers. Although employment of self-employed home appliance repairers is projected to decline, employment of wage and salary workers will increase about as fast as average. The number of home appliances in use is expected to increase with growth in the numbers of households and businesses. Appliances are also becoming more technologically advanced and will increasingly require a skilled technician to diagnose and fix problems.

In recent years, many consumers have tended to purchase new appliances when existing warranties expired rather than invest in repairs on old appliances. However, over the next decade, as more consumers purchase higher priced appliances designed to have much longer lives, they will be more likely to use repair service than to purchase new appliances. Employment is relatively steady during economic downturns because there is still demand for appliance repair services. In addition to new jobs created over the 2002-12 period, openings will arise as home appliance repairers retire or transfer to other occupations.

Self-employment of home appliance repairers will continue to decline due to the availability of manufacturer-sponsored training programs. Manufacturers often make these programs available only to large equipment dealers, thereby discouraging repairers from becoming self-employed or working for small shops. Many self-employed repairers are forced to join larger shops so that they can stay abreast of developments in the industry. Jobs are expected to be increasingly concentrated in larger companies as the numbers of smaller shops and family-owned businesses decline. However, repairers who maintain strong industry relationships may still go into business for themselves.

Nature of Work: Home appliance repairers, often called service technicians, keep home appliances working and help prevent unwanted breakdowns. Some repairers work specifically on small appliances such as microwave ovens and vacuum cleaners; others specialize in major appliances such as refrigerators, dishwashers, washers, and dryers.

Home appliance repairers visually inspect appliances and check for unusual noises, excessive vibration, fluid leaks, or loose parts to determine why the appliances fail to operate properly. They use service manuals, troubleshooting guides, and experience to diagnose particularly difficult problems. Repairers disassemble the appliance to examine its internal parts for signs of wear or corrosion. They follow wiring diagrams and use testing devices to check electrical systems for shorts and faulty connections.

After identifying problems, home appliance repairers replace or repair defective belts, motors, heating elements, switches, gears, or other items. They tighten, align, clean, and lubricate parts as necessary. When repairing appliances with electronic parts, they may replace circuit boards or other electronic components. Home appliance repairers generally install household durable goods such as refrigerators, washing machines, and cooking products. Repairers also answer customers' questions about the care and use of appliances. Repairers write up estimates of the cost of repairs for customers, keep records of parts used and hours worked, prepare bills, and collect payments. Self-employed repairers also deal with the appliance manufacturers to recoup monetary claims for work performed on appliances still under warranty.

Working Conditions: Home appliance repairers handling portable appliances usually work in repair shops that are generally quiet and adequately lighted and ventilated. Those who repair major appliances usually make service calls to customers' homes. They carry their tools and a number of commonly used parts with them in a truck or van for use on service calls. Repairers may spend several hours a day driving to and from appointments and emergency calls. They may work in clean comfortable rooms such as kitchens, or in damp, dirty, or dusty areas of a home. Repairers sometimes work in cramped and uncomfortable positions when they are replacing parts in hard-to-reach areas of appliances. Repairer jobs are generally not hazardous, but workers must exercise care and follow safety precautions to avoid electrical shocks and injuries when lifting and moving large appliances. When repairing gas appliances and microwave ovens, repairers must be aware of the dangers of gas and radio frequency energy leaks.

Home appliance repairers usually work with little or no direct supervision, a feature of the job that is appealing to many people. Many home appliance repairers work a standard 40-hour week, but they may work overtime and weekend hours in the summer months when they are in high demand to fix air conditioners and refrigerators. Some repairers work early morning, evening, and weekend shifts and may remain on call in case of emergency.

Education, Training, & Qualifications: Employers generally require a high school diploma for home appliance repairer jobs. Repairers of small appliances commonly learn the trade on the job; repairers of large household appliances often receive training in a formal trade school, community college, or directly from the appliance manufacturer. Mechanical and electrical aptitudes are desirable, and those who work in customers' homes must be courteous and tactful.

Employers prefer to hire people with formal training in appliance repair and electronics. Many repairers complete 1- or 2-year formal training programs in appliance repair and related subjects in high school, private vocational schools, and community colleges. Courses in basic electricity and electronics are increasingly important as more manufacturers install circuit boards and other electronic control systems in home appliances.

The U.S. Environmental Protection Agency (EPA) has mandated that all repairers who buy or work with refrigerants must be certified in their proper handling; a technician must pass a written examination to become certified. Exams are administered by organizations approved by the EPA, such as trade schools, unions, and employer associations. Though no formal training is required for certification, many organizations offer training programs designed to prepare workers for the certification examination.

Repairers in large shops or service centers may be promoted to supervisor, assistant service manager, or service manager. Some repairers advance to managerial positions such as regional service manager or parts manager for appliance or tool manufacturers. Experienced repairers who have sufficient funds and knowledge of small-business management may open their own repair shop.

Earnings: Median hourly earnings, including commission, of home appliance repairers were $16.28 ($33,862 annually) in May 2006. Some earned less than $9.37; the highest 10 percent earned more than $25.84. Median hourly earnings of home appliance repairers in the electronics and appliance stores industry, which employs the largest number of these workers, were $15.18 in electronics and appliance stores and $17.02 in personal and household goods repair and maintenance.

Earnings of home appliance repairers vary according to the skill level required to fix equipment, geographic location, and the type of equipment repaired. Because many repairers receive commissions along with their salary, earnings increase along with the number of jobs a repairer can complete in a day. Many larger dealers, manufacturers, and service stores offer typical benefits such as health insurance, sick leave, and retirement and pension programs. Some of these workers belong to the International Brotherhood of Electrical Workers.

Key Contacts: For general information about the work of home appliance repairers contact any of the following.

- **National Appliance Service Association**: P.O. Box 2514, Kokomo, IN 46904. Website: www.nasa1.org.

- **United Servicers Association, Inc.**: P.O. Box 31006, Albuquerque, NM 87190. Website: www.unitedservicers.com.

For information on the National Appliance Service Technician Certification program, contact:

- **National Appliance Service Technician Certification**: 3608 Pershing Avenue, Fort Worth, TX 76107. Website: www.nastec. org.

For information on the Certified Appliance Professional program, contact:

- **Professional Service Association**: 71 Columbia St., Cohoes, NY 12047. Website: www. psaworld.com.

Line Installers and Repairers

- ⇨ **Annual Earnings:** $50,773
- ⇨ **Education/Training:** High school diploma
- ⇨ **Outlook:** Slow growth but good

Employment Outlook: Overall employment of line installers and repairers is expected to grow more slowly (6 percent) than average during the 2006-2016 decade, but retirements are expected to create very good job opportunities for new workers, particularly for electrical power-line installers. Growth will reflect an increasing demand for electricity and telecommunications services as the population grows. However, productivity gains – particularly in maintaining these networks – will keep employment growth slow. With the increasing competition in electrical distribution, many companies are contracting out construction of new lines. The introduction of new technologies, especially fiber optic cable, has increased the transmission capacity of telephone and cable television networks. Job growth also will stem from the maintenance and modernization of telecommunications networks. Jobs will be generated as telephone and cable television companies expand and improve networks that provide customers with high-speed access to data, video, and graphics. Line installers and repairers will be needed not only to construct and install networks, but also to maintain the ever-growing systems of wires and cables. Besides those due to employment growth, many job openings will result from the need to replace the large number of older workers reaching retirement age.

Employment of electrical power line installers and repairers is expected to grow about as fast as the average for all occupations. Despite consistently rising demand for electricity, power companies will cut costs by shifting more work to outside contractors and hire fewer installers and repairers. Most new jobs for electrical power line installers and repairers are expected to arise among contracting firms in the construction industry. Because electrical power companies have reduced hiring and training in past years, opportunities are best for workers who possess experience and training.

Growth of wireless communications will also slow job increases for line installers and repairers in the long run. More households are switching to wireless delivery of their communications, video, and data services.

Nature of Work: Vast networks of wires and cables provide customers with electrical power and communication services. Networks of electrical power lines deliver electricity from generating plants to customers. Communication networks of telephone and cable television lines provide voice, video, and other communication services. These networks are constructed and maintained by line installers and repairers.

Line installers install new lines by constructing utility poles, towers, and underground trenches to carry the wires and cables. They use a variety of construction equipment, including digger derricks, trenchers, cable plows, and borers. When construction is complete, line installers string cable along the poles, towers, tunnels, and trenches. Other installation duties include setting up service for customers and installing network equipment.

In addition to installation, line installers and repairers also are responsible for maintenance of electrical, telecommunications, and cable television lines. Workers periodically travel in trucks, helicopters, and airplanes to visually inspect the wires and cables. Sensitive monitoring equipment can automatically detect malfunctions on the network, such as loss of current flow. When line repairers identify a problem, they travel to the location of the malfunction and repair or replace defective cables or equipment. Bad weather or natural disasters can cause extensive damage to networks. Line installers and repairers must respond quickly to these emergencies to restore critical utility and communication services. This can often involve working outdoors in adverse weather conditions.

Installation and repair work may require splicing, or joining together, separate pieces of cable. Many communication networks now use fiber optic cables instead of conventional wire or metal cables. Splicing fiber optic cable requires specialized equipment that carefully slices, matches, and aligns individual glass fibers. The fibers are joined by either electrical fusion (welding) or a mechanical fixture and gel (glue).

Working Conditions: Line installers and repairers must climb and maintain their balance while working on poles and towers. They lift equipment and work in a variety of positions, such as stooping or kneeling. Their work often requires that they drive utility vehicles, travel long distances, and work outdoors under a variety of weather conditions. Many line installers and repairers work a 40-hour week; however, emergencies may require overtime work. For example, when severe weather damages electrical and communication lines, line installers and repairers may work long and irregular hours to restore service.

Line installers and repairers encounter serious hazards on their jobs and must follow safety procedures to minimize potential danger. They wear safety equipment when entering utility holes and test for the presence of gas before going underground. Electric power line workers have the most hazardous jobs. High-voltage power lines can cause electrocution, and line installers and repairers must consequently use electrically insulated protective devices and tools when working with live cables. Power lines are typically higher than telephone and cable television lines, increasing the risk of severe injury due to falls. To prevent these injuries, line installers and repairers must use fall-protection equipment when working on poles or towers.

Education, Training, & Qualifications: Line installers and repairers are trained on the job, and employers require at least a high school diploma. Employers also prefer technical knowledge of electricity, electronics, and experience obtained through vocational/technical programs, community colleges, or the Armed Forces. Prospective employees should possess a basic knowledge of algebra and trigonometry, and mechanical ability. Customer service and interpersonal skills also are important. Because the work entails lifting heavy objects (many employers require applicants to be able to lift at least 50 pounds), climbing, and other physical activity, applicants should have stamina, strength, and coordination, and must be unafraid of heights. The ability to distinguish colors is necessary because wires and cables may be color-coded.

Many community or technical colleges offer programs in telecommunications, electronics, and/or electricity. Some schools, working with local companies, offer 1-year certificate programs that emphasize hands-on field work; graduates get preferential treatment in the hiring process at companies participating in the program. More advanced 2-year associate degree programs provide students with a broader knowledge of telecommunications and electrical utilities through courses in electricity, electronics, fiber optics, and microwave transmission.

Electrical line installers and repairers complete formal apprenticeships or employer training programs. These are sometimes administered jointly by the employer and the union representing the workers. Government safety regulations strictly define the training and education requirements for apprentice electrical line installers.

Line installers and repairers in telephone and cable television companies receive several years of on-the-job training. They also may attend training or take courses provided by equipment manufacturers, schools, unions, or industry training organizations.

Entry-level line installers may be hired as ground workers, helpers, or tree trimmers, who clear branches from telephone and power lines. These workers may advance to positions stringing cable and performing service installations. With experience, they may advance to more sophisticated maintenance and repair positions responsible for increasingly larger portions of the network. Promotion to supervisory or training positions also is possible, but more advanced supervisory positions often require a college diploma.

Earnings: Earnings for line installers and repairers are higher than those in most other occupations that do not require postsecondary education. Median hourly earnings for electrical power line installers and repairers were $24.41 ($50,773 annually) in May 2006. Some earned less than $13.96, and the highest 10 percent earned more than $32.80. Median hourly earnings for telecommunications line installers and repairers were $22.25. The lowest 10 percent earned less than $11.88, and the highest 10 percent earned more than $32.80.

Most line installers and repairers belong to unions, principally the Communications Workers of America, the International Brotherhood of Electrical Workers, and the Utility Workers Union of America. For these workers, union contracts set wage rates, wage increases, and the time needed to advance from one job level to the next.

Key Contacts: For more details about employment opportunities, contact the telephone, cable television, or electrical power companies in your community. For general information and some educational resources on line installer and repairer jobs, contact:

- **Communication Workers of America**: 501 3rd Street NW, Washington, DC 20001. Website: www.cwa-union.org/jobs.

- National Joint Apprenticeship and Training Committee: 301 Prince George's Blvd., Suite D, Upper Marlboro, MD 20774. Website: www.njatc.org.

Maintenance and Repair Workers

⇨ **Annual Earnings:** $31,907
⇨ **Education/Training:** High school and training
⇨ **Outlook:** Average

Employment Outlook: General maintenance and repair workers held 1.4 million jobs in 2006. They were employed in almost every industry. About one in five worked in manufacturing industries, almost evenly distributed through all sectors. About 19 percent worked in manufacturing industries, almost evenly distributed through all sectors, while about 10 percent worked for federal, state, and local governments. Others worked for wholesale and retail firms and for property management firms that operate office and apartment buildings.

Employment of general maintenance and repair workers is expected to grow about as fast as average (10 percent during the 2006-2016 decade) for all occupations. However, job openings should be plentiful. Maintenance and repair is a large occupation with significant turnover, and many job openings should result from the need to replace workers who transfer to other occupations or stop working for other reasons.

Employment is related to the number of buildings – for example, office and apartment buildings, stores, schools, hospitals, hotels, and factories – and the amount of equipment needing repair. However, as machinery becomes more advanced and requires less maintenance, the need for general maintenance and repair workers diminishes.

Nature of Work: Most craft workers specialize in one kind of work, such as plumbing or carpentry. General maintenance and repair workers, however, have skills in many different crafts. They repair and maintain machines, mechanical equipment, and buildings, and work on plumbing, electrical, and air-conditioning and heating systems. They build partitions, make plaster or drywall repairs, and fix or paint roofs, windows, doors, floors, woodwork, and other parts of building structures. They also maintain and repair specialized equipment and machinery found in cafeterias, laundries, hospitals, stores, offices, and factories. Typical duties include troubleshooting and fixing faulty electri-

cal switches, repairing air-conditioning motors, and unclogging drains. New buildings sometimes have computer-controlled systems, requiring workers to acquire basic computer skills.

General maintenance and repair workers inspect and diagnose problems and determine the best way to correct them, frequently checking blueprints, repair manuals, and parts catalogs. They replace or fix work or broken parts, where necessary, or make adjustments to correct malfunctioning equipment and machines. General maintenance and repair workers also perform preventive maintenance and ensure that machines continue to run smoothly, building systems operate efficiently, and the physical condition of buildings does not deteriorate. Employees in small establishments, where they are often the only maintenance worker, make all repairs, except for very large or difficult jobs. In larger establishments, their duties may be limited to the general maintenance of everything in a workshop or a particular area.

Working Conditions: General maintenance and repair workers often carry out several different tasks in a single day, at any number of locations. They may work inside a single building or in several different buildings. They may have to stand for long periods, lift heavy objects, and work in uncomfortably hot or cold environments, in awkward and cramped positions, or on ladders. They are subject to electrical shock, burns, falls, cuts, and bruises. Most general maintenance workers put in a 40-hour week. Some work evening, night, or weekend shifts or are on call for emergency repairs. Those employed in small establishments often operate with only limited supervision. Those working in larger establishments frequently are under the direct supervision of an experienced worker.

Education, Training, & Qualifications: Many general maintenance and repair workers learn their skills informally on the job. They start as helpers, watching and learning from skilled maintenance workers. Some learn their skills by working as helpers to other repair or construction workers, including carpenters, electricians, or machinery repairers. Necessary skills also can be learned in high school shop classes and postsecondary trade or vocational schools. It generally takes from one to four years of on-the-job training or school, or a combination of both, to become fully qualified – depending on the skill level.

Graduation from high school is preferred for entry into this occupation. High school courses in mechanical drawing, electricity, woodworking, blueprint reading, science, mathematics, and computers are useful. Mechanical aptitude, the ability to use shop mathematics, and manual dexterity are important. Good health is necessary because the job involves a great of walking, standing, reaching, and heavy lifting. Many positions require the ability to work without direct supervision. Many general maintenance and repair workers in large organizations advance to maintenance supervisor or become a craftworker such as an electrician, a heating and air conditioning mechanic, or a plumber. Promotion opportunities are limited within small organizations.

Earnings: Median hourly earnings of general maintenance and repair workers were $15.34 in May 2006. The highest 10 percent earned more than $24.44. Median hourly earnings in the industries employing the largest numbers of general maintenance and repair workers in 2006 were:

- Local government $14.83
- Elementary and secondary schools $14.01
- Activities related to real estate $11.79
- Lessors of real estate $11.54
- Traveler accommodations $10.58

Some general maintenance and repair workers are members of unions.

Key Contacts: Information about job opportunities may be obtained from local employers and local offices of the state employment service. For information related to maintenance managers, contact:

- **International Maintenance Institute Online:** P.O. Box 751896, Houston, TX 77275. Website: www.imionline.org.

Small Engine Mechanics

⇨ **Annual Earnings:** $30,056
⇨ **Education/Training:** Vocational training program/on-the-job training
⇨ **Outlook:** Excellent

Employment Outlook: Employment of small engine mechanics is expected to grow higher than average for all occupations during the 2006-2016 decade – 12 percent growth. Most of the job openings are expected to be replacement jobs, because many experienced small engine mechanics are expected to transfer to other occupations, retire, or stop working for other reasons. Job prospects should be especially favorable for persons who complete formal training programs. Growth of personal disposal income should provide consumers with more

discretionary dollars to buy motorboats, lawn and garden power equipment, and motorcycles. While advancements in technology will lengthen the interval between routine maintenance, the need for qualified mechanics to perform this service will increase. Employment of motorcycle mechanics should increase as the popularity of motorcycles rebounds. More people will be entering the 40-and-older age group – those responsible for the largest segment of marine craft purchases. These potential buyers will expand the market for motorboats, maintaining the demand for qualified mechanics.

Nature of Work: Small engine repair mechanics repair and service power equipment ranging from racing motorcycles to chain saws. Like large engines, small engines require periodic service to minimize the chance of breakdowns and keep them operating at peak performance. When a piece of equipment breaks down, mechanics use various techniques to diagnose the source and extent of the problem. The mark of a skilled mechanic is the ability to diagnose mechanical, fuel, and electrical problems and to make repairs in a minimal amount of time. Quick and accurate diagnosis requires problem-solving ability and a thorough knowledge of the equipment's operation.

In larger repair shops, mechanics may use special computerized diagnostic testing equipment as a preliminary tool in analyzing equipment. After pinpointing the problem, the mechanic makes the needed adjustments, repairs, or replacements. Some jobs require minor adjustments. A complete engine overhaul, on the other hand, requires a number of hours to disassemble the engine and replace worn valves, pistons, bearings, and other internal parts.

Working Conditions: Small engine mechanics usually work in repair shops that are well lighted and ventilated, but are sometimes noisy when engines are tested. Motorboat mechanics may work outdoors at docks or marinas, as well as in all weather conditions, when making repairs aboard boats. They may work in cramped or awkward positions to reach a boat's engine.

During the winter months in the northern United States, mechanics may work fewer than 40 hours a week, because the amount of repair and service work declines when lawnmowers, motorboats, and motorcycles are not in use. Many mechanics work only during the busy spring and summer seasons. However, many schedule time-consuming engine overhauls or work on snowmobiles and snow-blowers during winter downtime. Mechanics may work considerably more than 40 hours a week when demand is strong.

Education, Training, & Qualifications:
Due to the increasing complexity of motorcycles and motorboats, most employers prefer to hire mechanics who graduate from formal training programs for small engine mechanics. Because the number of these specialized post-secondary programs is limited, most mechanics learn their skills on the job or while working in related occupations. For trainee jobs, employers hire persons with mechanical aptitude who are knowledgeable about the fundamentals of small two- and four-stroke engines. Many trainees develop an interest in mechanics and acquire some basic skills through working on automobiles, motorcycles, motorboats, or outdoor power equipment as a hobby. Others may be introduced to mechanics through vocational automotive training in high school or one of many postsecondary institutions.

Most employers prefer to hire high school graduates for trainee mechanic positions, but will accept applicants with less education if they possess adequate reading, writing, and arithmetic skills.

Knowledge of basic electronics is essential for small engine mechanics, because electronic components control an engine's performance, the vehicle's instruments displays, and a variety of other functions of motorcycles, motorboats, and outdoor power equipment. The skills used as a small engine mechanic generally transfer to other occupations, such as automobile, diesel, or heavy vehicle and mobile equipment mechanics, Experienced mechanics with leadership ability may advance to shop supervisor or service manager jobs. Mechanics with sales ability sometimes become sales representatives or open their own repair shops.

Earnings: Median hourly earnings of motorcycle mechanics were $14.45 ($30,056 annually) in May 2006. Median earnings of motorboat mechanics were $15.96, and for outdoor power equipment mechanics median earnings were $12.94. The lowest 10 percent averaged $8.31 and the highest paid earned more than $19.31.

Key Contacts: To learn about work opportunities, contact local motorcycle, motorboat, and lawn and garden equipment dealers, boatyards, and marinas. Local offices of the state employment service also may have information about employment and training opportunities.

6

Science, Math, Engineering, and Technology Jobs

WHILE THE U.S. ECONOMY is by no means experiencing a shortage of scientists and engineers, nonetheless, job opportunities for scientists and engineers should be good to excellent throughout the coming decade. The U.S. economy should continue to move in the direction of more science and technology. The electronics revolution will continue unabated as it spreads through all areas of life. More and more money is expected to be invested by both government and private industry in research and development in order to develop a more internationally competitive economy.

While decreased defense spending in the 1990s did have an adverse effect on some scientific and engineering jobs tied to defense industries, the overall picture for the coming decade looks good, especially for those in the biological sciences, chemistry, mathematics, geology, meteorology, and civil, electronics, and mechanical engineering. As more public money is spent on developing national security and a more adequate infrastructure of roads, bridges, airports, tunnels, rapid transit, and water supply and sewage systems, opportunities for engineering technicians should improve considerably. Assuming manufacturing industries will continue to grow in the decade ahead, opportunities for mechanical engineering technicians should be good. The future especially looks good for electronics and environmental engineering technicians.

Ex-offenders who have the educational training and aptitude to pursue careers in these fields should do very well in the decade ahead. Most are stable, good paying jobs.

Drafters

⇨ **Annual Earnings:** $41,960
⇨ **Education/Training:** Technical training to associate degree
⇨ **Outlook:** Good – about average

Employment Outlook: Employment of drafters is expected to grow slower than average for occupations in the coming decade. Industrial growth and increasingly complex design problems associated with new products and manufacturing processes will increase the demand for drafting services. Drafters also are beginning to break out of the traditional drafting role and increasingly do work traditionally performed by engineers and architects, thus also increasing demand for drafters. However, the greater use of CADD equipment by drafters, as well as by architects and engineers, should limit demand for less skilled drafters, resulting in slower-than-average overall employment growth.

Nature of Work: Drafters prepare technical drawings and plans used by production and construction workers to build everything from manufactured products, such as toys, toasters, industrial machinery, and spacecraft, to structures, such as houses, office buildings, and oil and gas pipelines. Their drawings provide visual guidelines, show the technical details of the products and structures, and specify dimensions, materials, and procedures. Drafters fill in technical details, using drawings, rough sketches, specifications, codes, and calculations previously made by engineers, surveyors, architects, or scientists.

Working Conditions: Most drafters work a standard 40-hour week; only a small number work part time. Drafters usually work in comfortable offices furnished to accommodate their tasks. Because they spend long periods in front of computer terminals doing detailed work, drafters may be susceptible to eyestrain, back discomfort, and hand and wrist problems.

Education, Training, & Qualifications: Employers prefer applicants who have completed postsecondary school training in drafting, which is offered by technical institutes, community colleges, and some four-year colleges and universities. Employers are most interested in applicants with well-developed drafting and mechanical-drawing skills; knowledge of drafting standards, mathematics, science, and engineering technology; and a solid background in computer-aided design and drafting (CADD) techniques.

Earnings: Earnings for drafters vary by specialty and level of responsibility. Median annual earnings of architectural and civil drafters were $41,960 in May 2006. The middle 50 percent earned between $33,550 and $52,220. Median annual earnings of mechanical drafters were $43,700 in 2006. The middle 50 percent earned between $34,680 and $55,130. Median annual earnings of electrical and electronics drafters were $46,830 in 2006. The middle 50 percent earned between $36,660 and $60,160.

Key Contacts: Information on training and certification for drafting and related fields is available from:

- **Accrediting Commission of Career Schools and Colleges of Technology:** 2101 Wilson Blvd., Suite 302, Arlington, VA 22201. Website: www.accsct.org.

- **American Design Drafting Association:** 105 E. Main Street, Newbern, TN 38059. Website: www.adda.org.

Engineering Technicians

⇨ **Annual Earnings:** $40,560 to $53,300
⇨ **Education/Training:** Associate degree
⇨ **Outlook:** Average growth

Employment Outlook: Overall employment of engineering technicians is expected to increase about as fast as average for all occupations in the coming decade. Competitive pressures will force companies to improve and update manufacturing facilities and product designs, resulting in more jobs for engineering technicians. However, the growing use of advanced technologies, such as computer simulation and computer-aided design and drafting (CADD) will continue to increase productivity and limit job growth.

Nature of Work: Engineering technicians use the principles and theories of science, engineering, and mathematics to solve technical problems in research and development, manufacturing, sales, construction, inspection, and maintenance. Their work is more limited in scope and more practically oriented than that of scientists and engineers. Many engineering technicians assist engineers and scientists, especially in research and development. Others work in quality control – inspecting products and processes, conducting tests, or collecting data. In manufacturing, they may assist in product design, development, or production. Most engineering technicians specialize in certain areas, learning skills and working in the same disciplines as engineers. Occupational titles, therefore, tend to reflect those of engineers. Engineering technicians held 511,000 jobs in 2006 in the following occupational fields:

▪ Electrical and electronic engineering technicians	170,000
▪ Civil engineering technicians	91,000
▪ Industrial engineering technicians	75,000
▪ Mechanical engineering technicians	48,000
▪ Electro-mechanical technicians	16,000
▪ Aerospace engineering and operations technicians	8,500
▪ Engineering technicians, except drafters, all other	82,000

Working Conditions: Most engineering technicians work at least 40 hours a week in laboratories, offices, or manufacturing or industrial plants, or on construction sites. Some may be exposed to hazards from equipment, chemicals, or toxic materials.

Education, Training, & Qualifications: Although it may be possible to qualify for certain engineering technician jobs without formal training, most employers prefer to hire someone with a least a two-year associate degree in engineering technology. Training is available at technical institutes, community colleges, extension divisions of colleges and universities, and public and private vocational-technical schools, and in the Armed Forces.

Earnings: Median annual earnings of engineering technicians vary by specialty:

- Aerospace engineering and
  operations technicians $53,300
- Electrical and electronic
  engineering technicians $50,660
- Industrial engineering
  technicians $46,810
- Mechanical engineering
  technicians $45,850
- Electro-mechanical technicians $44,720
- Civil engineering technicians $40,560
- Environmental engineering
  technicians $40,560

Key Contacts: For more information on training and certification of engineering technicians, contact:

- **National Institute for Certification in Engineering Technologies (NICET):** 1420 King Street, Alexandria, VA 22314. Website: www.nicet.org.

- **Accreditation Board for Engineering and Technology, Inc.:** 111 Market Place, Suite 1050, Baltimore, MD 21202. Website: www. abet.org.

Electrical and Electronics Installers and Repairers

⇨ **Annual Earnings:** $45,178
⇨ **Education/Training:** Postsecondary training
⇨ **Outlook:** Good

Employment Outlook: Overall employment of electrical and electronics installers and re-pairers is expected to grow more slowly than the average for all occupations in the decade ahead, but varies by occupational specialty. Average employment growth is projected for electrical and electronics installers and repairers of commercial and industrial equipment. Employment of motor vehicle electronic equipment installers and repairers also is expected to grow as fast as the average. Employment of electric motor, power tool, and related repairers is expected to grow more slowly than average. Employment of electrical and electronic installers and repairers of transportation equipment is expected to grow more slowly than the average, due to declining industry employment in rail transportation, aerospace product and parts manufacturing, and ship- and boatbuilding. Employment of electrical and electronics installers and repairers of powerhouse, substation, and relay is expected to decline slightly.

Nature of Work: Electrical and electronics installers and repairers install, maintain, and repair complex pieces of electronic equipment used in business, government, and other organizations. The nature of their work varies depending on their occupational specialty. In 2,006 electrical and electronics installers and repairers held about 169,000 jobs in their occupational specialties:

- Electrical and electronics repairers,
  commercial and industrial
  equipment   80,000
- Electric motor, power tool,
  and related repairers   25,000
- Electrical and electronics repairers,
  powerhouse, substation, and relay   22,000
- Electrical and electronics installers
  and repairers, transportation
  equipment   21,000
- Electrical and electronics installers
  and repairers, motor vehicles   20,000

Many repairers worked for utilities, building equipment contractors, machinery and equipment repair shops, wholesalers, the federal government, retailers of automotive parts and accessories, rail transportation companies, and manufacturers of electrical, electronic, and transportation equipment.

Working Conditions: Many electrical and electronics installers and repairers work on factory floors, where they are subject to noise, dirt, vibration, and heat. Bench technicians work primarily in repair shops, where the surroundings are relatively quiet, comfortable, and well lighted. Installers and repairers may have to do heavy lifting and work in a variety of positions.

Education, Training, & Qualifications: Knowledge of electrical equipment and electronics is necessary for employment. Many applicants gain this knowledge through programs lasting one to two years at vocational schools or community colleges, although some less skilled repairers may have only a high school diploma. Entry-level repairers may work closely with more experienced technicians who provide technical guidance. Various organizations provide certification, including ACES International, the Consumer Electronics Association, the Electronics Technicians Association International, and the International Society of Certified Electronics Technicians. Repairers may specialize – in industrial electronics, for example. To receive certification, repairers must pass qualifying exams corresponding to their level of training and experience.

Earnings: Median hourly earnings of electrical and electronics repairers, commercial and industrial equipment, were $21.72 in May 2006 ($45,178 per year). Median hourly earnings of electric motor, power tool, and related repairers were $17.18). Median hourly earnings of electrical and electronics repairers, powerhouse, substation, and relay, were $27.60. Median hourly earnings of electronics installers and repairers, motor v ehicles, were $13.57. Median hourly earnings of electrical and electronics repairers, transportation equipment, were $20.72.

Key Contacts: For information on careers and certification, contact the following organizations:

- **Association of Communications and Electronics School International:** 5381 Chatham Lake Drive, Virginia Beach, VA 23464. Website: www.acesinternational.org.

- **Electronics Technicians Association International:** 5 Depot Street, Greencastle, IN 46135. Website: www.eta-i.org.

- **International Society of Certified Electronics Technicians:** 3608 Pershing Avenue, Fort Worth, TX 76107-4527. Website: www.iscet.org.

Laser Technicians

- ➪ **Annual Earnings:** $41,000
- ➪ **Education/Training:** Associate degree
- ➪ **Outlook:** Excellent

Employment Outlook: Job opportunities for laser technicians are expected to be excellent in the decade ahead. The increased use of laser technology in industry, including the fast-growing field of fiber optics, will generate numerous job opportunities for laser technicians. Expect increased demand for laser technicians in entertainment, defense, medicine, construction, manufacturing, and telecommunications.

Nature of Work: Laser technicians, also called laser/electro-optics technicians or LEOTs, work in a variety of occupational settings – manufacturing, medicine, research, communication, military, and defense – where they build, operate, repair, install, and test lasers, fibers, and systems that use lasers. Working under the direct supervision of scientists or engineers, they calculate measurements and clear, inspect, adjust, and operate lasers. Some laser technicians primarily work with semiconductor systems relating to computers and telecommunications. Others primarily work with gas-type systems in the fields of robotics, manufacturing, and medicine.

Working Conditions: Laser technicians work in clean and well-equipped laboratories and assembly areas. When working on delicate electronic and optical assemblies, laser technicians work in environmentally controlled areas, known as "clean rooms," where temperature, humidity, and dust content of air is carefully controlled. The work requires a great deal of attention to detail and special safety precautions since the work can be dangerous, especially in handling hazardous manufacturing materials (dye solutions, gas-filled discharge tubes, high-voltage power sources) and working with dangerous laser beams.

Education, Training, & Qualifications: Laser technicians need a certificate or associate degree in electrical or electronic technology. Many laser technicians complete a two-year associate degree in laser/electro-optics technology, which is offered by some community colleges. These institutions usually work closely with employers who hire directly from these programs. Some laser technicians receive training in laser technology through the Armed Forces.

Earnings: The median annual earnings of laser technicians were around $41,000 in 2006. Starting salaries begin at $25,000.

Key Contacts: For information on laser technology jobs and careers, including training programs, contact:

- **Laser Institute of America:** 13501 Ingenuity Drive, Suite 128, Orlando, FL 32826. Website: www.laserinstitute.org.

- **Laser and Electro-Optics Society:** 445 Hoes Lane, Piscataway, NJ 08855-1331. Website: www.i-leos.org.

Marine Service Technicians

- ➪ **Annual Earnings:** $30,000
- ➪ **Education/Training:** High school diploma and training
- ➪ **Outlook:** Good

Employment Outlook: Employment opportunities for marine service technicians, also known as marine mechanics, should be good in the decade ahead, assuming the economy continues to grow. During good economic times, when boat ownership increases, the demand for marine services technicians increases accordingly. In many parts of the country this is often a seasonal job. The best opportunities are found in affluent marine-oriented communities where boating is a year-round activity.

Nature of Work: Marine service technicians primarily test, service, and repair powerboats and sailboats. They work on both inboard and outboard engines, electrical and plumbing systems, fuel and water pumps, transmissions, rigging, masts, sails, navigation equipment, propellers, steering gear, sanitation systems, and hulls. They work with metal, wood, and fiberglass materials. Some marine service technicians are trained to service particular brands of two- and four-stroke cycle engines as well as particular types of vessels. Mechanics work on engines, transmissions, propellers, and navigational systems. Fiberglass/wood technicians focus on cleaning and repairing damaged boat hulls. Painters mix and apply paint or gel coats to boats with hand and spray equipment.

Working Conditions: Marine service technicians work in a variety of repair shops, marinas, and boat yards. Working conditions will vary depending on the particular employer.

Education, Training, & Qualifications: Most employers prefer applicants with a high school diploma. They also seek candidates who have completed marine service technician training programs. Some trade schools, career and technical schools, and community colleges offer six-month to two-year programs for marine service technicians. Employers also may send marine service technicians to special training programs offered by equipment manufacturers or distributors which may last up to two weeks.

Earnings: The median annual earnings of marine service technicians in 2006 were around $30,000. Keep in mind, however, that this is a seasonal job in many parts of the country.

Key Contacts: For more information on certification and careers for marine service technicians, contact:

- **Marine Retailers Association of America:** P.O. Box 1127, Oak Park, IL 60304. Website: www.mraa.com.

- **National Marine Electronics Association:** 7 Riggs Avenue, Severna Park, MD 21146. Website: www.nmea.org.

- **Association of Marine Technicians:** 455 Knollwood Terrace, Roswell, GA 30075-3416. Website: www.am-tech.org.

- **National Marine Manufacturers Association:** 200 E. Randolph Dr., Suite 5100, Chicago, IL 60601. Website: www.nmma.org.

- **Marine Advanced Technology Education Center:** The Monterey Peninsula College, 980 Fremont Street, Monterey, CA 93940. Website: www.marinetech.org.

Science Technicians

- ➪ **Annual Earnings:** $30,867 to $65,500
- ➪ **Education/Training:** Certificate, associate degree, or BA
- ➪ **Outlook:** Good to excellent

Employment Outlook: Job opportunities for science technicians are expected to increase as fast as the average for all occupations in the decade ahead. Continued growth of scientific and medical research, particularly research related to biotechnology, as well as the development and production of technical products, should stimulate demand for science technicians in many industries.

Nature of Work: Science technicians use the principles and theories of science and mathematics to solve problems in research and development and to investigate, invent, and help improve products. Their jobs are more practically oriented than those of scientists. They set up, operate, and maintain laboratory instruments, monitor experiments, make observations, calculate and record results, and often develop conclusions. They must keep detailed logs of all of their work-related activities. They make extensive use of computers, computer-interfaced equipment, robotics, and high-technology industrial applications such as biological engineering. They encompass a variety of occupations such as agricultural technicians, biological technicians, chemical technicians, nuclear technicians, and petroleum technicians.

Working Conditions: Science technicians work in a variety of settings. Many work indoors, usually in laboratories, and have regular hours. Others, such as agricultural and petroleum technicians, work outdoors, sometimes in remote locations, and may be exposed to hazardous conditions. Chemical technicians sometimes work with toxic chemicals, nuclear technicians may be exposed to radiation, and biological technicians sometimes work with disease-causing organisms or radioactive agents.

Education, Training, & Qualifications: Science technicians have at least two years of specialized training. Many junior and community colleges offer associate degrees in specific technology or a more general education in science and mathematics. Many science technicians have a bachelor's degree in science or mathematics, or have had science and math courses in four-year colleges. Some companies offer formal or on-the-job training for science technicians.

Earnings: The median annual earnings for science technicians ranged from a low of $30,867 to a high of $65,500 in 2006. The median hourly earnings of science technicians in 2002 were as follows for various occupations:

- Nuclear technicians $31.46
- Geological and petroleum technicians $22.19
- Forensic science technicians $21.79
- Chemical technicians $18.87
- Environmental science and protection technicians, including health $18.31
- Biological technicians $17.17
- Agricultural and food science technicians $15.26
- Forest and conservation technicians $14.84

In 2006, the average annual salary in nonsupervisory, supervisory, and managerial positions in the federal government was $40,629 for biological science technicians; $53,026 for physical science technicians; $54,081 for geodetic technicians; $50,337 for hydrologic technicians; and $63,396 for meteorological technicians.

Key Contacts: For information on career opportunities for science technicians, contact:

- **American Chemical Society:** Education Division, Career Publications, 1155 16th Street, NW, Washington, DC 20036. Website: www.acs.org.

- **American Academy of Forensic Sciences:** 410 North 21st Street, Colorado Springs, CO 80904. Website: www.aafs.org.

7

Production Occupations

THIS CHAPTER OUTLINES a six production jobs for people re-entering the workforce. Many ex-offenders find good job opportunities in what are often high turnover occupations, which constantly demand more workers. Most of these jobs require some postsecondary education and training. Some are best entered through on-the-job training and apprenticeships. Most are skilled occupations that pay modest wages.

Since most of our production jobs are plentiful, you should have little difficulty finding and changing jobs in these fields. Similar to the jobs outlined in Chapter 5, the jobs profiled here are relatively safe from offshoring. Most of these jobs also are becoming increasingly technical and automated. Technology will continue to transform these workplaces, and workers will be required to learn new skills through on-the-job training programs.

Computer-Control Programmers and Operators

⇨ **Annual Earnings:** $31,678
⇨ **Education/Training:** Prefer technical and vocational school training
⇨ **Outlook:** Average growth/excellent opportunities

Employment Outlook: Computer-control programmers and operators should have excellent job opportunities. Due to the limited number of people entering training programs, employers are expected to continue to have difficulty finding workers with the necessary skills and knowledge, which means good job opportunities for those with the necessary skills. Employment of computer-controlled machine tool operators is projected to grow more slowly than the average for all occupations through 2012, but employment of numerical tool and process control programmers is expected to grow about as fast as average for all occupations through 2012. Job growth in both occupations will be driven by the increasing use of computer numerically controlled (CNC) machine tools. Advances in CNC machine tools and manufacturing technology will further automate production, boosting CNC operator productivity and limiting employment growth.

Nature of Work: Computer-control programmers and operators use numerically controlled (CNC) machines to cut and shape precision products, such as automobile parts, machine parts, and compressors. CNC machines include machining tools such as lathes, multiaxis spindles, milling machines, and electrical discharge

75

machines (EDM), but the functions formerly performed by human operators are performed by a computer-control module. CNC machines cut away material from a solid block of metal, plastic, or glass – known as a workpiece – to form a finished part. Computer-control programmers and operators normally produce large quantities of one part, although they may produce small batches or one-of-a-kind items.

Before CNC programmers machine a part, they must carefully plan and prepare the operation. First, these workers review three-dimensional computer aided/automated design (CAD) blueprints of the part. Next, they calculate where to cut or bore into the workpiece, how fast to feed the metal into the machine, and how much metal to remove. They then select tools and materials for the job and plan the sequence of cutting and finishing operations.

Next, CNC programmers turn the planned machining operations into a set of instructions. These instructions are translated into a computer aided/automated manufacturing (CAM) program containing a set of commands for the machine to follow. These commands normally are a series of numbers (hence, numerical control) that describes where cuts should occur, what type of cut should be used, and the speed of the cut. CNC programmers and operators check new programs to ensure that the machinery will function properly and that the output will meet specifications. Because a problem with the program could damage costly machinery and cutting tools, computer simulations may be used to check the program instead of a trial run.

After the programming work is completed, CNC operators perform the necessary machining operations. CNC operators position the metal stock on the CNC machine tool – spindle, lathe, milling machine, or other – set the controls, and let the computer make the cuts. Heavier objects may be loaded with the assistance of other workers, autoloaders, a crane, or a forklift. CNC operators detect some problems by listening for specific sounds – for example, a dull cutting tool or excessive vibration. Dull cutting tools are removed and replaced. Operators listen for vibrations and then adjust the cutting speed to compensate. CNC operators also ensure that the workpiece is being properly lubricated and cooled, because the machining of metal products generates a significant amount of heat.

Working Conditions: Most machine shops are clean, well lit, and ventilated. Most modern CNC machines are partially or totally enclosed, minimizing the exposure of workers to noise, debris, and the lubricants used to cool workpieces during machining. Nevertheless, working around high-speed machine tools presents certain dangers, and workers must follow safety precautions. The job requires stamina because operators stand most of the day and, at times, may need to lift moderately heavy workpieces.

Numerical tool and process control programmers work on desktop computers in offices that typically are near, but separate from, the shop floor. These work areas usually are clean, well-lit, and free of machine noise. Numerical tool and process control programmers occasionally need to enter the shop floor to monitor CNC machining operations. On the shop floor, CNC programmers encounter the same hazards and exercise the same safety precautions as do CNC operators.

Most computer-control programmers and operators work a 40-hour week. CNC operators increasingly work evening and weekend shifts as companies justify investments in more expensive machinery by extending hours of operation. Overtime is common during peak production periods.

Education, Training, & Qualifications: Computer-control programmers and operators train in various ways – in apprenticeship programs, informally on the job, and in secondary, vocational, or postsecondary schools. Due to a shortage of qualified applicants, many employers teach introductory courses, which provide a basic understanding of metalworking machines, safety, and blueprint reading. A basic knowledge of computers and electronics also is helpful. Experience with machine tools is extremely important. In fact, many entrants to these occupations have previously worked as machinists or machine setters, operators, and tenders. Persons interested in becoming computer-control programmers or operators should be mechanically inclined and able to work independently and do accurate work.

High school courses or vocational school courses in mathematics (algebra and trigonometry), blueprint reading, computer programming, metalworking, and drafting are recommended. Apprenticeship programs consist of shop training and related classroom instruction. In shop training, apprentices learn filing, handtapping, and dowel fitting, as well as the operation of various machine tools. Classroom instruction includes math, physics, programming, blueprint reading, CAD software, safety, and shop practices. Skilled computer-control programmers and operators need an understanding of the machining process, including the complex physics that occur at the cutting point. Thus, most training programs teach CNC operations on manual machines prior to operating CNC machines. A growing number of computer-control programmers and operators receive most of their formal training from community or technical colleges. Less skilled CNC operators may need only a couple of weeks of on-the-job training. Qualifications for CNC programmers vary widely depending on the complexity of the job. Employers often prefer skilled machinists or those with technical school training.

Earnings: Median hourly earnings of computer-controlled machine tool operators, metal and plastic, were $15.23 ($31,678 annually) in 2006. Some earned less than $9.91, whereas the top 10 percent earned more than $22.45. Median hourly earnings of numerical tool and process control programmers were $20.42. The lowest 10 percent earned less than $13.11, while the top 10 percent earned more than $31.85.

Key Contacts: For general information about computer-control programmers and operators, contact:

- **Precision Machined Products Association**: 6700 West Snowville Rd., Brecksville, OH 44141. Website: www.pmpa.org.

For a list of training centers and apprenticeship programs, contact:

- **National Tooling and Machining Association**: 9300 Livingston Road, Fort Washington, MD 20744. Website: www.ntma.org.

Food-Processing Occupations

- ➪ **Annual Earnings:** $22,580 to $28,570
- ➪ **Education/Training:** Education/on-the-job training
- ➪ **Outlook:** Average growth

Employment Outlook: Overall employment in the food-processing occupations is expected to grow as fast as average for all occupations through 2016. Increasingly, cheaper meats from abroad will have a negative effect on domestic employment in many food-processing occupations. Job growth will be concentrated at the manufacturing level, as more cutting and processing of meat shifts from retail stores to food-processing plants. Nevertheless, job opportunities should be available at all levels of the occupation due to the need to replace experienced workers who transfer to other occupations or leave the labor force.

As the nation's population grows, the demand for meat, poultry, and seafood should continue to increase. Marketing by the poultry industry is likely to increase the demand for chicken and ready-to-heat products. Similarly the development of prepared food products that are lower in fat and more nutritious is likely to stimulate the consumption of red meat. The trend toward preparing case-ready meat at the processing level also should contribute to demand for animal slaughterers and meatpackers. Employment growth of lesser skilled meat, poultry, and fish cutters and trimmers – who work primarily in animal slaughtering and processing plants – is expected to increase about as fast as the average for all occupations in coming years. Fish cutters will be in demand, as the task of preparing ready-to-heat fish goods gradually shifts from retail stores to processing plants. Advances in fish farming, or "aquaculture," should help meet the growing demand for fish and produce opportunities for fish cutters.

Employment of more highly skilled butchers and meatcutters, who work primarily in retail stores, is expected to decline. Automation and the consolidation of the animal slaughtering and processing industries are enabling employers to transfer employment from higher paid butchers to lower-wage slaughterers and meatpackers in meatpacking plants. At present, most red meat arrives at grocery stores partially cut up, but a growing share of meat is being delivered prepackaged, with additional fat removed, to wholesalers and retailers. This trend is resulting in less work and, thus, fewer jobs for retail butchers.

While high-volume production equipment limits the demand for bakers in manufacturing, overall employment of bakers is expected to increase about as fast as average due to growing numbers of large wholesale bakers, in-store and specialty shops, and traditional bakeries. The numbers of specialty bread and bagel shops have been growing, spurring demand for bread and pastry bakers.

Employment of food batchmakers, food and tobacco cooking and roasting machine operators and tenders is expected to grow more slowly than average. As more of this work is being done at the manufacturing level rather than at the retail level, potential gains will be offset by productivity gains from automated cooking and roasting equipment. All other food processing workers should experience average growth in their occupational field.

Nature of Work: Food-processing occupations include many different types of workers who process raw food products into the finished goods sold by grocers or wholesalers, restaurants, or institutional food services. Butchers and meat, poultry and fish cutters and trimmers are employed at different stages in the process by which animal carcasses are converted into manageable pieces of meat, known as boxed meat, that are suitable for sale to wholesalers and retailers. Meat, poultry, and fish cutters and trimmers commonly work in animal slaughtering and processing plants, while butchers and meatcutters usually are employed at the retail level. As a result, the nature of these jobs varies significantly.

In animal slaughtering and processing plants, slaughterers and meatpackers slaughter cattle, hogs, goats, and sheep and cut the carcasses into large wholesale cuts, such as rounds, loins, ribs, and chucks, to facilitate the handling, distribution, and marketing of meat. In some plants, slaughterers and meatpackers also further process the large parts into cuts that are ready for retail use. These workers also produce hamburger meat and meat trimmings which are used to prepare sausages, luncheon meats, and other fabricated meat products. Slaughterers and meatpackers usually work on assembly lines, with each individual responsible for only a few of the many cuts needed to process a carcass.

In grocery stores, butchers and meatcutters separate wholesale cuts of meat into retail cuts or individually sized servings. They cut meat into steaks and chops, shape and tie roasts, and grind beef for sale as chopped meat. Butchers and meatcutters in retail food stores may also weigh, wrap, and label the cuts of meat, arrange them in refrigerated cases for display, and prepare special cuts to fill unique orders.

Poultry cutters and trimmers slaughter and cut up chickens, turkeys, and other types of poultry. Although the poultry-processing industry is becoming increasingly automated, many jobs, such as trimming, packing, and deboning, are still done manually. Most perform routine cuts on poultry as it moves along production lines. Fish cutters and trimmers are likely to be employed in both manufacturing and retail establishments. These workers primarily scale, cut, and dress fish by removing the head, scales, and other inedible portions and cutting the fish into steaks or fillets.

Bakers mix and bake ingredients in accordance with recipes to produce varying quantities of breads, pastries, and other baked goods. Bakers are commonly employed in grocery stores and specialty shops and produce small quantities of breads, pastries, and other baked goods for consumption on premises or for sale as specialty baked goods. In manufacturing, bakers produce goods in large quantities, using high-volume mixing machines, ovens, and other equipment. Goods produced in large quantities usually are available for sale through distributors, grocery stores, or manufacturers' outlets.

Working Conditions: Working conditions vary by type and size of establishment. In animal slaughtering and processing plants and large retail food establishments, butchers and meatcutters work in large meatcutting rooms equipped with power machines and conveyors. In small retail markets, the butcher (or fish cleaner) may work in a cramped space behind the meat or fish counter. To prevent viral and bacterial infections, work areas must be kept clean and sanitary.

Butchers and meatcutters, poultry and fish cutters and trimmers, and slaughterers and meatpackers often work in cold, damp rooms, which are refrigerated to prevent meat from spoiling and are damp because meat cutting generates large amounts of blood, condensation, and fat. Cool, damp floors increase the likelihood of slips and falls. In addition, cool temperatures, long periods of standing, and repetitious physical tasks make the work tiring. As a result, butchers and meat, poultry, and fish cutters are more susceptible to injury than are most other workers. Meatpacking plants had one of the highest incidences of work-related injury and illness of any industry in 2002. Injuries include cuts and occasional amputations, which occur when knives, cleavers, or power tools are used improperly. Also, repetitive slicing and lifting often lead to cumulative trauma injuries, such as carpal tunnel syndrome. Employers promote ways to reduce injury, but workers in this occupation still face the serious threat of disabling injuries.

Most traditional bakers work in bakeries, cake shops, hot-bread shops, hotels, restaurants, and cafeterias. They also may work in the bakery departments of supermarkets and cruise ships. Bakers may work under hot and noisy conditions. Also, bakers typically work under strict order deadlines and critical time-sensitive baking requirements, both of which can induce stress. Bakers usually work in shifts and may work early mornings, evenings, weekends, and holidays, While many bakers often work as part of a team, they also may work alone when baking particular items. Bakers in retail establishments may be required to serve customers.

Other food processing workers, such as food batchmakers, food and tobacco roasting, baking, and drying machine operators, and food cooking machine operators and tenders, typically work in production areas that are specially designed for food preservation or processing. Food batchmakers, in particular, work in kitchen-type, assembly-line production facilities. Because this work involves food, work areas must meet governmental sanitation regulations. The ovens, as well as the motors of blenders, mixers, and other equipment, often make work areas very warm and noisy. There are some hazards, such as burns, created by the equipment that these workers use. Those who work as food batch-makers, food and tobacco roasting, baking, and drying machine operators, and food cooking machine operators and tenders spend a great deal of time on their feet and generally work a regular 40-hour week that may include evening and night shifts.

Education, Training, & Qualifications: Training varies widely among food-processing occupations. However, most manual food-processing workers require little or no training prior to being hired.

Most butchers and poultry and fish cutters and trimmers acquire their skills on the job through formal and informal training programs. The length of training varies significantly. Simple cutting operations require a few days to learn, while more complicated tasks, such as eviscerating slaughtered animals, generally require several months to learn. The training period for highly skilled butchers at the retail level may be one or two years.

Generally, on-the-job trainees begin by doing less difficult jobs, such as making simple cuts or removing bones. After demonstrating skill with various meatcutting tools, trainees learn to divide carcasses into wholesale cuts and whole-sale cuts into retail and individual portions. Trainees may also learn to roll and tie roasts, prepare sausage, and cure meat. Th ose employed in retail food establishments often are taught operations such as inventory control, meat buying, and record keeping. In addition, growing concern about the safety of meats has led employers to offer their employees numerous safety seminars and extensive training in food safety.

Skills that are important to meat, poultry, and fish cutters and trimmers include manual dexterity, good depth perception, color discrimination, and good hand-eye coordination. Physical strength often is needed to lift and move heavy pieces of meat. Butchers and fish cleaners who wait on customers should have a pleasant personality, a neat appearance, and the ability to communicate clearly. In some states, a health certificate is required for employment.

Bakers often start as apprentices or trainees. Apprentice bakers usually start in craft bakeries, while in-store bakeries, such as those in super-markets, often employ trainees. Bakers need to be skilled in baking, icing, and decorating. They also need to be able to follow instructions, have

an eye for detail, and communicate well with others. Knowledge of bakery products and ingredients, as well as mechanical mixing equipment, is important. Many apprentice bakers participate in correspondence study and may work towards a certificate in baking. The complexity of skills required for certification as a baker is often underestimated. Bakers need to know about applied chemistry, ingredients and nutrition, government health and sanitation regulations, business concepts, and production processes, including how to operate and maintain machinery. Modern food plants typically use high-speed, automated equipment that often is operated by computers.

Food-machine operators and tenders usually are trained on the job, a process that can last anywhere from a month to a year, depending on the complexity of the tasks and the number of products involved. A degree in the appropriate area – dairy processing for those working in dairy product operations, for example – is helpful for advancement to lead worker or a supervisory role. Most food batchmakers participate in on-the-job training, usually from about a month to a year. Some food batchmakers learn their trade through an approved apprenticeship program.

Food-processing workers in retail or wholesale operations may progress to supervisory jobs, such as department managers or team leaders in supermarkets. A few of these workers may become buyers for wholesalers or supermarket chains. Some may open their own markets or bakeries. In processing plants, workers may advance to supervisory positions or become team leaders.

Earnings: Earnings vary by industry, skill, geographic region, and educational level. Median annual earnings of butchers and meat-cutters were $26,930 in May 2006. Some earned less than $16,520 and the highest-paid 10 percent earned more than $43,260 annually. Butchers and meatcutters employed at the retail level typically earn more than those employed in manufacturing.

Meat, poultry, and fish cutters and trimmers typically earn less than butchers and meat-cutters. In 2006, median annual earnings for these lower skilled workers were $20,370. The highest 10 percent earned more than $29,070, while the lowest 10 percent earned less than $14,960

Median annual earnings of bakers were $22,030 in 2006. The highest paid earned more than $33,470 and the lowest 10 percent earned less than $13,930. Median annual earnings of food batchmakers were $23,100 in 2006. Me-dian annual earnings for slaughterers and meatpackers were $21,690; for food cooking machine operators, $21,280; and for food and tobacco roasting, baking, and drying machine operators and tenders, $23,510.

Food-processing workers generally received typical benefits, including pension plans for union members or those employed by grocery stores. However, poultry workers rarely earned substantial benefits. In 2006, 21 percent of all butchers and other meat, poultry, and fish processing workers were union members or were covered by a union contract.

Key Contacts: State employment service offices can provide information about job openings for food-processing occupations. For information on various levels of certification as a baker, contact:

- **Retail Bakers of America:** 8400 Westpark Drive, 2nd Floor McLean, VA 22102. Website: www.rbanet.com.

Machinists

⇨ **Annual Earnings:** $34,757
⇨ **Education/Training:** Apprenticeship program/high school, community, or technical program
⇨ **Outlook:** Slower than average growth/ good job opportunities

Employment Outlook: Despite projected slower-than-average employment growth, job opportunities for machinists should continue to be excellent. The number of workers obtaining the skills and knowledge necessary to fill machinist jobs is expected to be less than the number of job openings arising each year from employment growth and from the need to replace machinists who transfer to other occupations or retire.

Employment of machinists is expected to grow more slowly than the average for all occupations over the 2002-12 period because of rising productivity among these workers. Machinists will become more efficient as a result of the expanded use of, and improvements in, technologies such as computer numerically controlled (CNC) machine tools, autoloaders, and high-speed machining. This allows fewer machinists to accomplish the same amount of work previously performed by more workers. Technology is not expected to affect the employment of machinists as significantly as that of most other production occupations because machinists monitor and maintain many automated systems.

Due to modern production techniques, employers prefer workers, such as machinists, who have a wide range of skills and are capable of performing almost any task in a machine shop.

Employment levels are influenced by economic cycles – as the demand for machined goods falls, machinists involved in production may be laid off or forced to work fewer hours.

Nature of Work: Machinists use machine tools, such as lathes, milling machines, and machining centers, to produce precision metal parts. They use their knowledge of the working properties of metals and their skill with machine tools to plan and carry out the operations needed to make machined products that meet precise specifications.

Before they machine a part, machinists must carefully plan and prepare the operation. These workers first review blueprints or written specifications for the job. They calculate where to cut or bore into the piece of metal being shaped, select the tools and materials for the job, plan the sequence of operations, and mark the metal to show where cuts should be made. After this layout work is completed, machinists perform the necessary machining operations. After the work is completed, machinists use both simple and highly sophisticated measuring tools to check the accuracy of their work against blueprints.

Some machinists may produce large quantities of one part, especially parts requiring the use of complex operations and great precision. Many modern machine tools are computer numerically controlled (CNC). Because most machinists train in CNC programming, they may write basic programs themselves and often modify programs in response to problems encountered during test runs.

Working Conditions: Today, most machine shops are relatively clean, well lit, and ventilated. Many computer-controlled machines are partially or totally enclosed, minimizing the exposure of workers to noise, debris, and the lubricants used to cool workpieces during machining. Nevertheless, working around machine tools presents certain dangers, and workers must follow safety precautions. Machinists wear protective equipment, such as safety glasses to shield against bits of flying metal and earplugs to reduce machinery noise. The job requires stamina, because machinists stand most of the day and, at times, may need to lift moderately heavy workpieces. Modern factories extensively employ autoloaders and overhead cranes, reducing heavy lifting.

Most machinists work a 40-hour week. Evening and weekend shifts are becoming more common as companies justify investments in more expensive machinery by extending hours of operation. Overtime is common during peak production periods.

Education, Training, & Qualifications: Machinists train in apprenticeship programs, informally on the job, and in high schools, vocational schools, or community or technical colleges. Experience with machine tools is helpful. Many entrants previously have worked as machine setters, operators, or tenders. Persons interested in becoming machinists should be mechanically inclined, have good problem-solving abilities, be able to work independently, and be able to do highly accurate work (tolerances may reach 1/10,000th of an inch) that requires concentration and physical effort.

High school or vocational school courses in mathematics (especially trigonometry), blueprint reading, metalworking, and drafting are highly recommended. Apprenticeship programs consist of shop training and related classroom instruction lasting up to four years. In shop training, apprentices work almost full time and are supervised by an experienced machinist while learning to operate various machine tools. Classroom instruction includes math, physics, materials science, blueprint reading, mechanical drawing, and quality and safety practices. In addition, as machine shops have increased their use of computer-controlled equipment, training in the operation and programming of CNC machine tools has become essential.

Apprenticeship classes are taught in cooperation with local community or vocational colleges. A growing number of machinists learn the trade through two-year associate degree programs at community or technical colleges. Graduates of these programs still need significant on-the-job experience before they are fully qualified. As new automation is introduced, machinists normally receive additional training to update their skills. This training usually is provided by a representative of the equipment manufacturer or a local technical school.

Earnings: Median hourly earnings of machinists were $16.71 ($34,757 annually) in May 2006. Some earned less than $10.29, while the top 10 percent earned more than $25.31. Median hourly earnings in the manufacturing industries employing the largest number of machinists in 2006 ranged from $17.36 in metalworking machinery manufacturing to $18.46 in aerospace product and parts manufacturing.

Key Contacts: For general information about machinists, contact:

- **Precision Machined Products Association**: 6700 West Snowville Road, Brecksville, OH 44141-3292. Website: www.pmpa.org.

For a list of training centers and apprenticeship programs, contact:

- **National Tooling and Machining Association**: 9300 Livingston Rd., Fort Washington, MD 20744. Website: www.ntma.org.

For more information on credential standards and apprenticeships, contact:

- **National Institute for Metalworking Skills**: 10565 Fairfax Blvd., Suite 203, Fairfax, VA 22030. Website: www.nims-skills.org.

Painting and Coating Workers, Except Construction and Maintenance

⇨ **Annual Earnings:** $26,832
⇨ **Education/Training:** On-the-job training
⇨ **Outlook:** Slow decline but good job opportunities

Employment Outlook: Overall employment of painting and coating workers is expected to decline slowly (by 4 percent from 2006 to 2016), but employment change will vary by specialty. Good job prospects are expected for those with painting experience. This decline is largely due to better spraying and coating machines and techniques that allow fewer workers to produce the same amount of work.

Nature of Work: Millions of items ranging from cars to candy are covered by paint, plastic, varnish, chocolate, or some other type of coating solution. Spray machine operators use spray guns to coat metal, wood, ceramic, fabric, paper, and food products with paint and other coating solutions. Some factories use automated painting systems that are operated by coating, painting, and spraying machine setters, operators, and tenders. Individuals who paint, coat, or decorate articles such as furniture, glass, pottery, toys, cakes, and books are known as painting, coating, and decorating workers. Transportation equipment painters, also called automotive painters, who work in repair shops are among the most highly skilled manual spray operators because they perform intricate, detailed work and mix paints to match the original color, a task that is especially difficult if the color has faded.

Painting and coating workers held about 192,000 jobs in 2006. Coating, painting, and spraying machine setters, operators, and tenders accounted for about 106,000 jobs, while transportation equipment painters constituted about 54,000. Another 31,000 jobs were held by painting, coating, and decorating workers.

Approximately 70 percent of wage-and-salary workers were employed by manufacturing establishments. Less that 4 percent were self-employed.

Working Conditions: Painting and coating workers typically work indoors and may be exposed to dangerous fumes from paint and coating solutions, although, in general, workers' exposure to hazardous chemicals has decreased because of regulations limiting emissions of volatile organic compound and other hazardous air pollutants.

Education, Training, & Qualifications: Most workers acquire their skills on the job; training usually lasts from a few days to several months, but becoming skilled in all aspects of painting can require 1 to 2 years of training.

Training for beginning painting and coating machine setters, operators, and tenders and for painting, coating, and decorating workers, may last from a few days to a couple of months.

Becoming skilled in all aspects of painting usually requires 1 to 2 years of on-the-job training and sometimes requires some formal classroom instruction.

Earnings: Median hourly earnings of wage-and-salary coating, painting, and spraying machine setters, operators, and tenders were $12.90 ($26,832 annually) in May 2006. The lowest 10 percent earned less than $8.67, and the highest 10 percent earned more than $19.87 an hour. Median hourly earnings of wage-and-salary transportation equipment painters were $17.15. Median hourly earnings of wage-and-salary painting, coating, and decorating workers were $11.04.

Many automotive painters employed by motor vehicle dealers and independent automotive repair shops receive a commission based on the labor cost charged to the customer. Under this method, earnings depend largely on the amount of work a painter does and how fast it is completed.

Key Contacts: For a director of certified automotive painting programs, contact:

- **National Automotive Technicians Education Foundation:** 101 Blue Seal Dr., SE, Suite 101, Leesburg, VA 20175. Website: www.natef.org.

Tool and Die Makers

⇨ **Annual Earnings:** $44,283
⇨ **Education/Training:** Apprenticeship/ postsecondary program
⇨ **Outlook:** Little growth/good job opportunities

Employment Outlook: Although employment of tool and die makers is expected to decline by 10 percent over the 2006-2016 decade, excellent job opportunities are expected as many employers report difficulty finding qualified applicants. Indeed, the number of workers receiving training in this field is expected to continue to be fewer than the number of openings created each year by workers who retire or transfer to other occupations.

The steady decline in employment for this field is due to advancements in automation, including CNC machine tools and computer-aided design. On the other hand, tool and die makers play a key role in building and maintaining advanced automated manufacturing equipment. As firms invest in new equipment, modify production techniques, and implement product design changes more rapidly, they will continue to rely heavily on skilled tool and die makers for retooling.

Nature of Work: Tool and die makers are among the most highly skilled workers in manufacturing. These workers produce tools, dies, and special guiding and holding devices that enable machines to manufacture a variety of products we use daily – from clothing and furniture to heavy equipment and parts for aircraft. Toolmakers craft precision tools and machines that are used to cut, shape, and form metal and other materials. They also produce jigs and fixtures (devices that hold metal while it is bored, stamped, or drilled) and gauges and other measuring devices. Die makers construct metal forms (dies) that are used to shape metal in stamping and forging operations. They also make metal molds for die casting and for molding plastics, ceramics, and composite materials.

To perform these functions, tool and die makers employ many types of machine tools and precision measuring instruments. As a result, tool and die makers are knowledgeable in machining operations, mathematics, and blueprint reading. In fact, tool and die makers often are considered highly specialized machinists. The main difference between tool and die makers and machinists is that machinists normally make a single part during the production process, while tool and die makers make parts and machines used in the production process.

Working from blueprints, tool and die makers first must plan the sequence of operations necessary to manufacture the tool or die. Next, they measure and mark the pieces of metal that will be cut to form parts of the final product. At this point, tool and die makers cut, drill, or bore the part as required, checking to ensure that the final product meets specifications. Finally, these workers assemble the parts and perform finishing jobs such as filing, grinding, and polishing surfaces. Modern technology has changed the ways in which tool and die makers perform their jobs. These works often use computer-aided design (CAD) to develop products and parts. Specifications entered into computer programs can be used to electronically develop drawings for the required tools and dies. Numerical tool and process control programmers use computer aided manufacturing (CAM) programs to convert electronic drawings into computer programs that contain instructions for a sequence of cutting tool operations.

After machining the parts, tool and die makers carefully check the accuracy of the parts using many tools, including coordinate measuring machines (CMM), which use software and sensor arms to compare dimensions of the part to the electronic blueprints. Next, they assemble the different parts into a functioning machine. Finally, they set up a test run using the tools or dies they have made to make sure the manufactured parts meet specifications. If problems occur, they compensate by adjusting the tools or dies.

Working Conditions: Tool and die makers usually work in tool rooms. These areas are quieter than the production floor because there are fewer machines in use at one time. They are also generally kept clean and cool to minimize heat-related expansion of metal workpieces and to accommodate the growing number of computer-operated machines. To minimize the exposure of workers to moving parts, machines have guards and shields. Most computer-controlled machines are totally enclosed, minimizing the exposure of workers to noise, dust, and the lubricants used to cool workpieces during machining. Tool and die makers also must follow safety rules and wear protective equipment, such as safety glasses to shield against bits of flying metal, earplugs to protect against noise, and gloves and masks to reduce exposure to hazardous lubricants and cleaners. These work-

ers also need stamina because they often spend much of their day on their feet and may do moderately heavy lifting.

Companies employing tool and die makers have traditionally operated only one shift per day. Overtime and weekend work are common, especially during peak production periods.

Education, Training, & Qualifications: Most tool and die makers learn their trade through four or five years of education and training in formal apprenticeships or postsecondary programs. Apprenticeship programs include a mix of classroom instruction and job experience and often require 10,400 hours, or about five years to complete. According to most employers, these apprenticeship programs are the best way to learn all aspects of tool and die making. A growing number of tool and die makers receive most of their formal classroom training from community and technical colleges, sometimes in conjunction with an apprenticeship program. Even after completing their apprenticeship, tool and die makers still need years of experience to become highly skilled. Most specialize in making certain types of tools, molds, or dies.

Tool and die makers learn to operate a variety of machines and hand tools. Classroom training usually consists of mechanical drawing, tool designing, tool programming, blueprint reading, and mathematics courses, including algebra, geometry, trigonometry, and basic statistics. Tool and die makers increasingly must have good computer skills to work with CAD technology, CNC machine tools, and computerized measuring machines.

Workers who become tool and die makers without completing formal apprenticeships generally acquire their skills through a combination of on-the-job training and classroom instruction at a vocational school or junior college. They often begin as machine operators and gradually take on more difficult assignments. Many machinists become tool and die makers.

Because tools and dies must meet strict specifications – precision to $1/10,000^{th}$ of an inch is common – the work of tool and die makers requires skill with precision measuring devices and a high degree of patience and attention to detail. Good eyesight is essential. Persons entering this occupation also should be mechanically inclined, able to work and solve problems independently, and capable of doing work that requires concentration and physical effort.

Earnings: Median hourly earnings of tool and die makers were $21.29 ($44,283 annually) in 2006. The lowest 10 percent had earnings of less than $ 13.85, while the top 1 0 pe rcent earned more than $32.41. Those working in motor vehicle parts manufacturing averaged the highest earnings at $26.45.

Key Contacts: For career information and to have inquiries on training and employment referred to member companies, contact:

- **Precision Machined Products Association**: 6700 West Snowville Road, Bresckville, OH 44141-3292. Website: www.pmpa.org.

For lists of schools and employers with tool and die apprenticeship and training programs, contact:

- **National Tooling and Machining Association**: 9300 Livingston Road, Ft. Washington, MD 20744. Website: www.ntma.org.

For information on careers, education and training, earnings, and apprenticeship opportunities in metalworking, contact:

- **Precision Metalforming Association Educational Foundation**: 6363 Oak Tree Blvd., Independence, OH 44131. Website: www.pmaef.org.

Welding, Soldering, & Brazing Workers

- ⇨ **Annual Earnings:** $31,408
- ⇨ **Education/Training:** On-the-job training/high school/vocational school
- ⇨ **Outlook:** Slow growth/excellent job opportunities

Employment Outlook: Employment of welding, soldering, and brazing workers is expected to grow about 5 percent over the 2006-2016 decade, which is slower than average for all occupations. However, job prospects should be excellent, as many potential entrants who could be welders may prefer to attend college or do work that has more comfortable working conditions. In addition, many openings will occur as workers retire or leave the occupation for other reasons.

The major factor affecting employment of welders is the economic health of the industries in which they work. Because almost every manufacturing industry uses welding at some stage of manufacturing or in the repair and maintenance of equipment, a strong economy will keep demand for welders high. A downturn affecting industries such as auto manufacturing,

construction, or petroleum, however, would have a negative impact on the employment of welders in those areas, and could cause some layoffs. Levels of government funding for shipbuilding as well as for infrastructure repairs and improvements are expected to be another important determinant of the future number of welding jobs.

Regardless of the state of the economy, the pressures to improve productivity and hold down labor costs are leading many companies to invest more in automation, especially computer-controlled and robotically controlled welding machinery. This will reduce the demand for some low-skilled welders, solderers, and brazers because these simple, repetitive jobs are being automated. The growing use of automation, however, should increase demand for higher skilled welding, soldering, and brazing machine setters, operators, and tenders. Welders working on construction projects or in equipment repair will not be affected by technology change to the same extent, because their jobs are not as easily automated.

Nature of Work: Welding is the most common way of permanently joining metal parts. In this process, heat is applied to metal pieces, melting and fusing them to form a permanent bond. Because of its strength, welding is used in shipbuilding, automobile manufacturing and repair, aerospace applications, and thousands of other manufacturing activities. Welding is also used to join beams when constructing buildings, bridges, and other structures, and to join pipes in pipelines, power plants, and refineries.

Welders use many types of welding equipment set up in a variety of positions, such as flat, vertical, horizontal, and overhead. They may perform manual welding, in which the work is entirely controlled by the welder, or semiautomatic welding, in which the welder uses machinery, such as a wire feeder, to perform welding tasks. Skilled welding, soldering, and brazing workers generally plan their work from drawings or specifications or use their knowledge of fluxes and base metals to analyze the parts to be joined. These workers then select and set up welding equipment, execute the planned welds, and examine welds to ensure that they meet standards or specifications. Highly skilled welders often are trained to work with a wide variety of materials in addition to steel, such as titanium, aluminum, or plastics. Some welders have more limited duties. They perform routine jobs that already have been planned and laid out and do not require extensive knowledge or welding techniques.

Working Conditions: Welding, soldering, and brazing workers often are exposed to a number of hazards, including the intense light created, poisonous fumes, and very hot materials. They wear safety shoes, goggles, hoods with protective lenses, and other devices designed to prevent burns and eye injuries and to protect them from falling objects. They normally work in well-ventilated areas to limit their exposure to fumes. Automated welding, soldering, and brazing machine operators are not exposed to as many dangers, however, and a face shield or goggles provide adequate protection for these workers.

Welders and cutters may work outdoors, often in inclement weather, or indoors, sometimes in a confined area designed to contain sparks and glare. Outdoors, they may work on a scaffold or platform high off the ground. In addition, they may be required to lift heavy objects and work in a variety of awkward positions, while bending, stooping, or standing to perform work overhead.

Although about 55 percent of welders, solderers, and brazers work a 40-hour week, overtime is common, and some welders work up to 70 hours per week. Welders also may work in shifts as long as 12 hours. Some welders, solderers, brazers, and machine operators work in factories that operate around the clock, necessitating shift work.

Education, Training, & Qualifications: Training for welding, soldering, and brazing workers can range from a few weeks of school or on-the-job training for low-skilled positions to several years of combined school and on-the-job training for highly skilled jobs. Formal training is available in high schools, vocational schools, and postsecondary institutions, such as vocational technical institutes, community colleges, and private welding schools. The military services operate welding schools as well. Some employers provide training. Courses in blueprint reading, shop mathematics, mechanical drawing, physics, chemistry, and metallurgy are helpful. Knowledge of computers is gaining importance, especially for welding, soldering, and brazing machine operators, who are becoming responsible for the programming of computer-controlled machines, including robots.

Welding, soldering, and brazing workers need good eyesight, hand-eye coordination, and manual dexterity. They should be able to concentrate on detailed work for long periods and be able to bend, stoop, and work in awkward positions. In addition, welders increasingly need to be willing to receive training and perform tasks in other production jobs.

Earnings: Median hourly earnings of welders, solderers, and brazers were $15.10 ($31,408 annually) in 2006. Some workers earned less than $10.08 while the highest 10 percent earned $22.50 or more. Median hourly earnings of welding, soldering, and brazing machine setters, operators, and tenders were $14.90. The lowest 10 percent earned less than $9.95 while the highest 10 percent earned more than $25.44. Median hourly earnings in motor vehicle parts manufacturing, the industry employing the largest numbers of welding machine operators in 2006, were $17.75.

Key Contacts: For information on training opportunities and jobs for welding, soldering, and brazing workers, contact local employers, the local office of the state employment service, or schools providing welding, soldering, and brazing training. Information on career opportunities in welding is available from:

- **American Welding Society**: 550 NW Lejeune Road, Miami, FL 33126. Website: www.aws.org.

Production Occupations in Decline

The following production occupations have long been popular with ex-offenders. However, in the coming decade, the U.S. Department of Labor projects significant declines in employment related to these fields. Much of the decline is due to increased productivity caused by automation and offshoring of jobs to countries offering cheap labor. While you'll still find excellent opportunities available in these fields, nonetheless, you need to be aware that finding and keeping a job in these fields may be difficult. Worst of all, many of these jobs do not have a good future for someone looking for career advancement in the long run.

Production Occupations

- Assemblers and Fabricators
- Machine Setters, Operators, and Tenders – Metal and Plastic

Printing Occupations

- Bookbinders and Bindery Workers
- Prepress Technicians and Workers
- Printing Machine Operators

Other Production Occupations

- Textile, Apparel, and Furnishings Occupations
- Photographic Process Workers and Processing Machine Operators
- Semiconductor Processors

For more information on these occupations, please review the current editions of the *Occupational Outlook Handbook* (OOH) and the *O*NET Dictionary of Occupational Titles* (O*NET). Online versions of these key reference books can be found here:

www.bls.gov/oco (*OOH*)
www.onetcenter.org (*O*NET*)

8

Transportation and Material Moving Occupations

IF MANY OF YOUR INTERESTS and skills relate to transportation and material moving occupations, be sure to survey the jobs outlined in this chapter. Many job and career opportunities are available for those who enjoy these lines of work. While these are not high-paying jobs, they are plentiful and can lead to long-term job security. Similar to many jobs profiled in previous chapters, the transportation and material moving occupations described here are some of today's safest jobs – relatively recession-proof and difficult to offshore.

Since most to the following jobs require a basic education and a limited amount of training, they are especially attractive for individuals re-entering the job market who need to quickly find a job but who may have limited work experience. Many of these jobs especially appeal to ex-offenders. Most of these jobs require a high school diploma and some specialized training. A few jobs, especially bus, truck, and taxi drivers, require a license and a good driving record.

If you are re-entering the job market with little work experience, few marketable skills, and red flags in your background, consider getting started in one of the jobs profiled in this chapter. They may provide an important first step for your new work life.

Bus Drivers

- ⇨ **Annual Earnings:** $32,095
- ⇨ **Education/Training:** Commercial driver's license
- ⇨ **Outlook:** Average growth

Employment Outlook: Persons seeking jobs as bus drivers should encounter many opportunities. Individuals who have good driving records and who are willing to work part time or an irregular schedule should have the best job prospects. School bus driving jobs, particularly in rapidly growing suburban areas, should be the easiest to acquire because most are part-time positions with high turnover and minimal training requirements. However, depending on one's offense, ex-offenders may be prohibited from acquiring jobs related to children and education. Those seeking higher paying intercity and public transit bus driver positions may encounter competition. Employment prospects for motorcoach drivers will fluctuate with the cyclical nature of the economy, as demand for motorcoach services is very dependent on tourism.

Employment of bus drivers is expected to increase about as fast as the average for all occupations through the year 2016, primarily to meet the transportation needs of the growing general population and the school-age population. Many additional job openings are expected to occur each year because of the need to replace workers who take jobs in other occupations or who retire.

Nature of Work: Bus drivers are essential in providing passengers with an alternative to their automobiles or other forms of transportation. Intercity bus drivers transport people between regions of a state or of the country; local-transit bus drivers do so within a metropolitan area or county; motorcoach drivers take clients on charter excursions and tours; and school bus drivers take youngsters to and from school and related events. Drivers pick up and drop off passengers at bus stops, stations, or, in the case of students, at regularly scheduled neighborhood locations based on strict time schedules. Drivers must operate vehicles safely, especially when traffic is heavier than normal. However, they cannot let light traffic put them ahead of schedule so that they miss passengers.

Local-transit and intercity bus drivers report to their assigned terminal or garage where they stock up on tickets or transfers and prepare trip report forms. In some transportation firms, maintenance departments are responsible for keeping vehicles in good condition. In other firms, drivers may be responsible for keeping their vehicles in good condition. During their shift these drivers collect fares; answer questions about schedules, routes, and transfer points; and sometimes announce stops.

Motorcoach drivers transport passengers on charter trips and sightseeing tours. Drivers routinely interact with clients and tour guides to make the trip as comfortable and informative as possible. They are responsible for keeping to strict schedules, adhering to the guidelines of the tour's itinerary, and ensuring the overall success of the trip. These drivers act as a customer service representative, tour guide, program director, and safety guide. Trips frequently last more than one day. The driver may be away for more than a week if assigned to an extended tour.

School bus drivers usually drive the same routes each day, stopping to pick up pupils in the morning and return them to their homes in the afternoon. Some school bus drivers also transport students and teachers on field trips or to sporting events. In addition to driving, some school bus drivers work part-time in the school system as janitors, mechanics, or classroom assistants when not driving buses.

Working Conditions: Driving a bus through heavy traffic while dealing with passengers is more stressful and fatiguing than physically strenuous. Intercity bus drivers may work nights, weekends, and holidays and often spend nights away from home, during which they stay in hotels at company expense. Drivers with seniority and regular routes have routine weekly work schedules, but others do not have regular schedules and must be prepared to work on short notice. They report for work only when called for a charter assignment or to drive extra buses on a regular route.

School bus drivers work only when school is in session. Many work 20 hours a week or less, driving one or two routes in the morning and afternoon. Drivers taking field or athletic trips, or who also have midday kindergarten routes, may work more hours a week.

Regular local-transit bus drivers usually have a five-day workweek; Saturdays and Sundays are considered regular workdays. Some drivers work evenings and after midnight. To accommodate commuters, many work "split shifts" – for example, 6am to 10am and 3pm to 7pm with time off in between. Tour and charter bus drivers may work any day and all hours of the day, including weekends and holidays. Their hours are dictated by the charter trips booked and the scheduled prearranged itinerary of tours. However, all bus drivers must comply with the limits placed on drivers by the Department of Transportation's rules and regulations concerning hours of service.

Education, Training, & Qualifications: Qualifications and standards for bus drivers are established by state and federal regulations. Federal regulations require drivers who operate commercial vehicles to hold a commercial driver's license (CDL) from the state in which they live. To qualify for a commercial driver's license, applicants must pass a written test on rules and regulations and then demonstrate that they can operate a bus safely. A national databank permanently records all driving violations incurred by persons who hold commercial licenses. A state may not issue a CDL to a driver who has already had a license suspended or revoked in another state. A driver with a CDL must accompany trainees until the trainees get their own CDL. There are physical requirements mandated for bus drivers as well. Age requirements may vary by state and employer.

All drivers must be able to read and speak English well enough to read road signs, prepare reports, and communicate with law enforcement officials and the public. Many employers prefer high school graduates and require a written test of ability to follow complex bus schedules. Because bus drivers deal with passengers, they must be courteous. They need an even temperament and emotional stability because driving in heavy, fast-moving, or stop-and-go traffic and dealing with passengers can be stressful.

Many companies and school systems give driver trainees instruction in Department of Transportation and company work rules, safety regulations, state and municipal driving regulations, and safe driving practices. During training, drivers practice driving on set courses.

Opportunities for promotion are generally limited. However, experienced drivers may become supervisors or dispatchers, assigning buses to drivers, checking whether drivers are on schedule, rerouting buses to avoid blocked streets or other problems, and dispatching extra vehicles and service crews to scenes of accidents and breakdowns. A few drivers may become managers. Promotion in publicly owned bus systems is often by competitive civil service examination. Some motorcoach drivers purchase their own equipment and open their own business.

Earnings: Median hourly earnings of transit and intercity bus drivers were $15.43 in May 2006. Some earned less than $9.26 an hour, while the highest 10 percent earned more than $24.08 an hour. The median hourly earnings of school bus drivers were $11.93 in 2006. Some earned less than $6.58 an hour, while the highest 10 percent earned more than $17.61 an hour.

The benefits bus drivers receive from their employers vary greatly. Most intercity and local-transit bus drivers receive paid health and life insurance, sick leave, vacation leave, and free bus rides on any of the regular routes of their line or system. School bus drivers receive sick leave, and many are covered by health and life insurance and pension plans. Because they do not generally work when school is not in session, they do not get vacation leave. Most intercity and many local transit bus drivers are members of the Amalgamated Transit Union.

Key Contacts: For information on employment opportunities, contact local transit systems, intercity bus lines, school systems, or the local office of the state employment service. General information on school bus driving is available from:

- **National School Transportation Association:** 43 South West Street, 4th Floor, Alexandria, VA 22314. Website: www.yellow buses.org.

General information on local-transit bus driving is available from:

- **American Public Transportation Association:** 1666 K Street NW, Suite 1100, Washington, DC 20006. Website: www.apta.com.

General information on motorcoach driving is available from:

- **United Motorcoach Association:** 113 S. West St., 4th Floor, Alexandria, VA 22314. Website: www.uma.org.

Cargo and Freight Agents

⇨ **Annual Earnings:** $37,110
⇨ **Education/Training:** High school diploma
⇨ **Outlook:** Good

Employment Outlook: Employment of cargo and freight agents is expected to grow faster than the average for all occupations in the decade ahead in response to the continuing growth of cargo traffic and next-day shipping services.

Nature of Work: Cargo and freight agents arrange for and track incoming and outgoing cargo and freight shipments in airline, train, or trucking terminals or on shipping docks. They expedite the movement of shipments by determining the route that shipments are to take and by preparing all necessary shipping documents.

Working Conditions: Cargo and freight agents work in a variety of settings. Some work in warehouses, stockrooms, or shipping and receiving rooms while others may spend time in cold storage rooms or outside on loading platforms, where they are exposed to the weather.

Education, Training, & Qualifications: A high school diploma is usually sufficient for entry in these positions.

Earnings: The median annual earnings in May 2006 for cargo and freight agents were $37,110.

Key Contacts: Information on job opportunities for cargo and freight agents is available from local employers and local offices of the state employment service.

Material Moving Occupations

⇨ **Annual Earnings:** varies – from $17,638 to $45,400
⇨ **Education/Training:** Prefer high school diploma
⇨ **Outlook:** Employment opportunities excellent

Employment Outlook: Job openings should be numerous because the occupation is very large and the turnover is relatively high – characteristic of occupations requiring little formal training. Many openings will arise from the need to replace workers who transfer to other occupations, retire, or leave the labor force for other reasons. However, overall employment in material moving occupations will increase more slowly than average for all occupations through 2016. Employment growth will stem from an expanding economy and increased spending on the nation's infrastructure, such as highways and bridges. However, equipment improvements, including the growing automation of material handling in factories and warehouses, will continue to raise productivity and moderate demand for material movers.

Job growth for material movers largely depends on growth in the industries employing them and the type of equipment the workers operate or the materials they handle. For example, employment of operators in manufacturing will decline due to increased automation and efficiency in the production process. On the other hand, employment will grow rapidly in temporary help organizations as firms contract out material moving services. Employment will grow in warehousing and storage as more firms contract out their warehousing to firms that specialize in them. Both construction and manufacturing are sensitive to changes in economic conditions, so the number of job openings in these industries may fluctuate from year to year. Although increasing automation may eliminate some manual tasks, new jobs will be created to operate and maintain material moving equipment.

Nature of Work: Material moving workers are categorized into two groups – operators and laborers. Operators use machinery to move construction materials, earth, petroleum products, and other heavy materials. Generally, they move materials over short distances – around a construction site, factory, or warehouse. Some move materials onto or off of trucks and ships. Operators control equipment by moving levers or foot pedals, operating switches, or turning dials. They may also set up and inspect equipment, make adjustments, and perform minor repairs when needed. Laborers and hand material movers manually handle freight, stock, or other materials; clean vehicles, machinery, and other equipment; and pack or package products and materials. Material moving occupations are classified by the type of equipment they operate or goods they handle. Each piece of equipment requires different skills to move different types of loads.

Working Conditions: Many material moving workers work outdoors in every type of climate and weather condition. The work tends to be repetitive and physically demanding. They may lift and carry heavy objects, and stoop, kneel, crouch, or crawl in awkward positions. Some work at great heights. Some jobs expose workers to harmful materials or chemicals, fumes, odors, loud noise, or dangerous machinery. To avoid injury, these workers wear safety clothing, such as gloves and hardhats, and devices to protect their eyes, mouth, or hearing. These jobs have become much safer as safety equipment such as overhead guards on forklift trucks has become common.

Material movers generally work eight-hour shifts, though longer shifts also are common. In many industries that work around the clock, material movers work evening or "graveyard" shifts. Some may work at night because the establishment may not want to disturb customers during normal business hours. Refuse and recyclable material collectors often work shifts starting at 5 or 6 am. Some material movers work only during certain seasons, such as when the weather permits construction activity.

Education, Training, & Qualifications: Most material moving jobs require little work experience or specific training. Some employers prefer applicants with a high school diploma, but most simply require workers to be at least 18 years old and physically able to do the work. For those jobs requiring physical exertion, employers may require that applicants pass a physical exam. Some employers also require drug testing or background checks before employment. Workers often are younger than workers in other occupations – reflecting the limited training but significant physical requirements of many of these jobs.

Material movers generally learn skills informally, on the job, from more experienced workers or supervisors. However, workers who use industrial trucks, other dangerous equipment, or handle toxic chemicals must receive specialized training in safety awareness and procedures.

This training is usually provided by the employer. Employers must also certify that each operator has received the training and evaluate each operator at least once every three years. Material moving equipment operators need a good sense of balance, distance judgment, and eye-hand-foot coordination. Most jobs require reading and basic math skills to read procedure manuals and billing and other documents. Mechanical aptitude and high school training in automobile or diesel mechanics are helpful because workers may perform some maintenance on their equipment. Experience operating mobile equipment, such as tractors on farms or heavy equipment in the military, is an asset. As material moving equipment becomes more automated, many workers will need basic computer and technical knowledge to operate the equipment.

Earnings: Median annual earnings of material moving workers in 2006 were relatively low – ranging from $17,638 a year ($8.48 an hour) for hand packers and packagers to $45,400 a year ($21.83 an hour) for gas compressor and gas pumping station operators. The largest number of workers tend to be found in lower paying positions. Pay rates vary according to experience and job responsibilities. Pay usually is higher in metropolitan areas. The seasonality of work may reduce earnings.

Key Contacts: For information about job opportunities and training programs, contact local state employment service offices, building or construction contractors, manufacturers, and wholesale and retail establishments. For information on safety and training requirements:

- **U.S. Department of Labor**: Occupational Safety and Health Administration (OSHA), 200 Constitution Ave. NW., Washington, DC 20210. Website: www.osha.gov.

Information on training and apprenticeships for industrial truck operators is available from:

- **International Union of Operating Engineers**: 1125 17ᵗʰ Street, NW, Washington, DC 20036. Website: www.iuoe.org.

Taxi Drivers and Chauffeurs

⇨ **Annual Earnings:** $20,342
⇨ **Education/Training:** Chauffeur/taxi driver's license
⇨ **Outlook:** Average growth

Employment Outlook: Persons seeking jobs as taxi drivers and chauffeurs should encounter good opportunities, because of the need to replace the many people who work in this occupation for short periods and then transfer to other occupations or leave the labor force. Opportunities should be best for persons with good driving records and the ability to work flexible schedules. Employment of taxi drivers and chauffeurs is expected to grow faster than average for all occupations through the year 2016, as local and suburban travel increases with population growth. Employment growth also will stem from federal legislation requiring services for persons with disabilities. Rapidly growing metropolitan areas should offer the best job opportunities. The number of job openings can fluctuate with the cycle of the overall economy because the demand for taxi and limousine transportation depends on travel and tourism. Extra drivers may be hired during holiday seasons and peak travel and tourist times.

Nature of Work: Taxi drivers help passengers get to and from their homes, workplaces, and recreational pursuits such as dining, entertainment, and shopping. At the start of their driving shift, taxi drivers usually report to a taxicab service or garage where they are assigned an automobile modified for commercial passenger use. Taxi drivers pick up passengers in one of three ways: "cruising" the streets to pick up random passengers; prearranged pickups; and picking up passengers from taxi stands established in highly trafficked areas.

Drivers should be familiar with the streets in the areas they serve so they can use the most efficient route to destinations. They should know the location of frequently requested destinations, such as airports, bus and railroad terminals, convention centers, hotels, and other points of interest. In case of emergency, the driver should also know the location of fire and police stations and hospitals. Upon reaching the destination, drivers determine the fare and announce it to the rider. Fares may include a surcharge for additional passengers, a fee for handling luggage, or a drop charge. Each jurisdiction determines the rate and structure of the fare system of zones through which the taxi passes during a trip. Passengers usually add a tip to the fare.

Chauffeurs operate limousines, vans and private cars for limousine companies, private businesses, government agencies, and wealthy individuals. Chauffeur service differs from taxi service in that all trips are prearranged. Many chauffeurs transport customers in large vans between hotels and airports, bus, or train terminals. Others drive luxury vehicles such as limousines, to business events, entertainment venues, and social events. Still others provide full-time personal transportation for wealthy families and private companies. Chauffeurs cater to passengers with attentive customer service and a special regard for detail. They help riders into the car by holding open doors, holding umbrellas when it is raining, and loading packages and luggage into the trunk of the car. A growing number of chauffeurs work as full-service executive assistants, simultaneously acting as driver, secretary, and itinerary planner.

Working Conditions: Taxi drivers and chauffeurs occasionally have to load and unload heavy luggage and packages. Driving for long periods can be tiring and uncomfortable, especially in densely populated urban areas. Drivers must be alert to conditions on the road, especially in heavy and congested traffic or in bad weather. Taxi drivers also risk robbery because they work alone and often carry large amounts of cash.

Work hours vary greatly. Some jobs offer full-time or part-time employment with work hours that can change from day to day or remain the same every day. It is often necessary for drivers to report to work on short notice. Chauffeurs who work for a single employer may be on call much of the time. Evening and weekend work are common for limousine and taxicab services. The needs of the client or employer dictate the work schedule for chauffeurs. The work of taxi drivers is much less structured. Working free of supervision, they may break for a meal or a rest whenever their vehicle is unoccupied. Many taxi drivers and chauffeurs like the independent, unsupervised work of driving their automobile. This occupation is attractive to individuals seeking flexible work schedules, such as college and postgraduate students, and to anyone seeking a second source of income.

Full-time taxi drivers usually work one shift a day, which may last from eight to 12 hours. Part-time drivers may work half a shift each day, or work a full shift once or twice a week. Drivers may work shifts at all times of the day and night, because most taxi companies offer services 24 hours a day. Early morning and late night shifts are common. Drivers work long hours during holidays, weekends, and other special times during which demand for their services may be heavier. Independent drivers, however, often set their own hours and schedules.

Design improvements in newer cabs have reduced some of the stress and increased the comfort and efficiency of drivers. Many regulatory bodies overseeing taxi and chauffeur services require standard amenities such as air-conditioning and general upkeep of the vehicles. Modern taxicabs also are equipped with sophisticated tracking devices, fare meters, and dispatching equipment. Satellites and tracking systems link many of these state-of-the-art vehicles with company headquarters. In a matter of seconds, dispatchers can deliver directions, traffic advisories, weather reports, and other important communication to drivers anywhere in the transporting area. The satellite link also allows dispatchers to track vehicle location, fuel consumption, and engine performance. Drivers can easily communicate with dispatchers to discuss delivery schedules and courses of action should there be mechanical problems. For instance, automated dispatch systems help dispatchers locate the closest driver to a customer in order to maximize efficiency and quality of service. When threatened with crime or violence, drivers may have special "trouble lights" to alert authorities to emergencies and ensure that help arrives quickly.

Taxi drivers and chauffeurs meet many different types of people. Dealing with rude customers and waiting for passengers requires patience.

Education, Training, & Qualifications: Persons interested in driving a limousine or taxicab must first have a regular automobile driver's license. They also must acquire a chauffeur or taxi driver's license, commonly called a "hack" license. Local governments set license standards and requirements for taxi drivers and chauffeurs that include minimum qualifications for driving experience and training. Local authorities generally require applicants for a hack license to pass a written exam or complete a training program that may require up to 80 hours of classroom instruction.

To qualify through either an exam or training program, applicants must know local geography, motor vehicle laws, safe driving practices, regulations governing taxicabs, and display some aptitude for customer service. Many taxi and limousine companies set higher standards than required by law. It is common for companies to review applicants' medical, credit, criminal, and driving records. In addition, many companies require a higher minimum age than that which is legally required and prefer that drivers be high school graduates.

In small and medium-sized communities, drivers are sometimes able to buy their taxi, limousine, or other type of automobile and go into business for themselves. These independent owner-drivers are required to have an additional permit allowing them to operate their vehicle as a company. Some big cities limit the number of operating permits. In these cities, drivers become owner-drivers by buying permits from owner-drivers who leave the business. Although many owner-drivers are successful, some fail to cover expenses and eventually lose their permit and automobile. Good business sense and courses in accounting, business, and business arithmetic can help an owner-driver to become successful. Knowledge of mechanics enables owner-drivers to perform their own routine maintenance and minor repairs to cut expenses.

Earnings: Earnings of taxi drivers and chauffeurs vary greatly, depending upon such factors as the number of hours worked, customers' tips, and geographic location. Median hourly earnings of salaried taxi drivers and chauffeurs, including tips, were $9.78 in May 2006. Some earned less than $6.85 an hour, and the highest 10 percent earned more than $15.80 an hour.

Key Contacts: Information on licensing and registration of taxi drivers and chauffeurs is available from local government agencies that regulate taxicabs. For information about work opportunities as a taxi driver or chauffeur, contact local taxi or limousine companies or state employment service offices or contact:

- **Taxicab, Limousine, and Paratransit Association:** 3849 Farragut Avenue, Kensington, MD 20895.

For general information about the work of limousine drivers, contact:

- **National Limousine Association:** 49 South Maple Ave., Marlton, NJ 08053. Website: www.limo.org

Truck Drivers

⇨ **Annual Earnings:** $35,048
⇨ **Education/Training:** Training and license
⇨ **Outlook:** Good

Employment Outlook: Employment is expected to grow about as fast as average for all occupations in the decade ahead. Job opportunities in this large occupation should be plentiful because of the growing demand for truck transportation services and the need to replace drivers who leave the occupation. The increased use of rail, air, and ship transportation requires truck drivers to pick up and deliver shipments. Demand for long-distance drivers will remain strong because these drivers transport perishable and time-sensitive goods more efficiently than do alternative modes of transportation.

Nature of Work: The work of truck drivers varies. Long-distance drivers may make short "turnaround" hauls where they deliver a load to a nearby city, pick up another loaded trailer, and drive back to their home base in one day. Other runs take an entire day or longer, and drivers remain away from home overnight. Local truck drivers may pick up a loaded truck in the morning and spend the rest of the day making deliveries or may make several trips between their dispatch point and customers to make deliveries.

Working Conditions: Truck driving has become less physically demanding because most trucks now have more comfortable seats, better ventilation, and improved cab designs. However, driving for many hours at a stretch, unloading cargo, and making deliveries can be tiring. Driving in bad weather, heavy traffic, or over mountains can be nerve-racking. Some self-employed long- distance truck drivers who own as well as operate their trucks spend over 240 days a year away from home. Local truck drivers frequently work 48 hours or more a week. Many who handle food for chain grocery stores, produce markets, or bakeries drive at night or early in the morning. Many load and unload their own trucks, which requires considerable lifting, carrying, and walking.

Education, Training, & Qualifications: Qualifications are established by state and federal regulations. All truck drivers must have a driver's license issued by the state in which they live, and most employers strongly prefer a good driving record. All drivers of trucks designed to carry at least 26,000 pounds are required to obtain a special commercial driver's license. Many firms require that drivers be at least 25 years old, be able to lift heavy objects, and have driven trucks for three to five years. Many prefer to hire high school graduates and require annual physical examinations. Since drivers often deal directly with the company's customers, they must get along well with people.

Earnings: As a rule, local truck drivers are paid by the hour and receive extra pay for working overtime – usually after 40 hours. Long-distance drivers are generally paid by the mile and their rate per mile can vary greatly. In May 2006, truck drivers had average straight-time hourly earnings of $16.85 ($35,048 annually). The middle 50 percent earned between $13.33 and $21.04 an hour.

Median hourly earnings in the industries employing the largest numbers of heavy truck and tractor-trailer drivers in 2002 were as follows:

- General freight trucking $18.38
- Grocery and related product
  wholesalers $18.01
- Specialized freight trucking $16.40
- Cement and concrete product
  manufacturing $15.26
- Other specialty trade contractors $14.94

Median hourly earnings of light or delivery services truck drivers were $12.17 in May 2006. The middle 50 percent earned between $9.13 and $16.16 an hour. Median hourly earnings in the industries employing the largest numbers of light or delivery service truck drivers in 2006 were as follows:

- Couriers $17.80
- General freight trucking $15.33
- Grocery and related product
  wholesalers $12.84
- Building material and supplies
  dealers $11.54
- Automotive parts, accessories, and
  tire stores $8.38

Median hourly earnings of driver/sales workers, including commissions, were $9.99 in 2006. The middle 50 percent earned between $7.12 and $15.00 an hour. Median hourly earnings in the industries employing the largest numbers of driver/sales workers in 2006 were as follows:

- Drycleaning and laundry services $14.81
- Direct selling establishments $13.72

- Grocery and related product
  wholesalers $12.37
- Full-service restaurants $7.11
- Limited-service eating places $7.02

Local truck drivers tend to be paid by the hour, with extra pay for working overtime. Employers pay long-distance drivers primarily by the mile. The per-mile rate can vary greatly from employer to employ and may even depend on the type of cargo being hauled. Some long-distance drivers are paid a percent of each load's revenue.

Most self-employed truck drivers are primarily engaged in long-distance hauling.

Key Contacts: Information on career opportunities in truck driving may be obtained from:

- **American Trucking Associations, Inc.:** 950 N. Glebe Road, Suite 210, Arlington, VA 22203. Website: www.truckline.com.

- **International Brotherhood of Teamsters:** 25 Louisiana Avenue, NW, Washington, DC 20001. Website: www.teamster.org.

A list of certified tractor-trailer driver training courses may be obtained from:

- **Professional Truck Driver Institute:** 555 E. Braddock Road, Alexandria, VA 22314. Website: www.ptdi.org.

9

Travel and Hospitality Jobs

F EW INDUSTRIES PROVIDE as many great job and career opportunities for people without a four-year degree and those re-entering the job market than the travel and hospitality industry. Highly segmented, this industry encompasses everything from airlines, cruise lines, tour operators, and car rental agencies to hotels, resorts, and rail services. The travel and hospitality industry is especially noted for focusing on performance and promoting talent from within its ranks. Indeed, many general managers of major hotels began their careers at the very bottom – doorman, front desk clerk, or porter – and were promoted within to increasingly responsible positions.

Many entry-level positions within this industry only require a high school diploma and a demonstrated ability to learn and achieve goals. Similar to other industries, employers within the travel and hospitality industry increasingly require candidates to have higher levels of education and training for entry into and advancement within this industry. Many vocational education schools, community colleges, and universities offer specialized short- and long-term programs in travel and hospitality. For anyone without a four-year degree, the travel and hospitality industry offers some of the more rewarding short- and long-term job and career opportunities.

Many of the jobs defining this exciting industry cross-cut other industries and only require basic skills, interest, motivation, drive, and a willingness to learn. If many of the jobs outlined in previous chapters are less than appealing to you, chances are you may find your dream job in one of the many segments that define the relatively open and inviting travel and hospitality industry. This also is an example of an industry undergoing tremendous economic stress and restructuring. It's often during such times that new opportunities arise for enterprising individuals who are willing to invest their futures in what may well be some exciting career opportunities.

The Industry and Its Many Players

The travel industry is much more than the stereotypical travel agent arranging tickets, tours, and hotels for tour groups and anxious tourists. This is a highly segmented industry consisting of a network of mutually dependent players – airlines, hotels, resorts, cruise lines, restaurants, wholesalers, incentive groups, retail tour agents, car rental companies, catering firms, meeting planners, corporate travel divisions, educators, journalists, photographers, and travel writers. These as well as a host of related organizations, individuals, and jobs are focused on the business of moving and managing people from one location to another.

The travel industry is a challenging, exciting, and highly entrepreneurial industry. Its many players report a high degree of job satisfaction. Indeed, many claim to have found *"the best job in the world"* – and with all the perks to prove it! Public relations directors in major hotels, for example, often meet and entertain celebrities, work closely with the local business community, and participate in numerous community activities – a worklife many still can't believe they "fell into" in the travel industry.

While many of the businesses, such as major airlines and hotel chains, are huge corporations, most travel-related businesses appear big but are actually small and highly entrepreneurial. They appear big because they are connected to one another through efficient communication and marketing systems which place everyone within a mutually interdependent network of business transactions. It's the type of business where there is a high degree of competition as well as a high degree of mutual dependence and cooperation. Individuals working in this industry manage to advance their careers by moving from one player to another with relative ease.

The major segments or sub-industries and players within the travel industry include operators, suppliers, promoters, and supporters:

- accommodations and lodging industry
- advertising
- advertising agencies
- airlines
- airport and aviation management groups
- bus lines
- car rentals
- computer support services
- convention and meeting planners
- corporate travel managers
- cruise lines
- culture and arts promotion groups
- government tourist promotion offices
- incentive travel companies
- public relations
- publishing and journalism
- rail services
- research and marketing groups
- resorts and spas
- restaurants
- sales and marketing
- theme parks
- tour guiding
- tour operators
- tourist sites and attractions
- travel agencies and operators
- travel clubs
- travel education and training
- travel insurance
- travel websites (e-travel)
- travel writers and photographers

Not surprisingly, the travel industry employs numerous types of workers from accountants, computer specialists, and lawyers to market researchers, artists, and doctors. Many people also are able to freelance in this industry as part- and full-time professionals serving as wholesalers, travel agents, writers, photographers, trainers, and consultants.

Air Traffic Controllers

⇨ **Annual Earnings:** $117,240
⇨ **Education/Training:** Work experience
⇨ **Outlook:** Good

Employment Outlook: Employment of air traffic controllers is expected to grow about as fast as the average in the decade ahead. Increas-

ing air traffic will require more controllers to handle the additional work. New computerized systems will assist the controller by automatically making many of the routine decisions. This will allow controllers to handle more traffic, thus increasing their productivity. Federal budget constraints also may limit hiring of air traffic controllers.

Air traffic controllers held about 25,000 jobs in 2006. The vast majority were employed by the Federal Aviation Administration (FAA) and work at airports – in towers and flight service stations – and in air route traffic control centers. A few serve as instructors at the FAA Academy in Oklahoma City; conduct research at the FAA national experimental center near Atlantic City, NJ; work for the Department of Defense; or work for private air traffic companies providing service to non-FAA towers.

Nature of Work: Air traffic controllers coordinate the movement of air traffic to ensure that planes stay a safe distance apart. Their primary concern is safety, but controllers also must direct plane efficiently to minimize delays. Some regulate airport traffic; others regulate flights between airports. Both airport tower and en route controllers usually control several planes at a time. Often they have to make quick decisions about completely different activities.

Working Conditions: Controllers work a basic 40-hour week; however, they may work additional hours for which they receive overtime pay or equal time off. Because most control towers and centers operate 24 hours a day, seven days a week, controllers rotate night and weekend shifts. During busy times, controllers must work rapidly and efficiently. Total concentration is required to keep track of several planes at the same time and to make certain that all pilots receive correct instructions. The mental stress of being responsible for the safety of several aircraft and their passengers can be exhausting for some persons.

Education, Training, & Qualifications: To become an air traffic controller, a person must enroll in an FAA-approved education program and pass a pre-employment test that measures his/her ability to learn the controller's duties in order to qualify for job openings in the air traffic control system. (Exceptions are air traffic controllers with prior experience and military veterans.) The pre-employment test is currently offered only to students enrolled in an FAA-approved education program. In addition, applicants must have three years of full-time work experience or four years of college, or an equivalent combination of both.

Upon successful completion of an FAA-approved program, individuals who receive a school recommendation and who meet the basic qualification requirements, including age limit and achievement of a qualifying score on the FAA pre-employment test, become eligible for employment as an air traffic controller. Candidates must also pass a medical exam, drug screening, and security clearance before they can be hired. Upon selection, employees attend the FAA Academy in Oklahoma City for 12 weeks of training, during which they learn the fundamentals of the airway system, FAA regulations, controller equipment, and aircraft performance characteristics, as well as more specialized tasks. After graduation, it takes several years of progressively more responsible work experience, interspersed with considerable classroom instruction and independent study, to become a fully licensed controller.

Earnings: This is one of the highest paid jobs for people without a four-year degree. Median annual earnings of air traffic controllers in May 2006 were $117,240. The middle 50 percent earned between $86,860 and $142,210. Both the worker's job responsibilities and complexity of the particular facility determine a controller's pay. For example, controllers who work at FAA's busiest air traffic control facilities earn higher pay.

Key Contacts: Career information on how to qualify and apply for a job as an air traffic controller is available through:

- **Federal Aviation Administration:** 800 Independence Avenue, SW, Washington, DC 20591. Website: www.faa.gov.

Aircraft and Avionics Equipment Mechanics and Service Technicians

⇨ **Annual Earnings:** Around $47,736
⇨ **Education/Training:** On-the-job training and certificate
⇨ **Outlook:** Excellent

Employment Outlook: Opportunities for aircraft and avionics equipment mechanics and service technician jobs should be excellent for persons who have completed aircraft mechanic training programs. Employment of aircraft mechanics is expected to increase about as fast as the average for all occupations in the decade ahead. As more and more people are expected to fly in the decade ahead, the number of aircraft requiring servicing will increase accordingly.

Aircraft and avionics equipment and service technicians held about 138,000 jobs in 2006; about one in six of these workers was an avionics technician. Nearly 40 percent of aircraft and avionics equipment mechanics and technicians worked for air transportation companies, and close to 20 percent worked for private maintenance and repair facilities. About 20 percent worked for the federal government, and about 13 percent worked fo r aerospace products and parts manufacturing firms. Most of the rest worked for companies that operate their own planes to transport executives and cargo.

Nature of work: To keep aircraft in peak operating condition, aircraft and avionics equipment mechanics and service technicians perform scheduled maintenance, make repairs, and complete inspections required by the Federal Aviation Administration (FAA). Some mechanics work on one of many different types of aircraft, such as jets, propeller-driven airplanes, or helicopters. Others specialize in one section of a particular type of aircraft, such as the engine, hydraulics, or electrical system.

Avionics systems are now an integral part of aircraft design and have vastly improved aircraft capability. Avionics technicians repair and maintain components used for aircraft navigation and radio communications, weather radar systems, and other instruments that control flight, engine, and other primary functions. Because of technological advances, an increasing amount of time is spent repairing electronic systems, such as computerized controls. Technicians may also be required to analyze and develop solutions to complex electronic problems.

Working Conditions: Mechanics usually work in hangars or in other indoor areas, although they can work outdoors – sometimes in unpleasant weather – when hangars are full or when repairs must be made quickly. Mechanics often work under time pressure to maintain flight schedules or, in general aviation, to keep from inconveniencing customers. At the same time, mechanics have a tremendous responsibility to maintain safety standards, and this can cause the job to be stressful. Frequently mechanics must lift or pull heavy objects weighing as much as 70 pounds. They occasionally must work in precarious positions on scaffolds or ladders. Aircraft mechanics usually work 40 hours a wcck on eight-hour shifts around the clock. Overtime work is frequent.

Education, Training, & Qualifications: The majority of mechanics who work on civilian aircraft are certified by the FAA as "airframe mechanic" or "power plant mechanic," or "avionics repair specialist." The FAA requires at least 18 months of work experience for an airframe, power plant or avionics repairer's certificate. Completion of a program at an FAA-certified mechanic school can substitute for the work experience requirement. Applicants for all certificates also must pass written and oral tests and demonstrate that they can do the work

authorized by the certificate. Although a few people become mechanics through on-the-job training, most learn their job in one of about 200 trade schools certified by the FAA. Some aircraft mechanics in the military acquire enough general experience to satisfy the work experience requirements for the FAA certificate. In general, however, jobs in the military services are too specialized to provide the broad experience required by the FAA. Courses in math and science are helpful, as they demonstrate many of the principles involved in the operation of aircraft. Development of writing skills is useful because mechanics are often required to submit reports.

Earnings: Median hourly earnings of aircraft mechanics and service technicians were about $22.95 in May 2006 ($47,736 annually). For avionics technicians, median earnings were about $46,945 per year). Mechanics who work on jets for the major airlines generally earn more than those working on other aircraft. Airline mechanics and their families receive reduced-fare transportation on their own and most other airlines. Almost four in 10 aircraft and avionics equipment mechanics and service technicians are members of unions or covered by union agreements.

Key Contacts: Information about jobs with a particular airline can be obtained by contacting the personnel manager of the company. For general information about aircraft and avionics equipment mechanics and service technicians, contact:

- **Professional Aviation Maintenance Association:** 400 Commonwealth Drive, Warrendale, PA 15096. Website: www.pama.org.

Chefs, Cooks and Food Preparation Workers

⇨ **Annual Earnings:** Varies greatly from $15,550 to over $50,000
⇨ **Education/Training:** High school diploma plus training
⇨ **Outlook:** Excellent

Employment Outlook: Overall employment of chefs, cooks, and food preparation workers is expected to increase about as fast as the average for all occupations in the decade ahead. Employment growth will be spurred by increases in population, household income, and leisure time that will allow people to dine out and take vacations more often. In addition, growth in the number of two-income households will lead more families to opt for the convenience of dining out. Competition for jobs in the top kitchens of higher end restaurants should be keen. Minimal education and training requirements, combined with a large number of part-time positions, make employment as chefs, cooks, and food preparation workers attractive to people seeking first-time or short-term employment, a source of additional income, or a flexible schedule.

Nature of Work: Chefs, cooks, and other food preparation workers prepare a wide range of foods – from soups, snacks, and salads to entrees, side dishes, and desserts – for restaurants, institutions, bakeries, and fast-food outlets. Chefs are the most highly skilled, trained, and experienced kitchen workers. Executive chefs coordinate the work of the kitchen staff and often direct certain kinds of food preparation. They decide the size of servings, sometimes plan menus, and buy food supplies. Larger restaurants and food service establishments tend to have varied menus and larger kitchen staffs. They often include several chefs and cooks, sometimes called assistant or line cooks, along with other less skilled kitchen workers, such as food preparation workers. Each chef or cook works an assigned station that is equipped with the types of stoves, grills, pans, and ingredients needed for the foods prepared at each station. Job titles often reflect the principal ingredient prepared or the type of cooking preformed – vegetable cook, fry cook, or grill cook.

Chefs, cooks, and food preparation workers held 3.1 million jobs in 2006. The distribution of jobs among the various types of chefs, cooks, and food preparation workers was as follows:

- Food preparation workers   902,000
- Cooks, restaurant   850,000
- Cooks, fast food   629,000
- Cooks, institution and
  cafeteria   401,000
- Cooks, short order   195,000
- Chefs and head cooks   115,000
- Cooks, private household   4,900
- Cooks, all other   16,000

Working Conditions: Many restaurant and institutional kitchens have modern equipment, convenient work areas, and air-conditioning; but others, particularly in older and smaller eating places, are frequently not as well equipped. Workers generally must withstand the pressure and strain of working in close quarters during busy periods, stand for hours at a time, lift heavy pots and kettles, and work near hot ovens and grills. Work hours in restaurants may include late evening, holiday, and weekend work, while hours in cafeterias in factories, schools, or other institutions may be more regular. The wide range in dining hours and the need for fully staffed kitchens during all open hours create work opportunities for individuals seeking supplemental income, flexible work hours, or variable schedules.

Education, Training, & Qualifications: Most kitchen workers start as fast-food or short-order cooks, or in one of the other less skilled kitchen positions that require little education or training and allow them to acquire their skills on the job. An increasing number of chefs and cooks obtain their training through high school or post-high school vocational programs and two- or four-year colleges. Chefs and cooks may also be trained in apprenticeship programs offered by professional culinary institutes, industry associations, and trade unions. Some large hotels and restaurants operate their own training programs for cooks and chefs. Executive chefs and head cooks who work in fine restaurants require many years of training and experience and an intense desire to cook. The American Culinary Federation accredits over 100 formal training programs and sponsors apprenticeship programs around the country.

Earnings: Wages of chefs, cooks, and other kitchen workers vary depending on where they work. Elegant restaurants and hotels pay the highest wages. Many executive chefs earn over $50,000 a year. Top chefs can earn twice that much. In 2006, median annual earnings for chefs and head cooks were $34,370. The middle 50 percent earned between $25,910 and $46,040. The highest 10 percent earned $60,730+ per year. Median hourly earnings of other cooks and food preparation workers in 2006 were:

- Restaurant cooks $9.16
- Institution and cafeteria cooks $8.72
- Food preparation workers $7.85
- Short-order cooks $7.82
- Fast-food cooks $6.90

Some employers provide employees with uniforms and free meals.

Key Contacts: For information on career opportunities and educational programs for chefs, cooks, and other kitchen workers, contact local employers, local offices of the state employment service, or:

- **American Culinary Federation:** 180 Center Place Way, St. Augustine, FL 32095. Website: www.acfchefs.org.

- **International Council on Hotel, Restaurant, and Institutional Education:** 2810 North Parham Road, Suite 230, Richmond, VA 23294. Website: www.chrie.org.

- **National Restaurant Association:** 1200 17th Street, NW, Washington, DC 20036-3097. Website: www.restaurant.org.

Cruise Line Jobs

- ⇨ **Annual Earnings:** Varies
- ⇨ **Education/Training:** High school diploma to college
- ⇨ **Outlook:** Excellent

Employment Outlook: Job opportunities with cruise lines should increase at a faster rate than most jobs for the decade ahead as more and more cruise ships come on line to accommodate the increased demand for cruise vacations. Indeed, the cruise industry has experienced phenomenal growth during the past decade as interest in cruise vacations has increased and as more and more mega-cruise ships have come on line. Each year cruise ships carry nearly 8 million North American passengers. The number of passengers is likely to double over the coming decade as more and more people choose cruise ships as their favorite mode of vacation-resort travel. In response to this projected growth in passengers, nearly 50 new cruise ships have come on line during the past five years. Such growth translates into more and more jobs in this much sought-after industry.

Cruise ship jobs are highly competitive. Operating like large resorts whose main purpose is to pamper their guests during short three- to 14-day cruises, most cruise ships maintain a high staff-per-passenger ratio. They hire for every type of department and position you would find in five-star resorts – housekeeping, kitchen, entertainment, health, fitness, tours, gaming, guest relations, engineering, maintenance, hair salon, and gift shop. They hire accountants, cooks, waiters, engineers, casino operators, pursers, photographers, massage therapists, cosmetologists, doctors, nurses, entertainers, youth counselors, water sports instructors, fitness instructors, and lecturers. However, they disproportionately hire crew members from Southern Europe and Asia who traditionally occupy these lower-paying jobs.

Nature of Work: There are many myths about cruise line jobs. The biggest myths are that these jobs are all fun and games, they pay well, and there are plenty of opportunities available onboard for Americans. The realities are that most cruise line jobs involve hard work and do not pay well, and few Americans find jobs onboard. Cruise ship jobs involve long hours, a great deal of stress, a willingness to work with a diverse multinational team, an ability to please all types of passengers, and the willingness to give exceptional and exacting service. Above all, you must be people-oriented, tolerant, flexible, and handle stress well. You must have the disposition of a servant – the customer is always right, even though he or she may be a jerk!

If you have a family, an onboard cruise ship job is likely to involve long separations. For many Americans, it's the type of job best enjoyed by young single individuals who regard these cruise ship jobs as short-term travel positions or entry-level positions for moving within the larger travel and hospitality industry. Many Americans will spend three to five years working with cruise lines – accumulating valuable travel and resort experience – before "settling down" to more stable family-oriented jobs on shore.

Few Americans work onboard, and those that do tend to be found in a very limited number of "American" positions – entertainment, gift shop, youth counselor, physical fitness, and sports. You won't find many Americans piloting ships, managing restaurants, serving tables, cooking food, or making beds. These positions tend to be dominated by other nationals. Most American involvement with the cruise ship industry tends to be on shore – in marketing, sales, and computer reservation systems.

Americans tend to be disproportionately found in the entertainment, physical fitness, public relations, youth counseling, spa, shop, casino, and marketing and sales end of cruise ship jobs. Despite all the glamour, cruise ship pay and lifestyles simply are not sufficiently attractive for many Americans to continue long-term in this industry. Americans also are not noted for their talent in dispensing exceptional, exacting, and high level service that is the hallmark of many cruise lines. Many Americans typically pursue cruise ship jobs in the hopes of moving on to other jobs within the travel and hospitality industry, especially with hotels, resorts, restaurants, casinos, and night clubs. A cruise ship job is often a short stop along the way to other more rewarding jobs and careers.

Breaking into the cruise industry is relatively easy given the high turnover rate of personnel and the availability of numerous entry-level positions. Functioning as a combination floating city, resort, and hotel, most cruise ships operate with a staff of 300 to 900 who provide a wide range of services. As a result, cruise lines are constantly hiring for all types of positions. The most common shipboard opportunities include:

- **Front desk/purser's desk:** Positions include chief purser, assistant purser, guest services staff members.

- **Boutiques/shops:** sales staff and cashiers.

- **Restaurants and bars:** Chef, sous chef pastry cook, baker, wine steward, buffet staff, food and beverage staff, bartender, Maitre d', wait staff, busboy, butcher, ice carver, dishwasher.

- **Casino:** Cashier, dealer, slot technician.

- **Salon and spa:** Massage therapist, cosmetologist, hair stylist, nail technician, masseur/masseuse.

- **Show lounges:** Dancer, singer, comedian, magician, lecturer, sound technician, band member, disk jockey, and other types of entertainers.

- **Activities:** Youth counselor, activities coordinator, instructor (yoga, chess, bridge, diving, golf, tennis, dance, water sports), shore excursion, sports director, swimming pool/deck attendant.

- **Operations:** Computer specialist, electrician, machinist, and painter.

- **Photography:** Photographer.

- **Medical:** Physician, dentist, and nurse.

The cruise industry is a great entry point into the travel industry. Most positions require little or no experience, though a few positions require many years of experience. If you target your job search, make the right contacts, and are persistent, you should be able to land a job with a cruise line.

As you conduct a job search, you should be aware that many onboard positions are not controlled by the cruise lines. Gift shops, beauty salons, casinos, sports and recreation, and entertainment are often concessions operated by contractors or concessionaires. For example, dancers, musicians, singers, massage therapists, cosmetologists, and medical doctors are often hired through firms that control these onboard concessions. If a position you desire relates to these concessions, you will need to make employment contacts with the appropriate concessionaire rather than the cruise line.

Most cruise lines require an online application or a mailed, faxed, or e-mailed resume and cover letter. Another approach is to send a copy of your resume, along with an accompanying cover letter, directly to the personnel office of a cruise line. Specify on the envelope whether you are applying for a "shipside" or a "shoreside" position, identify which department you wish to work for, and/or call ahead to get the name of the department or person you should address your correspondence to.

Cruise lines recruit individuals for both shoreside and shipboard positions. The three largest cruise lines, which employ the largest staffs, include the following:

- **Carnival Cruise Lines**
  www.carnival.com
- **Princess Cruises**
  www.princess.com
- **Royal Caribbean International**
  www.royalcaribbean.com

Be sure to familiarize yourself with each cruise line's operations. For example, the Disney Cruise Lines and Carnival Cruises are very family- and youth-oriented, requiring many youth counselors. Crystal and Seabourn Cruises are very upscale, offering many five-star amenities and the services of spa personnel and academic lecturers. Norwegian Cruise Lines is noted for its sports programs and theme cruises. If you survey the companies' websites, you'll get a good idea of various opportunities available with such companies. Best of all, you can apply for jobs online 24 hours a day!

Key Contacts: Several websites offer books and application packages for cruise ship jobs which include job search tips and addresses of major cruise employers and employment firms:

- **Cruise Jobs**
  www.cruisejobs.com
- **Cruise Line Jobs**
  www.cruiselinejobs.com
- **Cruise Ship Entertainment Jobs**
  www.cruiseshipentertainment.com
- **Cruise Ship Jobs**
  www.shipjobs.com
- **CruiseJobFinder**
  www.cruisejobfinder.com

Flight Attendants

⇨ **Annual Earnings:** $53,780
⇨ **Education/Training:** High school diploma plus training
⇨ **Outlook:** Good

Employment Outlook: Opportunities for flight attendants should improve considerably in the decade ahead as the airline industry continues to recover from a major downturn attendant with the effects of the 9/11 terrorist attacks on the United States and the oil crisis of 2008. Employment of flight attendants is expected to grow about as fast as the average for all occupations in the decade ahead. Population growth and an improving economy are expected to boost the number of airline passengers.

Flights attendants held about 97,000 jobs in 2006. Commercial airlines employed the vast majority of flight attendants, most of whom lived in their employer's home base city. A small number of flight attendants worked for large companies that operated corporate aircraft for business purposes.

Nature of Work: Major airlines are required by law to provide flight attendants for the safety of the traveling public. Although the primary job of flight attendants is to ensure that safety regulations are followed, they also try to make flights comfortable and enjoyable for passengers. As passengers board the plane, flight attendants greet them, check their tickets, and tell them where to store coats and carry-on items. Flight attendants instruct all passengers in the use of emergency equipment and check that seat belts are fastened, trays upright, and personal items properly stowed. During the flight, flight attendants reassure passengers, assist any who need help or become ill, and heat and distribute precooked meals or snacks. Prior to landing, flight attendants collect headsets, and take inventory of alcoholic beverages and moneys collected.

Working Conditions: Because airlines operate around the clock, year-round, flight attendants may work nights, holidays, and weekends. On-duty time is usually limited to 12 hours per day, with a daily maximum of 14 hours. Attendants usually fly 65 to 85 hours a month and, in addition, generally spend 50 hours a month on the ground preparing flights, writing reports, and waiting for planes to arrive. They may be away from their home base at least one-third of the time. During this time, the airlines provide hotel accommodations and an allowance for meals. Flight attendants must be flexible, reliable, and willing to relocate. Flight attendants are susceptible to injury because of the job demands in a moving aircraft. Flight attendants are kept busy – especially on short flights – and must stand for long periods. No matter how tiring the job, they must remain pleasant and efficient.

Education, Training, & Qualifications: Although nearly 50 percent of flight attendants have a college degree and over 70 percent have some college education, entry into this occupation only requires a high school diploma. Those with several years of college and experience dealing with people are preferred. Applicants who attend schools and colleges that offer flight attendant training may have an advantage over other applicants. Highly desirable areas of study include psychology and education – people-oriented disciplines. Applicants must be at least 18 to 21 years old. There are height requirements for the purpose of reaching overhead bins, and most airlines want weight proportionate to height. Vision must be correctable to 20/30 or better with glasses or contact lenses (uncorrected no worse than 20/200).

Once hired, all candidates undergo training ranging from three to eight weeks, depending on the size and type of carrier. Training takes place at the airline's flight training center. New trainees are not considered employees of the airline until they successfully complete the training program. Some airlines charge individuals for training. Toward the end of their training, students go on practice flights. Flight attendants are required to go through periodic retraining and pass an FAA safety examination in order to continue flying. Because assignments are based on seniority, usually only the most experienced attendants get their choice of assignments. Advancement takes longer than in the past, because flight attendants are remaining in this career longer than they used to.

Earnings: Median annual earnings of flight attendants were $53,780 in May 2006. The middle 50 percent earned between $33,320 and $77,410. New hires usually begin at the same pay scale regardless of experience, and all flight attendants receive the same future pay increases. Flight attendants receive extra compensation for night and international flights and for increased hours. Some airlines offer incentive pay for working holidays or taking positions that require additional responsibility or paperwork. Most airlines guarantee a minimum of 65 to 85 hours per month, with the option to work additional hours. Flight attendants also receive a "per diem" allowance for meals and expenses while on duty away from home. In addition, flight attendants and their immediate families are entitled to free fares on their own airline and reduced fares on most other airlines. The majority of flight attendants hold union membership.

Key Contacts: Information about job opportunities and qualifications required for work at a particular airline may be obtained by contacting the airline's human resources office. For further information on flight attendant careers, contact:

- Association of Flight Attendants: 501 Third Street, NW, Washington, DC 20001. Website: www.afanet.org.

Food and Beverage Service Workers

◇ **Annual Earnings:** Varies with hourly wages and tips
◇ **Education/Training:** None required
◇ **Outlook:** Excellent

Employment Outlook: Employment is expected to grow faster than average due to the anticipated increase in the population, personal income, and leisure time. Replacement needs because of high turnover will result in plentiful job openings.

Nature of Work: This is one of the largest categories of workers – 7.4 million employed in 2006 and 8.4 million projected to be employed in 2016. Waiters and waitresses take customers' orders, serve food and beverages, prepare itemized checks, and sometimes accept payments. In some establishments waiters and waitresses may perform additional duties such as escorting guests to tables, setting and clearing tables, or cashiering.

Bartenders fill drink orders taken by waiters from customers seated in the restaurant as well as take orders from customers seated at the bar. Most bartenders must know dozens of drink recipes and be able to mix drinks accurately, quickly, and without waste. Bartenders collect payment, operate the cash register, clean up after customers have left, and may also serve food to customers seated at the bar.

Hosts and hostesses welcome guests, direct patrons to where they may leave coats, and indicate where they may wait until their table is ready. Hosts and hostesses assign guests to tables, escort them to their seats, and provide menus.

Dining room attendants and bartender helpers assist waiters, waitresses, and bartenders by keeping the serving area stocked with supplies, cleaning tables, and removing dirty dishes to the kitchen.

Fast-food workers take orders, get the ordered items, serve the customer, and accept payment. They may cook and package French fries, make coffee, and fill beverage cups.

Working Conditions: Food and beverage workers are on their feet most of the time and often have to carry heavy trays of food, dishes, and glassware. During busy dining periods, they are under pressure to serve customers quickly.

Many food and beverage workers are expected to work evenings, weekends, and holidays; some work split shifts. Although some food and beverage workers work 40 hours or more per week, the majority are employed part-time.

Education, Training, & Qualifications: There are no specific educational requirements for food and beverage service jobs. Although many employers prefer to hire high school graduates for waiter, waitress, bartender, host, and hostess positions, completion of high school is generally not required for fast-food workers, or dining room attendants and bartender helpers. For many persons, these jobs serve as a source of immediate income rather than a career. Most food and beverage workers pick up their skills on the job by observing and working with more experienced workers.

Earnings: Food and beverage service workers derive their earnings from a combination of hourly wages and customer tips. In 2006, median hourly earnings (including tips) of waiters and waitresses were $7.14. The middle 50 percent earned between $6.42 and $9.14. Waiters at some of the very top restaurants are known to make over $50,000 a year. For most waiters and waitresses, higher earnings are primarily the result of receiving more in tips rather than higher wages. Tips generally average 10-20 percent of the guests' checks. Those working in busy, expensive restaurants earn the most.

In 2006, full-time bartenders had median hourly earnings (including tips) of $7.86. The middle 50 percent earned between $6.77 and $10.10. Like waiters and waitresses, bartenders employed in public bars may receive more than half of their earnings as tips. Service bartenders often are paid higher hourly wages to offset their lower tip earnings.

Median hourly earnings (including tips) other food and beverage workers in 2006 were:

• Nonrestaurant food servers	$8.70
• Hosts and hostesses	$7.78
• Counter attendants in cafeterias, food concessions, and coffee shops	$7.76
• Dishwashers	$7.57
• Dining room and cafeteria attendants	$7.36
• Combined food preparation and serving workers	$7.24

Many beginning or inexperienced workers start earning the federal minimum wage of $5.85 an hour. However, a few states set minimum wages higher than the federal minimum.

Key Contacts: For information on food and beverage service jobs contact:

- **International Council on Hotel, Restaurant, and Institutional Education:** 2810 North Parham Road, Suite 230, Richmond, VA 23294. Website: www.chrie.org.

- **National Restaurant Association:** 1200 17th Street, NW, Washington, DC 20036-3097. Website: www.restaurant.org.

Hotel, Motel, and Resort Desk Clerks

- **Annual Earnings:** $18,460
- **Education/Training:** On-the-job training
- **Outlook:** Excellent

Employment Outlook: Employment is expected to grow faster than average for most occupations in the decade ahead as the number of hotels, motels, and other lodging establishments increases in response to increased business travel and tourism. Opportunities for part-time work should be plentiful. Employment of desk clerks is sensitive to cyclical swings in the economy. During recessions, vacation and business travel declines, and hotels and motels need fewer clerks.

Nature of Work: Hotel and motel desk clerks may register guests, assign rooms, and answer questions about available services, checkout times, the local community, and other matters. Because most smaller hotels and motels have minimal staffs, the clerk also may function as a bookkeeper, advance reservation agent, cashier, and/or telephone operator.

Working Conditions: Hotel and motel desk clerks are on their feet most of the time. During holidays and other busy periods, these clerks may find the work hectic due to the large number of guests or travelers who must be served. When service does not flow smoothly – because of mishandled reservations, for example – these clerks act as a buffer between the establishment and its customers.

Education, Training, & Qualifications: A high school diploma or its equivalent usually is required. Hotel and motel desk clerk job orientation is usually brief and includes an explanation of the job duties and information about the establishment, such as room location and available services. They start work on the job under the guidance of a supervisor or experienced clerk. They may need additional training in data processing or office machine opera-

tions to use computerized reservation, room assignment, and billing systems.

Earnings: In 2006, the average annual earnings of full-time hotel and motel clerks were around $18,460. Earnings depend on the location, size, and type of establishment in which they work. Large luxury hotels and those located in metropolitan and resort areas generally pay clerks more than less expensive ones and those located in less populated areas. In general, hotels pay higher salaries than motels or other types of lodging establishments.

Key Contacts: Information on careers in the lodging industry may be obtained from:

- **The Educational Institute of the American Hotel and Lodging Association:** 800 N. Magnolia A venue, Suite 3 00, O rlando, FL 32803. Website: www.ei-ahla.org.

- **American Hotel & Lodging Association:** 1201 New York Ave.,, NW, Suite 600, Washington, DC 20005. Website: www.ahla.com.

Restaurant and Food Service Managers

- **Annual Earnings:** $43,020
- **Education/Training:** Training and college
- **Outlook:** Good

Employment Outlook: Food manager jobs are expected to grow 5 percent, or more slowly than the average for all occupations through 2016. However, job opportu nities should be good because, in addition to job growth, many more openings will arise from the need to replace managers who leave the occupation. Job opportunities will be especially good for those with an associate or bachelor's degree in restaurant and institutional food service management.

Projected employment growth varies by industry. Most new jobs will arise in full-service restaurants and limited-service eating places as the number of these establishments increases along with the population. Manager jobs in special food services, an industry that includes food service contractors, will increase as hotels, schools, health care facilities, and other businesses contract out their food services to firms in this industry. Food service manager jobs still are expected to increase in hotels, schools, and health care facilities, but growth will be slowed as contracting out becomes more common.

Nature of Work: Efficient and profitable operation of restaurants and institutional food service facilities requires that managers and assistant managers select and appropriately price interesting menu items, efficiently use food and other supplies, achieve consistent quality in food preparation and service, recruit and train adequate numbers of workers and supervise their work, and attend to the administrative aspects of the business. In larger establishments, much of the administrative work is delegated to a bookkeeper, but in others the manager must keep accurate records of the hours and wages of employees, prepare the payroll, and do paperwork to comply with licensing laws and reporting requirements of tax, wage and hour, unemployment compensation, and Social Security laws. They must also ensure that accounts with suppliers are paid on a regular basis. Today many managers are able to ease the burden of recordkeeping through the use of computers.

In most full-service restaurants and institutional food service facilities, the management team consists of a general manager, one or more assistant managers, and an executive chef. The executive chef is responsible for all food preparation activities, including running kitchen operations, planning menus, and maintaining quality standards for food service. One of the most important tasks of food service managers is assisting executive chefs as they select successful menu items. Many restaurants rarely change their menus while others make frequent alterations. Managers or executive chefs estimate food needs, place orders with distributors, and schedule the delivery of fresh food and supplies. Managers interview, hire, train, and, when necessary, fire employees. They also tally the cash and charge receipts received and balance them against the record of sales. They are responsible for depositing the day's receipts at the bank or securing them in a safe place. Finally, managers are responsible for locking up the establishment, checking that ovens, grills, and lights are off, and switching on alarm systems.

Working Conditions: Since evenings and weekends are popular dining periods, night and weekend work is common. Many restaurant and food service mangers work 50 hours or more per week. However, some managers of institutional food service facilities work more conventional hours because factory and office cafeterias are often open only on weekdays for breakfast and lunch.

When problems occur it is the responsibility of the manager to resolve them with minimal disruption to customers. The job can be hectic during peak dining hours, and dealing with irritable customers or uncooperative employees can be particularly stressful.

Education, Training, & Qualifications: Many restaurant and food service manager positions are filled by promoting experienced food and beverage preparation and service workers. Waiters, waitresses, chefs, and fast-food workers who have demonstrated their potential for handling increased responsibility sometimes advance to assistant manager or management trainee jobs when openings occur. However, most food service management companies and restaurant chains recruit management trainees from among graduates of two- and four-year college programs. They prefer to hire persons with degrees in restaurant and institutional food service management. A bachelor's degree in restaurant and food service management provides especially strong preparation for a career in this occupation.

Earnings: Earnings vary greatly according to the type and size of the establishment. In 2006, the median annual earnings of salaried food service managers were $43,020. The middle 50 percent earned between $34,210 and $55,100. Median annual earnings in the industries employing the largest numbers of food service managers in 2006 were as follows:

- Traveler accommodation $48,890
- Special food services $48,712
- Elementary and secondary
  schools $39,650
- Full-service restaurants $45,650
- Limited-service eating places $39,070

In addition to receiving typical benefits, most salaried food service managers are provided free meals and the opportunity for additional training, depending on their length of service.

Key Contacts: For additional information on education, training, and a career as a food service manager, contact:

- **International Council on Hotel, Restaurant, and Institutional Education:** 2810 North Parham Road, Suite 230, Richmond, VA 23294. Website: www.chrie.org.

- **National Restaurant Association Educational Foundation:** 175 West Jackson Blvd., Suite 1500, Chicago, IL 60604-2814. Website: www.nraef.org.

10

49 More Jobs for Ex-Offenders

THIS FINAL CHAPTER SUMMARIZES in abbreviated form 49 additional jobs ex-offenders should consider as possible career alternatives. Detailed information on each of these jobs can be found in the U.S. Department of Labor's *Occupational Outlook Handbook* (www.bls.gov/oco) and the *O*NET Dictionary of Occupational Titles* (www.onetcenter.org).

Computer and Internet Jobs

Despite a great deal of talk about the offshoring of information technology jobs, the computer and Internet industries will generate a large number of jobs within the United States during the coming decade. These remain some of the hottest industries for anyone wishing to hitch themselves to a very promising career future. Indeed, next to health care, the fastest growing occupations – increasing the number of jobs by over 35 percent – will be in the computer industry:

- network systems and data communications analysts
- computer software engineers
- database administrators
- computer systems analysts
- network and computer systems administrators
- computer and information systems managers

That's the good news. The bad news affects people without a four-year degree, because most of these growing computer- and Internet-related occupations require at least a bachelor's degree. In fact, entry into these high-demand fields requires a great deal of formal education at the bachelor's level and beyond. Computer software engineers, for example, must have a bachelor's degree to qualify for the more than 200 certification programs that constitute part of the formal continuing education track for computer software engineers. Given the right education and training in various computer fields, one should experience long-term job security, career advancement, job mobility, and relatively high salaries and generous benefits in these fields. Computer engineers and computer systems analysts in particular rank near the very top on most lists of the 10 or 25 hottest jobs in the decade ahead. If you want to fast-track your career, make good money, and experience long-term job security, these are the fields to be in for the coming decade.

There's also good news here for people with less than a bachelor's degree. Thousands of computer-related job opportunities are available for those without a four-year degree. Many of these jobs require short-term training courses, certification, or a two-year associate degree acquired through a junior or community college. For the most part, these jobs relate to the serving and maintenance of computers, computer support services, and computer applications. Given the rapidly changing nature of computer technology, individuals in these fields are constantly being retrained in the latest hardware and systems applications. Consequently, the distinction between people with or without a four-year degree becomes less important than the distinction between people with or without the latest training.

Computer Service Technicians

⇨ **Annual Earnings:** $36,483
⇨ **Education/Training:** Certificate or associate degree
⇨ **Outlook:** Slower than average

Employment of computer service technicians (computer repairers) is expected to grow more slowly than average for all occupations in the decade ahead. Limited growth will be driven by the increasing dependence of business and individuals on computers and other sophisticated office machines. The need to maintain this equipment will create new jobs for repairers.

Computer-Control Programmers and Operators

⇨ **Annual Earnings:** $31,678
⇨ **Education/Training:** Apprenticeships and training programs
⇨ **Outlook:** Excellent

Despite the projected slow decline in employment of computer control programmers and operators, job opportunities should be excellent, as employers are expected to continue to have difficulty finding qualified workers. The demand for computer-control programmers will be negatively affected by the increasing use of software that automatically translates part and product designs into CNC machine tool instructions.

Computer Support Specialists and Systems Administrators

⇨ **Annual Earnings:** $51,800
⇨ **Education/Training:** Certificate, associate degree, or BS
⇨ **Outlook:** Excellent

Employment of computer support specialists is expected to increase much faster than average as organizations continue to adopt increasingly sophisticated technology. Employment of systems administrators is expected to increase much faster than average as firms continue to invest heavily in securing computer networks. Demand for computer security specialists will grow as businesses and government continue to invest heavily in cyber-security, protecting vital computer networks and electronic infrastructures from attack. As businesses continue to expand their electronic commerce in conducting business online, they will increasingly require the services of information technology specialists who can help them use technology to communicate with employees, clients, and consumers.

Web Developer/Designer

⇨ **Annual Earnings:** $54,750 to $81,500
⇨ **Education/Training:** Certificate, associate degree, or BS
⇨ **Outlook:** Good

The explosive growth of the Internet, intranets, and online commerce make this one of the fastest growing high-tech occupations in the decade ahead. However, times are changing. Like many other computer fields, this one is becoming more and more competitive. Many of these jobs have moved overseas.

Webmaster

⇨ **Annual Earnings:** $38,293 to
   $62,954, depending on experience
⇨ **Education/Training:** Certificate,
   associate degree, or BS
⇨ **Outlook:** Excellent

As the number of websites continues to expand and as corporations develop intranets, the position of webmaster has been in great demand. The demand for webmasters will be great in the coming decade as more and more businesses, nonprofit organizations, and government agencies further develop Internet and intranet sites. However, like Web developers, this position is becoming more and more competitive.

Health and Medical Care Jobs

Health and medical care jobs represent some of the fastest growing and best paying opportunities for people re-entering the workforce. This is an enormous industry, which consumes over $2 trillion a year in the United States, representing 15 percent of the gross domestic product! If you don't know what you want to do, seriously consider whether you would enjoy working in this field. Opportunities are numerous and the rewards are many. Entry into the medical field will most likely result in a rewarding long-term career.

If you don't have the necessary educational background and credentials to qualify for entering health and medical fields, you should survey various options for acquiring basic qualifications for breaking into these high-demand fields. Most jobs require some form of postsecondary education, training, or certification. Many jobs require two-year associate degrees provided by community or junior colleges, while other jobs only require on-the-job training or a nine- to 24-month training program offered by hospitals, vocational schools, or community colleges.

Five of the 10 fastest growing jobs in the decade ahead are projected to be in the health care field. Altogether, nearly 15 million people work in the health care industry. While major restructuring of health care financing and services may negatively affect some jobs in this field, especially nurses in hospitals and physicians in private practice, medicine and health care are hot career fields for the decade ahead.

In general, jobs in the medical and health care industries pay better than in most other industries. They also offer good advancement opportunities for those who seek additional training and certification within or between related medical fields. The best paying jobs will go to those with high levels of education and specialized training, such as surgeons, radiologists, gynecologists, and anesthesiologists. These fields also will generate hundreds of thousands of lower paying entry-level support positions, especially for medical assistants, technicians, technologists, nursing aides, and home health aides, which require the least amounts of medical education and training.

Seven of the jobs appearing in this section are usually included on most lists of the "50 best jobs." While not necessarily the best paying jobs, they are in high demand and offer excellent entry into the expanding health care industry.

Dental Assistants

⇨ **Annual Earnings:** $30,222
⇨ **Education/Training:** 9-12 month
   training programs
⇨ **Outlook:** Excellent.

The employment outlook for dental assistants should be excellent in the decade ahead as more individuals use dental services. More and more dentists hire dental assistants to perform routine dental tasks so they can concentrate on performing more profitable procedures. Dentists currently employ nearly 280,000 dental assistants. This number should increase by 29% between 2006 and 2016.

Medical Assistants

⇨ **Annual Earnings:** $26,290
⇨ **Education/Training:** 1- to 2-year training program
⇨ **Outlook:** Excellent – faster than average

This will be one of the fastest growing occupations in the decade ahead. Employment growth will be driven by the increase in the number of group practices, clinics, and other health care facilities that need a high proportion of support personnel, particularly the flexible medical assistant who can handle both administrative and clinical duties. Medical assistants work primarily in outpatient settings.

Medical Records and Health Information Technicians

⇨ **Annual Earnings:** $28,030
⇨ **Education/Training:** Associate degree
⇨ **Outlook:** Excellent

This occupational field should experience excellent job growth due to the rapid growth in the number of medical tests, treatments, and procedures that will be increasingly scrutinized by third-party payers, regulators, courts, and consumers. Technicians with a strong background in medical coding will be in high demand.

Occupational Therapists

⇨ **Annual Earnings:** $60,470
⇨ **Education/Training:** Master's degree in occupational therapy
⇨ **Outlook:** Good to excellent

Employment of occupational therapists is expected to increase faster than average. Growth in demand for occupational therapists should continue due to the increasing number of individuals with disabilities or limited functions who require therapy services. The increased number of heart attacks and strokes among middle-aged people as well as a growing over-75 population will ensure the continuing demand for occupational therapy services. Hospitals will continue to employ a large number of occupational therapists to provide therapy services to acutely ill inpatients as well as to staff their outpatient rehabilitation programs.

Occupational Therapist Aides

⇨ **Annual Earnings:** $25,020
⇨ **Education/Training:** High school diploma
⇨ **Outlook:** Faster than average growth

Employment of occupational therapist aides is expected to grow much faster than average due to the growth in the number of individuals with disabilities or limited function. An aging population will need more occupational therapy services. Third-party payers will encourage occupational therapists to delegate more hands-on therapy work to occupational therapist aides.

Occupational Therapist Assistants

⇨ **Annual Earnings:** $42,060
⇨ **Education/Training:** Associate degree or certificate
⇨ **Outlook:** Much faster than average

Employment of occupational therapists is expected to grow much faster than average due to growth in the number of individuals with disabilities. Job growth will result from an aging population, which will need more occupational therapy services. Increasing demand also will result from advances in medicine that allow more people with critical problems to survive and then need rehabilitative therapy.

Personal and Home Care Aides

⇨ **Annual Earnings:** $17,763
⇨ **Education/Training:** On-the-job training
⇨ **Outlook:** Excellent job opportunities

Excellent job opportunities are expected for this occupation since the number of elderly, an age group characterized by mounting health problems and requiring some assistance, is projected to rise substantially. Other patient groups will increasingly rely on home care, a trend that reflects several developments, including efforts to contain costs by moving patients out of hospitals and nursing care facilities as quickly as possible. The relatively low skill requirements, low pay, and high emotional demands of the work result in high replacement needs.

Physical Therapists

- ⇨ **Annual Earnings:** $66,200
- ⇨ **Education/Training:** Graduation from an accredited physical therapist education program and passing a licensure exam
- ⇨ **Outlook:** Good to excellent

Employment of physical therapists is expected to grow faster than average due to the growing number of individuals with disabilities, injuries, or limited functions requiring therapy services. The growing elderly population is particularly vulnerable to chronic and debilitating conditions that require therapeutic services. Employers also are using physical therapists to evaluate work sites, develop exercise programs, and teach safe work habits to reduce injuries.

Physical Therapy Assistants and Aides

- ⇨ **Annual Earnings:** $41,360 (assistants) and $22,060 (aides)
- ⇨ **Education/Training:** On-the-job training to associate degree
- ⇨ **Outlook:** Excellent

Employment of physical therapy assistants is expected to grow much faster than average due to the growing number of elderly patients with chronic and debilitating conditions who require therapeutic services as well as the growing number of heart attack and stroke victims who require cardiac and physical rehabilitation. Job opportunities will be good, especially in acute hospital, rehabilitation, and orthopedic settings.

Physician Assistants

- ⇨ **Annual Earnings:** $74,980
- ⇨ **Education/Training:** Bachelor's degree/ graduation from a PA program
- ⇨ **Outlook:** Much faster than average

Employment of physician assistants (PAs) is expected to grow much faster than the average due to anticipated expansion of the health services industry and an emphasis on cost containment, resulting in increasing utilization of PAs by physicians and health care institutions. Physicians and institutions are expected to

employ more PAs to provide primary care and to assist with medical and surgical procedures because PAs are cost-effective members of the health care team. Telemedicine – using technology to facilitate interaction between physicians and physician assistants – also will expand the use of physician assistants. Job opportunities for PAs should be good, particularly in rural and inner city clinics, because those settings have difficulty attracting physicians.

Registered Nurses

- ⇨ **Annual Earnings:** $57,280
- ⇨ **Education/Training:** Associate to bachelor's degrees
- ⇨ **Outlook:** Excellent

Registered nurses are the largest health care occupation with about 2.5 million jobs in 2006. These jobs will grow much faster than other occupational gro ups – projected to generate 587,000 new jobs, among the largest number of new jobs for any occupation. This increase corresponds to the overall growth in health care and the increased demand for new nurses in home health, long-term, and ambulatory care.

Respiratory Therapists

- ⇨ **Annual Earnings:** $47,420
- ⇨ **Education/Training:** Associate degree
- ⇨ **Outlook:** Excellent

Employment for respiratory therapists is expected to be very good in the coming decade. The number of jobs is expected to increase substantially due to an increasingly middle-aged and elderly population. Older people are more likely to suffer from cardiopulmonary diseases such as pneumonia, chronic bronchitis, emphysema, and heart disease.

Veterinary Technologists and Technicians

- ⇨ **Annual Earnings:** $26,790
- ⇨ **Education/Training:** Two- to four-year programs
- ⇨ **Outlook:** Excellent

Employment of veterinary technologists and technicians is expected to grow much faster than the average for all occupations during the coming decade. Keen competition is expected for veterinary technologist and technician jobs in zoos, due to expected slow growth in zoo capacity, the low turnover among workers, and a limited number of openings. As pet owners become more affluent, they are more willing to pay for advanced care of their pets. The rapidly growing number of cat owners should boost the demand for feline medicine, off-setting any reduced demand for veterinary care for dogs. Biomedical facilities, diagnostic laboratories, wildlife facilities, humane societies, animal control facilities, drug or food manufacturing companies, and food safety inspection facilities will provide more jobs for veterinary technologists and technicians.

Sales and Related Jobs

Many people re-entering the workforce can look toward a variety of sales positions to start new careers. These are some of the most recession-proof jobs. After all, even in tough times, companies are always looking to maintain and expand their market shares through good sales representatives. These jobs also are ideal for people who prefer flexible work schedules or enjoy operating as independent contractors. However, you'll need to check to see if you might be barred from any sales jobs because of past convictions, especially any that relate to drugs (pharmaceuticals) and finances (banks, insurance, investments).

Are you born to sell? Not many people are, but you may find you have many hidden talents that would be perfect for re-entering the job market as a salesperson. If, for example, you are self-motivated and goal-oriented, enjoy meeting strangers, can handle rejections, and are good at persuading others to buy a product or perform a service, a job or career in one of many sales fields may be right for you. While a college degree is often a plus for individuals who deal with highly technical and scientific products and services, such as pharmaceuticals, computers, weapons systems, and financial services, many sales fields, such as automotive, real estate, and insurance, are open to anyone who has demonstrated the ability to learn about a product, network for clients, and present and close deals. Regardless of their educational backgrounds, talented salespeople working in commission-based fields selling high-ticket items can realize substantial annual earnings.

You don't need formal education credentials to be a good and productive salesperson. Effective selling skills often center on attitude, personality, communication, prospecting, perseverance, organization, and follow-through. Good salespeople can often transfer their skills from one occupational field to another because of the generic nature of their skills. For example, an individual who starts out selling automobiles may later move into insurance and real estate.

Earnings for salespeople can vary considerably depending on the economy, their industry, their products/services, and their talent. The least compensated tend to be part-time salespeople in retail establishments, especially in clothing and merchandising. The best compensated are generally salespeople in the financial and pharmaceutical industries.

Since most salespeople receive a base salary plus commission, their income largely depends on a combination of factors that may or may not be within their control, such as the state of the economy and their industry. Many real estate agents, for example, realized substantial increases in incomes during the hot real estate market of 2003-2005. That situation changed dramatically during 2007-2008 when the real estate market cooled down and declined substantially.

Nonetheless, sales is a very talent-driven type of occupation involving a great deal of hard work, self-motivation, and persistence. If you are born to sell, you'll most likely do very well in any sales field. You will be sought after by many employers who readily seek such talent that immediately contributes to increasing their company's bottom line. Better still, employers will overlook your past record if you can produce a stellar sales record!

Advertising Sales Agents

- ⇨ **Annual Earnings:** $42,750
- ⇨ **Education/Training:** Moderate-term on-the-job training
- ⇨ **Outlook:** Good

In 2006, there were 170,000 persons working as advertising sales agents soliciting advertisements for inclusion in publications such as newspapers and magazines, television/radio advertising time, and custom-made signs. Employment for advertising sales agents in the decade ahead is expected to grow faster than average, assuming the economy grows at a relatively steady state.

Insurance Sales Agents

- ⇨ **Annual Earnings:** $43,870
- ⇨ **Education/Training:** High school diploma to college degree
- ⇨ **Outlook:** Good

Average employment growth is expected among insurance agents in the decade ahead. But opportunities for agents will be favorable for persons with the right qualifications and skills. Multilingual agents should be in high demand because they can serve a wider range of customers.

Real Estate Brokers and Sales Agents

- ⇨ **Annual Earnings:** $39,760 (agents) and $60,790 (brokers)
- ⇨ **Education/Training:** Experience and training
- ⇨ **Outlook:** Good

Although real estate experienced hard times in recent years, employment of real estate brokers and sales agents is expected to grow in the coming decade as this sector rebounds.

Retail Salespersons

- ⇨ **Annual Earnings:** Varies greatly, from minimum wage on up – $19,760 annual average ($8.53 an hour for clothing to $18.70 for auto sales)
- ⇨ **Education/Training:** High school diploma or equivalent
- ⇨ **Outlook:** Good

Employment of retail salespersons is expected to be good because of the need to replace the large number of workers who transfer to other occupations or leave the labor force each year. Employment is expected to grow about as fast as the average for all occupations. Opportunities for part-time work should be abundant, and demand will be strong for temporary workers during peak selling periods, such as the end-of-year holiday season.

Sales Representatives, Wholesale and Manufacturing

- ⇨ **Annual Earnings:** $64,440
- ⇨ **Education/Training:** Some college helpful
- ⇨ **Outlook:** Excellent

Employment is expected to grow about as fast as average due to continued growth in the variety and number of goods sold and from openings resulting from the need to replace workers who transfer to other occupations or leave the labor force. Job prospects for wholesale sales representatives will be better than those for manufacturing sales representatives because manufacturers are expected to continue contracting out sales duties to independent agents rather than using in-house or direct sales personnel.

Travel Agents

- ⇨ **Annual Earnings:** $29,210
- ⇨ **Education/Training:** High school diploma and training
- ⇨ **Outlook:** Fair to excellent

While employment of travel agents is expected to decline in the decade ahead, many opportunities will be available for those who specialize in a particular area of travel – travel destination, type of traveler, or mode of transportation. As more people travel and seek special travel experiences, specialty travel agents should be in demand. The future looks very bright for entrepreneurial travel agents who use the Internet to promote their services as well as offer unique travel programs to their clients.

Sports, Entertainment, and Media Jobs

Few job and career fields have such a mass appeal as sports, entertainment, and the media. Many people would love to get paid playing their favorite sport, starring in a movie, or being before the television camera. Others would like to become a famous artist, musician, singer, or designer. And still others dream of working behind the scenes, where they put together and market productions.

In many respects, these fields generate a disproportionate number of glamour jobs that place primary emphasis on special skills and demonstrated talents rather than education credentials. Talented and entrepreneurial individuals, who demonstrate a great deal of creativity and imagination, will find many opportunities in these fields.

Be forewarned, however, that jobs in sports, entertainment, and the media often pay much less than expected. While the top talent in these fields earn top dollar, many others working in these fields struggle for years on a part-time basis as they attempt to acquire experience and connections for making a rewarding career in a field that allows them to pursue their passions. If you have the necessary talent and drive, you'll find numerous jobs opportunities in these exciting fields.

Actors

⇨ **Annual Earnings:** $24,149
⇨ **Education/Training:** High school diploma to college degree
⇨ **Outlook:** Good

Employment of actors is expected to grow about as fast as average. Although many people will aspire to enter this profession, many will leave the field early because the work is hard, the hours are long, and the pay is low. Competition for jobs will be stiff. Only performers with the most stamina and talent will find regular employment. In 2006, actors (including producers and directors) held about 163,000 jobs, primarily in motion picture and video, performing arts, and broadcast industries.

Athletes, Coaches, Umpires, and Related Workers

⇨ **Annual Earnings:** Varies greatly (umpires, $22,880; coaches, $26,950; athletes, $41,060)
⇨ **Education/Training:** Experience and training
⇨ **Outlook:** Good

Employment of athletes, coaches, umpires, and related workers is expected to increase faster than average for all occupations. Employment will grow as the general public continues to increasingly participate in organized sports as a form of entertainment, recreation, and physical conditioning. Job growth also will be driven by the growing numbers of baby boomers approaching retirement, during which they are expected to become more active participants of leisure-time activities, such as golf and tennis, and require instruction. Expanding opportunities are expected for coaches and instructors, as a higher value is being placed upon physical fitness in our society.

Artists and Related Workers

⇨ **Annual Earnings:** Varies greatly (craft artists, $24,090 to art directors, $68,100)
⇨ **Education/Training:** Training and experience
⇨ **Outlook:** Good

Employment of artists and related workers is expected to grow faster than average. Because the arts attract many talented people with creative ability, the number of aspiring artists continues to grow. Consequently, competition for both salaried jobs and freelance work in some areas is expected to be keen. The need for artists to illustrate and animate materials for magazines, journals, and other printed or electronic productions will spur demand for illustrators and animators of all types. Growth in the motion picture and video industries will provide new job opportunities for illustrators, cartoonists, and animators. Competition for most jobs, however, will be strong.

Broadcast and Sound Engineering Technicians and Radio Operators

- ⇨ **Annual Earnings:** $30,690 to $43,010
- ⇨ **Education/Training:** Technical school to college training
- ⇨ **Outlook:** Good

People seeking entry-level jobs as technicians in broadcasting are expected to face strong competition in major metropolitan areas, where pay generally is higher and the number of qualified job seekers is plentiful. Overall employment of broadcast and sound engineering technicians and radio operators is expected to grow faster than average. Projected job growth will vary among occupations in this field.

Designers

- ⇨ **Annual Earnings:** Varies (graphic designers, $39,900, to interior designers, $42,260)
- ⇨ **Education/Training:** Experience to bachelor's degree
- ⇨ **Outlook:** Good to excellent

Overall employment of designers should grow about as fast as average as the economy expands and consumers, businesses, and manufacturers continue to rely on designer services. Graphic designers are projected to provide the most new jobs. Rising demand for interior design of private homes, offices, restaurants and other retail establishments, and institutions that care for the rapidly growing elderly population should spur employment growth of interior designers.

Desktop Publishers

- ⇨ **Annual Earnings:** $34,130
- ⇨ **Education/Training:** High school diploma/related certificate or coursework helpful
- ⇨ **Outlook:** Average growth

Employment of desktop publishers is expected to experience little or no change because more people are learning basic desktop publishing skills as a part of their regular job functions in other occupations and because more organizations are formatting materials for display on the web rather than designing pages for print publication.

Gaming Services

- ⇨ **Annual Earnings:** Varies from $14,730 to $62,820
- ⇨ **Education/Training:** High school or GED plus training
- ⇨ **Outlook:** Excellent

With demand for gaming showing no sign of waning, employment in gaming services occupations is projected to grow faster than average. Even during the recent downturn in the economy, profits at casinos have risen. Opportunities will be best for those with previous casino gaming experience, a degree or technical or vocational training in gaming or a hospitality-related field, and strong customer service skills.

Musicians, Singers, and Related Workers

- ⇨ **Annual Earnings:** $39,750 to $41,038
- ⇨ **Education/Training:** Experience, training, and college
- ⇨ **Outlook:** Good

Competition for jobs for musicians, singers, and related workers is expected to be keen. The vast number of persons with the desire to perform will exceed the number of openings. Overall employment of musicians, singers, and related workers is expected to grow about as fast as average. Most new wage and salary jobs for musicians will arise in religious organizations. Slower-than-average growth is expected for self-employed musicians, who generally perform in nightclubs, concert tours, and other venues.

Photographers

- ⇨ **Annual Earnings:** $26,170
- ⇨ **Education/Training:** Experience to associate degree
- ⇨ **Outlook:** Good

Photographers can expect keen competition for job openings because the work is attractive to many people. Employment of photographers is expected to increase about as fast as average. Demand for portrait photographers should increase as the population grows. Job growth, however, will be constrained somewhat by the widespread use of digital photography and the falling price of digital equipment.

Public Relations Specialists

⇨ **Annual Earnings:** $47,350
⇨ **Education/Training:** Internships or associate degree
⇨ **Outlook:** Excellent

Employment of public relations specialists is expected to increase faster than average. Keen competition will likely continue for entry-level public relations jobs. Many people are attracted to this profession due to the high-profile nature of the work. While college graduates will have the best opportunities, individuals without a four-year degree can also succeed in this field.

Recreation and Fitness Workers

⇨ **Annual Earnings:** Recreation workers, $20,470; fitness trainers, $25,910
⇨ **Education/Training:** High school to graduate degree, depending on the position
⇨ **Outlook:** Faster than average growth

Jobs for fitness workers are expected to increase much faster than the average. Fitness workers should have good opportunities due to the rapid job growth in health clubs, fitness facilities, and other settings where fitness workers are concentrated.

Television, Video, and Motion Picture Camera Operators and Editors

⇨ **Annual Earnings:** $40,060 to $46,670
⇨ **Education/Training:** Experience and training
⇨ **Outlook:** Good

Television, video, and motion picture camera operators and editors can expect keen competition for job openings because the work is attractive to many people. Employment of camera operators and editors is expected to grow about as fast as the average for all occupations in the decade ahead. Rapid expansion of the entertainment market, especially motion picture production and distribution, will spur growth of camera operators. In addition, computer and Internet services will provide new outlets for interactive productions. Growth will be tempered, however, by the increased off-shore production of motion pictures. Camera operators will be needed to film made-for-the-Internet broadcasts, such as live music videos, digital movies, sports features, and general information on entertainment programming.

Office and Administrative Support Jobs

Numerous job opportunities are available in office and administrative support occupations that would be appropriate for ex-offenders. Many of these jobs encompass back office operations that large corporations have been increasingly outsourcing to cheap labor markets abroad. Some of the best opportunities in these occupational fields will be found with small businesses that employ fewer than 100 individuals. These companies tend to rely on in-house personnel rather than outsource such jobs abroad.

Most of the jobs profiled in this section require a high school diploma and some additional training. Two jobs that appear on the U.S. Department of Labor's list of 20 jobs with high median earnings and a significant number of job openings in the decade ahead are executive secretaries and administrative assistants.

Bill and Account Collectors

⇨ **Annual Earnings:** $29,057
⇨ **Education/Training:** High school diploma
⇨ **Outlook:** Faster than average growth

Employment of bill and account collectors is expected to grow faster than average. Cash flow is becoming increasingly important to companies, which are now placing greater emphasis on collecting bad debts sooner. As more companies in a wide range of industries get involved in lending money and issuing their own credit cards, they will need to hire collectors, because debt levels will inevitably rise.

Bookkeeping, Accounting, and Auditing Clerks

- ⇨ **Annual Earnings:** $30,560
- ⇨ **Education/Training:** High school and training
- ⇨ **Outlook:** Average

Job growth is projected to be average through 2016, and job prospects should be good as a large number of bookkeeping, accounting, and auditing clerks are expected to retire or transfer to other occupations.

Customer Service Representatives

- ⇨ **Annual Earnings:** $28,329
- ⇨ **Education/Training:** High school diploma
- ⇨ **Outlook:** Excellent

Employment of customer service representatives is expected to grow much faster than average. Job prospects should be excellent. Bilingual job seekers, in particular, may enjoy favorable job prospects. Replacement needs are expected to be significant in this large occupation because many young people work as customer service representatives before switching to other jobs. This occupation is well suited to flexible work schedules, and many opportunities for part-time work will continue to be available, particularly as organizations attempt to cut labor costs.

Dispatcher

- ⇨ **Annual Earnings:** $32,190
- ⇨ **Education/Training:** High school diploma
- ⇨ **Outlook:** Average to slow growth

Employment of dispatchers is expected to grow more slowly (6%) than average during the 2006 to 2016 decade. In addition to those positions resulting from job growth, many openings will arise from the need to replace workers who transfer to other occupations or leave the labor force. The growing and aging population will increase demand for emergency services and stimulate employment growth of police, fire, and ambulance dispatchers.

File Clerks

- ⇨ **Annual Earnings:** $22,089, but varies by occupational setting
- ⇨ **Education/Training:** High school diploma or equivalent
- ⇨ **Outlook:** Declining opportunities

The employment outlook for different types of file clerks is expected decline rapidly in the decade ahead. Job prospects should be best for jobseekers who have general office skills and who are familiar with personal computers and other office machines.

Order Clerks

- ⇨ **Annual Earnings:** $26,333
- ⇨ **Education/Training:** High school diploma
- ⇨ **Outlook:** Decline

Overall employment of order clerks is expected to decline rapidly through the year 2016 due to improvements in technology and office automation. However, numerous job openings are expected because some of the clerks who leave the occupation will need to be replaced.

Secretaries and Administrative Assistants

- ⇨ **Annual Earnings:** Secretaries ($27,240), executive secretaries and administrative assistants ($37,240), legal secretaries ($38,190)
- ⇨ **Education/Training:** High school diploma
- ⇨ **Outlook:** Average growth

Overall employment of secretaries and administrative assistants is expected to grow as fast as average. Opportunities should be best for applicants, particularly experienced secretaries, with extensive knowledge of software applications. Projected employment of secretaries will vary by occupational specialty. Employment growth in the health care and social assistance and legal services industries should lead to average growth for medical and legal secretaries. Employment of executive secretaries and administrative assistants is projected to grow more slowly than the average for all occupations.

Shipping, Receiving, and Traffic Clerks

⟳ **Annual Earnings:** $26,240
⟳ **Education/Training:** High school diploma
⟳ **Outlook:** Good

Slower-than-average employment growth is expected as a result of increasing automation. However, many additional job openings will result from the need to replace shipping, receiving, and traffic clerks who leave the occupation.

Stock Clerks and Order Fillers

⟳ **Annual Earnings:** $26,070
⟳ **Education/Training:** High school diploma
⟳ **Outlook:** Good

Employment is projected to decline as a result of automation in factories, warehouses, and stores. However, numerous job openings will occur each year due to the need to replace workers who leave the occupation. Applicants familiar with computers and other electronic office and business equipment will have the best job prospects.

Weighers, Measurers, Checkers, and Samplers, Recordkeeping

⟳ **Annual Earnings:** $25,376
⟳ **Education/Training:** High school diploma
⟳ **Outlook:** Good

Despite rapid declines in overall employment (11% in the 2006-2016 decade) due primarily to automation, job opportunities should arise from the need to replace workers who leave the labor force or transfer to other occupations.

Military, Government, and Nonprofit Jobs

The military, government, and nonprofit organizations offer millions of jobs that crosscut many of the possible opportunities outlined throughout this book. Ex-offenders should be aware of the following employment opportunities related to this very large and exciting complex of organizations:

1. **The military does hire ex-offenders.** If you think the military is closed to ex-offenders, think again. Indeed, between 2003 and 2006 the military recruited more than 100,000 ex-offenders as part of its "moral waiver" program. This program allows the various services to recruit individuals who have a record. While most of those recruited were convicted of minor drug offenses, some individuals also had felony convictions. The military generally passes on violent offenders. If you are interested in a career with the military, be sure to see if you are eligible to join under the moral waiver program. The military, and especially the U.S. Army, has aggressively and quietly recruited ex-offenders since 2003 in order to achieve their demanding monthly recruitment goals. In fact, in 2008 more than 1 of every 10 recruits in the army were given moral waivers.

2. **Government employment is restricted for ex-offenders but by no means closed.** Most prohibitions to hiring ex-offenders in government relate to police and security jobs. Some federal, state, and local governments agencies may have a blanket prohibition on hiring ex-offenders, but these prohibitions are by no means uniform. You need to know the hiring practices of various government agencies. If, for example, you want to become an FBI agent, it's best to move on with your dreams since employment is very restrictive and selective with this high-profile agency. At the same time, many city, county, and state governments,

which literally employ most public servants (20+ million), do hire ex-offenders for certain positions. For example, at the state level, many departments of corrections are open to hiring ex-offenders for non-security-related positions (see the brief discussion and accompanying chart on pages 23-24). Many local governments will hire ex-offenders for public works and social welfare positions. Indeed, many transitional work experiences (see discussion on pages 13-18) are sponsored by local governments, especially in the public works departments. Do check out **contracting opportunities** with private firms that do business with government agencies. Many of these semi-public organizations hire ex-offenders.

3. **Many nonprofit organizations regularly hire ex-offenders.** Many organizations within the nonprofit sector (which employs 10+ million people) regularly hire ex-offenders. These include faith-based, drug and alcohol rehabilitation, housing/homeless, family, health, HIV/AIDS, social welfare, and mental health organizations – in other words, nonprofit organizations that are closely associated with the corrections system and related recovery and re-entry issues. Some ex-offenders end up working for nonprofits that relate to their own addictions – the classic "major in your own problem" career choice phenomenon! When considering a career with nonprofits, keep in mind that many of these organizations are very poor and thus pay little and are constantly looking for resources to keep in operation. In other words, many are struggling organizations that mirror many of the struggles their targeted constituents are dealing with on a daily basis. For more information on employment with nonprofits, check out these excellent gateway websites, which focus on jobs with the nonprofit sector:

   - GuideStar   www.guidestar.org
   - Action Without Borders   www.idealist.org
   - Foundation Center   www.foundationcenter.org
   - Independent Sector   www.independentsector.org
   - Nonprofit Charitable Organizations   http://nonprofit.about.com
   - Nonprofit Jobs   www.opportunityknocks.org

Start Your Own Business

While most of this book focuses on jobs with other people's organizations, you may also be interested in working for yourself. Indeed, each year nearly seven percent of Americans strike out on their own to start their own business. They do so for a variety of positive and negative reasons. Like many other ex-offenders who seek true freedom, you may want to become your own boss as you pursue dreams of operating your own business.

The fact that you may have little or no business experience should not dissuade you from considering an entrepreneurial option to employment. If you have the right combination of skills, some great ideas, and the necessary drive to be an entrepreneur, you should consider working for yourself.

While nearly 900,000 new businesses are started each year, another 700,000 to 800,000 businesses fail each year; 50 percent fail within the first 38 months; and nearly 90 percent fail within 10 years. Unfortunately, starting your own business is risky; the statistical odds are against becoming a successful entrepreneur.

You should approach business opportunities the same way you approach the job market: do research, develop networks, and conduct informational and referral interviews.

Most business people will tell you similar stories about the realities of running one's own business. Do your market research, work long hours, plan, and be persistent. They also will give you advice on businesses to avoid and essential business routines.

Many service and high-tech businesses will be growing in the decade ahead. Given major issues, such as energy, the environment, health care, fitness, and leisure, and the changing demographic structure (fewer young people, more elderly, the two-career family) numerous opportunities are arising for small personal-service businesses to meet the needs of the elderly and career-oriented families. Businesses relating to restaurants, home maintenance, health care, housing for the elderly, green technologies, energy, the environment, and mortuaries and cemeteries should expand considerably in the future.

Opportunities are also available for inventive business people who can make more productive use of busy people's time – for example, fast food, financial planning, and mail-order Internet and catalog shopping. The information and high-tech revolutions are taking place at the same time two-career families do not have time to waste standing in lines at banks, grocery stores, and department stores. Mail-order or Internet-based home and office-based shopping should increase dramatically during the next decade.

A service business is especially attractive. It's easy to establish; many require a small initial investment; and the accounting is often simple. You may be able to operate from your home and thus keep the costs of operation down.

If you decide to go into business, make sure you choose the right business for your particular skills, abilities, motivation, and interests. A good starting point is the Small Business Administration's website, especially the useful section on determining whether or not you are best suited for the entrepreneurial life:

www.sba.gov/smallbusinessplanner/index.html

You also should visit this section of their website, which includes a listing of several free online courses on starting a business:

www.sba.gov/services/training/index.html

One of the most popular and useful such courses recommended by the Small Business Administration is entitled "Entrepreneurship: Starting and Managing Your Business":

www.myownbusiness.org/course_sba.html

Available in 13 sessions, it's offered as both a free or enhanced fee-based course. Whatever you do, make sure you take this course.

Several other websites also can provide useful assistance on how to start and run a successful business:

- **Small Business Administration**   www.sba.gov/index.html
- **BizMove.com**   http://bizmove.com
- **Business Know-How**   http://businessknowhow.com
- **AllBusiness**   www.allbusiness.com
- **Business Owner's Toolkit**   http://toolkit.com
- **CEO Business Express**   www.ceoexpress.com
- **Entrepreneur.com**   www.entrepreneur.com
- **Entrepreneurship**   www.entrepreneurship.org

Career Resources

THE FOLLOWING CAREER RESOURCES are available directly from Impact Publications. Full descriptions of each title, as well as numerous downloadable catalogs, videos, software, and other products, can be found at www.impactpub lications.com. Complete the following form or list the titles, include shipping (see formula at the end of page 123), enclose payment, and send your order to:

IMPACT PUBLICATIONS
9104 Manassas Drive, Suite N
Manassas Park, VA 20111-5211 USA
1-800-361-1055 (orders only)
Tel. 703-361-7300 or Fax 703-335-9486
Email address: query@impactpublications.com
Quick & easy online ordering: www.impactpublications.com

Orders from individuals must be prepaid by check, money order, or major credit card. We accept telephone, fax, and email orders.

Qty.	TITLES	Price	TOTAL
Ex-Offender Re-Entry Titles by the Author			
____	Best Jobs for Ex-Offenders	$9.95	____
____	Best Resumes and Letters for Ex-Offenders	$19.95	____
____	The Ex-Offender's Job Hunting Guide	$17.95	____
____	The Ex-Offender's Job Interview Guide	$9.95	____
____	The Ex-Offender's Quick Job Hunting Guide	$9.95	____
____	The Ex-Offender's Re-Entry Success Guide	$9.95	____
____	Job Interview Tips for People With Not-So-Hot Backgrounds	$14.95	____
____	No One Will Hire Me!	$15.95	____
____	Overcoming Barriers to Employment	$17.95	____
Other Titles By the Author			
____	201 Dynamite Job Search Letters	$19.95	____
____	America's Top Jobs for People Re-Entering the Workforce	$19.95	____
____	Blue-Collar Resume and Job Hunting Guide	$15.95	____
____	Change Your Job, Change Your Life	$21.95	____
____	Complete Guide to Public Employment	$19.95	____
____	High Impact Resumes and Letters	$19.95	____
____	Get a Raise in 7 Days	$14.95	____
____	Give Me More Money!	$17.95	____
____	I Can't Believe They Asked Me That!	$17.95	____
____	I Want to Do Something Else, But I Don't Know What It Is	$15.95	____
____	The Job Hunting Guide	$14.95	____
____	Job Hunting Tips for People With Hot and Not-So-Hot Backgrounds	$17.95	____
____	Job Interview Tips for People With Not-So-Hot Backgrounds	$14.95	____

_____	Jobs for Travel Lovers	$19.95 _____
_____	Military-to-Civilian Resumes and Letters	$21.95 _____
_____	Military Transition to Civilian Success	$21.95 _____
_____	Nail the Cover Letter	$17.95 _____
_____	Nail the Job Interview	$14.95 _____
_____	Nail the Resume	$17.95 _____
_____	Overcoming 101 More Barriers to Employment	$17.95 _____
_____	Resume, Application, and Letter Tips for People With Hot and Not-So-Hot Backgrounds	$17.95 _____
_____	Salary Negotiation Tips for Professionals	$16.95 _____
_____	Savvy Interviewing: The Nonverbal Advantage	$10.95 _____
_____	The Savvy Networker	$13.95 _____
_____	The Savvy Resume Writer	$12.95 _____
_____	Win the Interview, Win the Job	$15.95 _____
_____	You Should Hire Me!	$15.95 _____

Ex-Offenders in Transition

_____	9 to 5 Beats Ten to Life	$15.00 _____
_____	99 Days and a Get Up	$9.95 _____
_____	Ex-Offender's Job Search Companion	$11.95 _____
_____	Man, I Need a Job	$7.95 _____

Testing and Assessment

_____	Career Tests	$12.95 _____
_____	Do What You Are	$18.95 _____
_____	I Don't Know What I Want, But I Know It's Not This	$15.00 _____
_____	Now, Discover Your Strengths	$30.00 _____
_____	What Should I Do With My Life?	$14.95 _____

Attitude, Motivation, and Goal Setting

_____	100 Ways to Motivate Yourself	$14.99 _____
_____	Attitude Is Everything	$14.95 _____
_____	Changing for Good	$12.95 _____
_____	Goals!	$16.95 _____
_____	The Power of Positive Thinking	$14.00 _____
_____	The Purpose-Driven Life	$14.99 _____
_____	Success Principles	$16.95 _____

Inspiration, Empowerment, and Addictions

_____	7 Habits of Highly Effective People (2nd Edition)	$15.95 _____
_____	17 Lies That Are Holding You Back and the Truth That Will Set You Free	$16.95 _____
_____	Awaken the Giant Within	$16.00 _____
_____	Change Your Thinking, Change Your Life	$18.95 _____
_____	Denial Is Not a River In Egypt	$13.95 _____
_____	Forgiveness	$13.95 _____
_____	Life Strategies	$13.95 _____
_____	Purpose-Driven Life	$19.99 _____
_____	Your Best Life Now	$19.99 _____

Career Exploration and Job Strategies

_____	25 Jobs That Have It All	$14.95 _____
_____	50 Cutting Edge Jobs	$15.95 _____
_____	95 Mistakes Job Seekers Make & How to Avoid Them	$13.95 _____
_____	100 Great Jobs and How to Get Them	$17.95 _____
_____	300 Best Jobs Without a Four-Year Degree	$16.95 _____
_____	Best Jobs for the 21st Century	$19.95 _____
_____	How to Get a Job and Keep It	$16.95 _____
_____	Occupational Outlook Handbook	$19.95 _____

_____ O*NET Dictionary of Occupational Titles	$39.95	_____
_____ What Color Is Your Parachute?	$18.95	_____

Resumes and Letters

_____ 101 Great Tips for a Dynamite Resume	$13.95	_____
_____ Best KeyWords for Resumes, Cover Letters, & Interviews	$17.95	_____
_____ Best Resumes for People Without a Four-Year Degree	$19.95	_____
_____ Cover Letters for Dummies	$16.99	_____
_____ Resumes for Dummies	$16.99	_____

Networking

_____ A Foot in the Door	$14.95	_____
_____ Little Black Book of Connections	$19.95	_____
_____ Masters of Networking	$16.95	_____

Start Your Own Business

_____ 101 Small Business Ideas for Under $5,000	$19.95	_____
_____ The $100,000+ Entrepreneur	$19.95	_____
_____ Small Business for Dummies	$21.99	_____
_____ Start Your Own Business	$24.95	_____

SUBTOTAL   _____

Virginia residents add 5% sales tax   _____

POSTAGE/HANDLING ($5 for first
product and 9% of SUBTOTAL) $5.00

9% of SUBTOTAL --- _____

TOTAL ENCLOSED ------------------------------------- _____

SHIP TO:

NAME _____

ADDRESS: _____

_____

_____

PAYMENT METHOD:

❑ I enclose check/money order for $ _____ made payable to
IMPACT PUBLICATIONS.

❑ Please charge $ _____ to my credit card:

❑ Visa   ❑ MasterCard   ❑ American Express   ❑ Discover

Card # _____ Expiration date: ____/____

Signature _____

New Re-Entry Success Programs

From Parole to Payroll:
A Process of Persistence

Our most popular ex-offender series is now available in this revised 2008 edition! The three videos (DVD or VHS), each running 25 minutes, contain solid, real-world content designed to help ex-offenders find satisfying work. Features informative interviews, helpful tips, and colorful graphics. English-language subtitled. **$89.95 each. SPECIAL: $269.85 for the set and workbook.**

- *Finding a Job*
- *Resumes and Job Applications*
- *The Job Interview*

Countdown to Freedom:
Ex-Offender Re-Entry and Re-Integration

This six-part video series takes offenders step-by-step through the transition process—from incarceration to community re-integration. Includes candid interviews with professionals and ex-offenders on what to expect. Ex-offenders learn what actions they must take, how to prevent relapse and overcome barriers, and much more. Available in **men's or women's versions** (we automatically ship the men's version unless specified otherwise). Each program runs 15-25 minutes. Close-captioned. 2007. **$129.00 (DVD) or $139.00 (VHS) each. SPECIAL: $695.00 (DVD) or $725.00 (VHS) for complete series of six programs:**

- *Preparation for Release: Part One*
- *Release and Beyond: Lifestyle Changes*
- *Preparation for Release: Part Two*
- *Release and Beyond: Relapse Triggers*
- *Day of Release*
- *Release and Beyond: Support Systems*

Starting Fresh With a Troubled Background

This three-part job-finding series is ideal for ex-offenders and others with troubled and not-so-hot backgrounds. Each program shows how an ex-offender can overcome the many obstacles in finding a job, from organizing and implementing each step of the job search to writing honest resumes and letters and disclosing a criminal past during interviews. 19 minutes each. 2007. Can purchase separately: **$98.00 (VHS) or $108.00 (DVD). SPECIAL: $269.95 (VHS) or $299.95 (DVD) for all three programs.**

- *Starting Fresh: Finding a Job With a Troubled Background*
- *Starting Fresh: Resumes and Cover Letters With a Troubled Background*
- *Starting Fresh: Interviewing With a Troubled Background*

Goin' Home: The Series

Delbert Boone takes a group of offenders at Chicago's Adult Transition Center (operated by the Safer Foundation) through the process of being honest about their life and future. They talk about where

their choices have taken them and how to empower themselves to understand what they must do to avoid returning to a life of addiction, crime, and incarceration. Includes engaging visuals and music. DVD or VHS. 33 minutes each. 2007. Can purchase each program separately for **$200.00. SPECIAL: $995.00 for the 6-part series.**

- *Taking a Look at You*
- *Empowering Yourself*
- *The Deception of Addiction*
- *The Rules of the Game*
- *Giving Up the Game*
- *The Art of Mainstreaming*

Ex-Offender's Guide to Job Fair Success

A job fair is one of the most effective methods ex-offenders can use for developing key contacts and finding employment. Instead of spending hours scouring the Internet or classifieds to find job leads, they can go to a single place to speak with many employers face to face. This program helps ex-offenders discover how to make the most of a job fair. Includes online instructor's guide (see www.impactpublications.com). 2007. **DVD only. $129.00**

Expert Job Search Strategies for the Ex-Offender

Assists ex-offenders creating a career plan and preparing for the most critical steps in the job search. Covers everything from putting together a powerful resume and preparing for the job interview to dressing properly and deciding what you want to do with the rest of your life. Each DVD contains interviews with correctional officials and offers advice tailored to the formerly incarcerated. Includes an online instructor's guide (see www.impactpublications.com). 2007. **DVD only. $399.00**

- *Career Planning and Goals*
- *Resume Realities*
- *Interview Techniques*

Living Free: Inspiring Ex-Offenders to Overcome Career and Life Barriers and Find Success

Addresses the challenges facing ex-offenders through the eyes of four ex-offenders who share their stories on their experiences after release. They explain how they overcame barriers, such as transportation and finding employment, and how they dealt with societal pressures. Stresses the importance of positive relationships, family, and the many things they've done to turn their lives around. 31 minutes. 2006. **$129.00 (DVD) or $139.00 (VHS).**

Parole – Getting Out and Staying Out

This program follows paroled prisoners as they re-enter civilian life and face challenges both large and small. Provides an eye-opening look at the typical parolee's struggle to find work, stay away from drugs and former friends, and maintain a positive attitude about the future. 16 minutes. Close-captioned. 2006. **DVD and VHS versions. $59.95**

Ex-Offender Re-Entry Kits

Ex-Offender's Job Finding and Re-Entry Kit

Many educators, career counselors, and workforce development professionals provide assistance to ex-offenders in prisons, detention centers, and community transition programs. If you are involved with this group, consider acquiring this unique collection of books and videos that addresses the transition needs of ex-offenders. **SPECIAL: $569.95 for complete kit!**

BOOKS

- *9 to 5 Beats Ten to Life* ($15.00)
- *99 Days and a Get Up* ($9.95)
- *Best Resumes and Letters for Ex-Offenders* ($19.95)
- *Ex-Offender's Job Hunting Guide* ($17.95)
- *Ex-Offender's Job Search Companion* ($11.95)
- *Job Interview Tips for People With Not-So-Hot Backgrounds* ($14.95)
- *Man, I Need a Job!* ($7.95)
- *No One Is Unemployable* ($29.95)
- *No One Will Hire Me!* ($15.95)
- *Putting The Bars Behind You Survival Guides* (7 books, $59.95)
- *Quick Prep Careers* ($18.95)

DVDS

- *Living Free* ($129.00)
- *Re-Entry* ($125.00)
- *Putting the Bars Behind You* ($99.00)

Top 10 Videos for Ex-Offenders

The following videos represent our 10 most popular videos used in correctional programs. Can purchase separately. For details on each video, please visit the Video/DVD section of our online bookstore, www.impactpublications. com. **SPECIAL: $995.00 for all 10 videos.**

- *Best 10¹ᐟ⁴ Tips for People With a Not-So-Hot Past* ($98.00)
- *An Ex-Offender's Guide to Job Fair Success. DVD only* ($129.00)
- *Finding a Job When Your Past Is Not So Hot* ($125.00)
- *Finding Employment: First Step for the Ex-Offender* ($98.00/108.00)
- *From Parole to Payroll: Finding a Job* ($89.95)
- *From Parole to Payroll: Resumes and Job Applications* ($89.95)
- *From Parole to Payroll: The Job Interview* ($89.95)
- *Living Free* ($129.00/139.00)
- *Parole: Getting Out and Staying Out* ($59.95)
- *Post-Prison Blues* ($129.00/139.00)

The Purpose-Driven Ex-Offender Kit

Many ex-offenders lack a sense of direction and purpose in their lives. Books in this unique kit focus on goals, purposes, attitudes, and principles of success. These inspirational books are responsible for changing the lives of millions of people who look within themselves for both spiritual and practical guidance. Can purchase separately. **SPECIAL: $199.95 for complete set of 14 books.**

- *7 Habits of Highly Effective People* ($15.95)
- *Attitude Is Everything* ($14.95)
- *Awaken the Giant Within* ($16.00)
- *Change Your Attitude* ($16.99)
- *Changing for Good* ($12.95)
- *Claiming Your Place at the Fire* ($16.95)
- *Goals!* ($16.95)
- *Life Strategies* ($13.95)
- *Power of Positive Thinking* ($14.00)
- *The Power of Purpose* ($15.95)
- *The Purpose-Driven Life* ($14.99)
- *The Success Principles* ($16.95)
- *You Can Heal Your Life* ($14.95)
- *Your Best Life Now Study Guide* ($9.99)

Change Your Attitudes and Behaviors Kit

Like bad habits, attitudes and behaviors are difficult to change. However, many people need to change their attitudes and behaviors in order to become more effective in their work and life. Without such changes, they are destined to repeat their same old patterns of behavior which are often dysfunctional. This set of outstanding resources addresses some of the most important habits for success and failure as well as shows how to make the necessary attitudinal and behavioral changes relating to addictions, anger, incarceration, and various life skills. Can purchase separately. **SPECIAL: $270.95 for all 19 resources.**

- *7 Habits of Highly Effective People* ($15.95)
- *7 Habits of Highly Effective Teens* ($14.95)
- *12 Bad Habits That Hold Good People Back* ($15.95)
- *The Addiction Workbook* ($18.95)
- *The Addictive Personality* ($14.00)
- *Angry Men* ($14.95)
- *Angry Women* ($14.95)
- *Attitude Is Everything* ($14.95)
- *Awaken the Giant Within* ($16.00)
- *Change Your Attitude* ($16.99)
- *Changing for Good* ($12.95)
- *Denial Is Not a River In Egypt* ($13.95)
- *The Ex-Offender's Job Hunting Guide* ($17.95)
- *The Habit Change Workbook* ($19.95)
- *Life Strategies* ($13.95)
- *Reinventing Yourself* ($18.99)
- *Sex, Drugs, Gambling, and Chocolate* ($15.95)
- *Simple Steps to Impossible Dreams* ($14.00)
- *The Success Principles* ($16.95)

ORDERS: TOLL FREE 800.361.1055 FAX 703.335.9486 ONLINE ORDERING: *www.impactpublications.com*

39092 08082414 9